ESSAYS IN HONOR OF

Russel B. Nye

ESSAYS IN HONOR OF

Russel B. Nye

edited by

Joseph Waldmeir

THE MICHIGAN STATE UNIVERSITY PRESS
EAST LANSING

Copyright © 1978

Michigan State University Press

Library of Congress Catalog Card Number: 78-61765

ISBN 0-87013-209-1

★
 ★
★
 ★
★

Manufactured in the United States of America

CONTENTS

Foreword   *vii*

C. David Mead   A SCHOLAR'S PROFILE   1

John Cawelti   THE JOYS OF BUCHANEERING   7

Robert Falk   HENRY JAMES' *The Ameri-*
                       can AS A CENTENNIAL
                       NOVEL   31

Louis Filler   CONSENSUS: HOW ACADEMICS
                       KEEP FROM MURDERING
                       EACH OTHER AT PRO-
                       FESSIONAL MEETINGS   43

M.W. Fishwick   THE THINGNESS OF THINGS   65

Norman Grabo   COLONIAL AMERICAN THEOL-
                       OGY: HOLINESS AND THE
                       LYRIC IMPULSE   74

Victor M. Howard   THE CANADIAN CRANK   92

Georges Joyaux   ROCK CARRIER'S TRILOGY: A
                       SECOND LOOK AT QUEBEC'S
                       DARK YEARS   105

Contents

William McCann   KIM HUBBARD AND JOURNAL-
ISTIC HUMOR IN THE MID-
WEST   129

Hugo McPherson   HOW HOT IS THE SCARLET
LETTER?   141

J.E. Morpurgo   RICHER IN ESTEEM: A RE-
APPRAISAL OF JOHN BUR-
GOYNE   151

Gilman M. Ostrander   LORD KAMES AND AMERICAN
REVOLUTIONARY CULTURE   168

A.J.M. Smith   NONSENSE POETRY AND RO-
MANTICISM   180

Milton R. Stern   NATHANIEL HAWTHORNE:
"CONSERVATIVE AFTER
HEAVEN'S OWN FASHION"   195

Linda Welshimer Wagner   JOHN DOS PASSOS: REACHING
PAST POETRY   226

Joseph Waldmeir   RABBIT REDUX REDUCED: RE-
DEDICATED? REDEEMED?   247

Notes on Contributors   263

Foreword

These essays were written to honor Russel B. Nye on the occasion of his retirement from teaching. The essayists were asked to contribute first of all as representatives of the five areas in which Nye has gathered honor to himself over a long and distinguished career—American History (including biography, the area of American history in which he took a Pulitzer award), American Literature, American Studies, Canadian Culture, and Popular Culture. Secondly, they were asked because they were all distinguished colleagues, or ex-students, and friends of his.

That they all agreed, and that each contribution is original and unique to this collection, is I think a further tribute to the man they are intended to honor.

I mentioned at the outset that the essays are presented upon the occasion of Nye's retirement from teaching. I must emphasize that qualification for, fortunately, he assures any who ask that he does not intend to retire from the other pleasures and duties of his profession. For which of course we all offer our profoundest thanks.

Grateful acknowledgements are also due to Mr. Leslie Scott and the M.S.U. Development Fund for support in this venture.

J.W.

ESSAYS IN HONOR
OF

Russel B. Nye

A Scholar's Profile

C. DAVID MEAD

For one who has known Russel Nye for many years, it is not altogether easy to view the man or his work objectively. And a person so innately modest as he would turn instinctively from expressions of praise. Those who know him are aware that, as much as he enjoys the discussion of men and books, he rarely mentions his own accomplishments. Indeed his colleagues are sometimes surprised to learn that another book or essay, or perhaps some honor or award, has been added to his record without his ever speaking of it. Although the remarks made here are doubtless more fulsome than he would wish, they are surely, in the opinion of his colleagues, something less than he deserves.

Student in Nye's classes or other readers of his scholarly writing frequently comment on the great store of information which he imparts both in his lectures and his books. After reading *The Unembarrassed Muse* (1970), one well-known critic wrote that "he seems to have read everything," and another called it a "feast of information." These are typical responses. Nye keeps no formal "savings bank," as Emerson called his voluminous journals, but he is a tireless reader with an extraordinary memory for meaningful details. Combined with these qualities is his insatiable curiosity, especially about the people and events forming the historical and social pattern of American culture. His knowledge is never merely decorative, but is the rich background for his insights into our life as a nation.

But more than curiosity, it is his deep desire for truth that has made Nye a lifelong explorer of museums, libraries and bookstores, as well as battlefields and other scenes of history. His books and classroom lectures are illuminated by the surprising, little-known details which come from his foraging among the obscure yet important events and places of human experience. They give authenticity to narrative and sometimes prove the wisdom of Melville's familiar comment on Queequeg's native island: "It is not down on any map; true places never are." In *A Baker's Dozen* (1956) Nye restored to our attention a whole group of once-famous Americans and events neglected or forgotten by later generations.

In a long series of books Nye has recorded America's historical changes and crises, especially those which have marked our intellectual life. There is an inherent optimism in his work, rooted in his trust in the diverse strength of the American people. There is also a kind of fascination with our native earth, with the vastness and beauty which moved the imagination of Cooper, Thoreau and countless other American authors. Moreover, in most of his writings there is a commitment to certain concepts of American faith which, perhaps simple in themselves, are so complicated in their relationship: belief in the worth of the individual man as expressed by Franklin, Emerson and Faulkner; and respect for the broad social democracy called for by Jefferson, Melville and Dreiser.

Despite his extensive scholarly achievements, Nye thinks of himself primarily as a teacher. His own scholarship supports his thorough, articulate knowledge, and his teaching reflects meticulous planning and organization. He is especially sensitive to the varied backgrounds of students. His classes illustrate his belief that the university teacher should encourage students to have responsible, critical minds, to think boldly and innovatively, and to apply their learning to the contemporary world. Students who meet and talk with him can readily feel his devotion to his work.

His enthusiastic involvement makes them more excited and hopeful about the possibilities of their own academic future. He is one of those exceptional teachers who satisfy the expectations of perceptive students that knowledge will be transformed, evaluated and made meaningful in their own lives. In 1960 he received Michigan State University's Distinguished Teacher Award, and in 1962 he was given the title of Distinguished Professor of English.

Nye's professional spirit is fostered by his high expectations for American education and culture. He is an ardent defender of the role of the teacher-scholar and of the importance of the humanities in a free society. Reading and writing books, and talking to others about literature and intellectual history, are more than vocational activities. They are the means of a personal fulfillment which is the best possible way to show the value of humanistic study. His wide learning and his committed practice would not be so important to others if they were not so important to him.

Russel Nye was born in Viola, Wisconsin, in 1913. After graduating from Oberlin College in 1934, he attended the University of Wisconsin in Madison, completing his M.A. in 1935 and the Ph.D. in 1940. At Wisconsin he studied both English and history and came under the pervasive influence of such important literary scholars as Harry Hayden Clark and Henry Pochman as well as the historians William B. Hesseltine and John D. Hicks. In the 1930's the study of American literature was emerging as a major area of teaching and research. Nye's natural interest in intellectual history was strongly encouraged by his teachers in Madison, who recognized the need for literary historians with a firm bibliographical and factual knowledge of our cultural background.

After a year of teaching at Adelphi College, Nye in 1940 went to Michigan State College, where he has been a member of the English faculty for nearly four decades. In 1944 he received a Knopf Fellowship and a year later the Pulitzer Prize in biography for *George Bancroft: Brahmin Rebel.* In 1947 he was awarded a Rockefeller Fellowship in American history; a Newberry Library

Fellowship in midwestern history followed in 1948, the year of his *Midwestern Progressive Politics*, a definitive study of its subject. In the meantime he became Head of the English Department, an office which from 1946 to 1960 he combined successfully with an increasingly active scholarly and professional career. For several years he served also as Director of the Division of Language and Literature, requiring his supervision of both the foreign language and English programs.

Although a complete list of Nye's publications is too extensive to include here, some of them are of such particular interest or merit that they deserve special notice. *Fettered Freedom: Civil Liberties and the Slavery Controversy 1830–1860* (1949) is an extensive investigation of the idea of freedom in American society in the antebellum period. Another expression of Nye's Civil War interest is his *William Lloyd Garrison and the Humanitarian Reformers* (1956). In the same year appeared *A History of the United States*, two volumes written with J. E. Morpurgo of England. Widely used in European universities, this work is translated into French and German editions. In *The Cultural Life of the New Nation 1776–1830* (1960), Nye demonstrated his unusual ability to synthesize and interpret the complex elements of our early cultural history. The book's sequel, *Society and Culture in America 1830–1860* (1974), is equally distinguished for its thorough research and articulate style. *This Almost Chosen People* (1966) defines and skillfully traces through our history some of the important ideas which have formed the American mind.

Nye's activities and influence extend far beyond the campus of Michigan State University. He has been an editorial consultant for professional journals, including *American Literature, Clio* and the *Journal of Popular Culture*. He has been active in the affairs of professional organizations, serving as president of the American Studies Association 1965–67, president of the Popular Culture Association 1970–71, and chairman of the American Literature Group of the Modern Language Association 1975–76. His early and continuous advocacy of programs in American studies and popular culture has given a strong impetus to their development as significant areas for teaching and research. He has also served as a member or advisor of such organizations as the National Endowment for the Humanities, the Canada Council, the Fulbright Advisory Committee, and the Governor's Commission on Higher Education in Michigan. From 1950 to 1968 he was a member of the Ferris State College Board of Control, receiving the honorary degree of L.L.D. from that institution in 1969. In that year he was honored also with the L.H.D. from Northern Michigan University.

Nye has been a lecturer or visiting professor at a number of American institutions, including Indiana University, George Washington University, and the Universities of Maine and Massachusetts. His major work outside the United States has been in France and Canada, where he has studied and taught extensively. He has been a guest lecturer on American literature and culture at such Canadian universities as McGill, Queen's, Western Ontario, Xavier, and Sackville, as well as the Universities of Nice and Aix-Marseilles in France. Active in the Canadian Association of American Studies, Nye has also developed a special interest in English-Canadian and French-Canadian literature, fields of study which he has extended to the literature program at Michigan State. The Canadian-American Studies Program at the University owes much to his energy and leadership.

Only rarely does an individual make so indelible an imprint on his department as Nye has made at Michigan State University. During his long and devoted service as an administrator he had a constant concern for his colleagues and their welfare. He guided his department from relative obscurity to a place of national prominence. During his term of office many programs, such as the comparative literature and doctoral programs, were undertaken and developed. He has given his time and energy generously and patiently to both undergraduate and graduate students, and has directed more doctoral programs than any other member of his department or college.

These remarks give only a partial view of this modest scholar who has contributed so much in so many ways to the search for knowledge, and whose learning and teaching have enriched the lives of so many people. "A teacher affects eternity," wrote Henry Adams; "he can never tell where his influence stops." Russel Nye's years at Michigan State University will end without conclusion, because he and his work will continue to influence others, especially the colleagues and students he has known. For them, this man of such unusual warmth, integrity and humanity has illustrated by his own career how learning can be a force giving meaning and fulfillment to life.

The Joys of Buchaneering

JOHN CAWELTI

If we are to take his own word for it, John Buchan would probably have written his stories whether they were successful or not. In his autobiography he tells us:

> It was huge fun playing with my puppets, and to me they soon became very real flesh and blood. I never consciously invented with a pen in my hand; I waited until the story had told itself and then wrote it down, and, since it was already a finished thing, I wrote it fast. The books had a wide sale, both in English and in translations, and I have always felt a little ashamed that profit should accrue from what had given me so much amusement. I had no purpose in writing except to please myself, and even if my books had not found a single reader I would have felt amply repaid.

There seems little reason to doubt that Buchan's account is essentially correct, that the stories were for him a pleasant and relaxing mode of fantasy, a refreshing escape from a life filled with problems, tensions, and achievements of a very wide range. The interesting thing is that Buchan's fantasies, coupled with his ability to put them in words, became the ground for a rich and various series of collective fantasies. Buchan, more than any other writer, assembled the formula for the modern secret agent story.

Of course, he had many precursors. Stories of spying and political intrigue like tales of crime go back to the fountainheads of western literature, the Bible and Homer; Joshua sent spies into Canaan, Odysseus returned to his palace disguised as a beggar in order to ascertain the situation, and the Philistines produced the first of a great tradition of dangerous but glamorous female agents. However, in spite of, or perhaps because of, this almost universal human fascination with spying and disguise, the professional spy remained a disreputable character well into the nineteenth century. When James Fenimore Cooper wrote the first novel with a spy as one of the central characters [*The Spy* (1821)], his ambivalence about the spy as hero shows in many ways. Though Harvey Birch is treated sympathetically as an American patriot who selflessly plays a role as double agent, scorned by all but the elusive Mr. Harper (George Washington) to whom he reports British secrets, Cooper also makes him a comic, déclassé character who hovers on the edges of the main plot. The central story of *The Spy* deals with the romantic reunion of two aristocratic families torn by their conflicting loyalties in the American Revolution. After Cooper, spies and political intrigue increasingly cropped up in the nineteenth century European novel—in Stendahl, Turgenev, Dostoyevsky, Zola, for example,—until at the beginning of the twentieth century in *The Secret Agent* (1907) and *Under Western Eyes* (1911) Joseph Conrad made espionage the subject of two great tragic novels.

But Conrad's dark, brooding portrayals of a modern world of intrigue and betrayal, of ceaseless but futile espionage between countries and the clash of rival ambitions within society, were hardly models for a literature of entertainment and escape based on spying. To create this, a writer had to combine the subject-matter of spying with the form and mood of romantic adventure, and to create a hero-type and cast of characters who could persuasively and effectively function in a world of this type. For skillfully written romantic adventure and mystery, there could have been no better models than the late nineteenth century

British writers Haggard, Stevenson, Kipling and Doyle. Haggard and Kipling had brilliantly spun out exciting tales of exotic adventure on the fringes of the Empire in Africa and India and they had shown how effectively the English gentleman could be set against a lush and glamorous background and made to embody heroic virtues. Haggard's Allan Quartermain, in particular, was certainly one important progenitor of the Buchan hero. Stevenson had not only done superb adventure stories with a historical and Scottish setting—the latter particularly important as a model for Buchan—but he had also explored the modern city as a locus for adventure. Doyle was also a dedicated historical romancer, but his most popular and successful stories, the various exploits of Sherlock Holmes, had shown how the theme of espionage could be used as a source of mystery and an object of detection. Finally, as international tensions increased in the first decade of the twentieth century, many writers turned to international intrigue for their adventure plots, most notably Erskine Childers and William LeQueux.

Buchan wove elements from all of these precursors into his tales, but the combination was distinctively his own, stamped with the power, and the peculiar limitations, of his own imagination. Perhaps the most striking quality of his spy stories has also marked his most popular later successor, Ian Fleming, who had something like Buchan's ability to stretch a thin skin of verisimilitude over the wildest kind of fantasy and allegory. This balance differentiates Buchan from his near contemporary and fellow secret agent romancer Saxe Rohmer. Rohmer's Fu Manchu stories have a compelling power of fantasy, but they are too absurdly and wildly implausible to appeal to readers of any degree of sophistication. Fu Manchu and his dauntless pursuers have led a thriving life in pulp novel and B film, but the comparison between Rohmer and Buchan is somewhat analogous to that between Mickey Spillane and Dashiell Hammett: Buchan, like Hammett, was the chief creator of a formulaic tradition which proved capable of complex and various development; Rohmer was, like Spillane, a prolific popular exponent of the formula in its simplest and most extreme form. Because of this, the study of Rohmer's writings can sometimes reveal to us in an exaggerated way the themes that lurk beneath the more balanced and controlled surface of Buchan's work. The terror of racial degeneration, for example, though never treated as obsessively by Buchan as in the symbolizing of the "yellow peril" through Fu Manchu and his minions, is unquestionably there.

Buchan effectively combined the fantasy of highly colorful villains, plots, and incidents, together with allegory, using characters to represent general moral and social traits thereby suggesting that the whole fate of society is somehow at stake. Generally, the most successful writers of spy thrillers have dealt in this sort of combination, though in some cases, like Graham Greene's, their sense of realism has been in tension with it. Of the other spy writers, perhaps only Eric Ambler has continually worked with the formula without possessing either a rather unrestricted fantasy or a need to transmute fantasy into allegory. Buchan seems to have had a remarkably clear perception of this aspect of his psyche. We noted above his frank statement that his tales were fantasy outlets strongly needed at certain periods of his life. Early in his autobiography, he notes that the earliest and strongest influences on his thought were the fairy tales which his father loved and collected and the strong Calvinistic discipline which was also part of his parson father's way of life. These two influences came together for Buchan when he discovered and read what would become for him the basic literary work:

> *The Pilgrim's Progress* became my constant companion. Even to-day I think that, if the text were lost, I could restore most of it from memory. My delight in it came partly from the rhythms of its prose, which, save in King James's Bible, have not been equalled in our literature; there are passages, such as the death of Mr. Valiant-for-Truth, which all my life have made music in my ear. But its spell was largely due to its plain narrative, its picture of life as a pilgrimage over hill and dale, where surprising adventures lurked by the wayside,

a hard road with now and then long views to cheer the
traveller and a great brightness at the end of it.

It is probably more revealing than exaggerated to suggest that
Buchan created the modern spy story out of his need to construct a contemporaneous fantasy that might have for him something of the feeling and meaning of *The Pilgrim's Progress.* In
any case, his stories exude Bunyanesque allusions and devices
at every pore. This is obvious in the case of *Mr. Standfast* where
one of the hero figures reads Bunyan throughout the novel and
attempts to pattern himself on a Bunyan character, finally going
to his death in emulation of Bunyan's Mr. Valiant-for-Truth. But
in an even deeper sense than such explicit references to *The
Pilgrim's Progress,* the fantasy world of Buchan's spy stories takes
on the basic form of the pilgrim's quest. In each of the novels,
a rather ordinary but courageous hero sets out on a quest which
takes him from the comfort and security of the city out into an
increasingly jagged and dangerous landscape. As he proceeds on
his quest he becomes more and more isolated and alone to face
the agents and the plots of the diabolical conspiracy which
threatens to overthrow the moral world. Finally, with the assistance of a few courageous friends, he succeeds in uncovering
the enemy and conspiracy and overthrowing them.

Thus, Buchan was able to take the situations of modern international intrigue and cast them in the forms of romantic adventure, permeating them with the particular allegorical intensity
of a Bunyanesque sense of the world. At his best, he was able
to clothe this allegorical fantasy with enough verisimilitude to
effectually disguise, at least from time to time, the weaknesses
inherent in his obsessive symbolic machinery and his tendency
toward a completely fantastic dependence on magical coincidence.
Perhaps the most important contributors to this surface verisimilitude are not such insights into the workings of government as
the novels offer us (for an experienced colonial administrator
Buchan writes surprisingly little about the actual processes of
politics—that may have been one of the things he was using his

powers of fantasy to get away from) but the moments of social comedy. Though basically a very serious man, Buchan apparently had a larky delight in social eccentricities and his best books are enlivened with incidents and characters which add an earthy touch of reality to the fantastic proceedings and remind us that the intense moral allegorizing of the story is not to be taken all that seriously. In fact, one of the weaknesses of Buchan's spy stories was his tendency to let the overinflated moral seriousness of his fantasy overpower these contrasting moments of eccentric humor.

Buchan usually achieved his most effective balance of fantasy, moral allegory and humor in his narrations of the pursuit across the landscape which always seemed to arouse him to his best efforts. His own insightful description of the peculiar narrative power of the chase reveals how compelled he was by it:

> I was especially fascinated by the notion of hurried journeys. In the great romances of literature they provide some of the chief dramatic moments, and since the theme is common to Homer and the penny reciter it must appeal to a very ancient instinct in human nature. We live our lives under the twin categories of time and space, and when the two come into conflict we get the great moment. Whether failure or success is the result, life is sharpened, intensified, idealized. A long journey, even with the most lofty purpose, may be a dull thing to read of if it is made at leisure; but a hundred yards may be a breathless business if only a few seconds are granted to complete it. For then it becomes a sporting event, a race; and the interest which makes millions read of the Derby is the same, in a grosser form, as when we follow an expedition straining to relieve a beleagured fort, or a man fleeing to sanctuary with the avenger behind him.

It was above all through his elaboration of the structure of the "hurried journey" or flight and pursuit that Buchan developed the basic formula of the twentieth century spy thriller. Since he first showed how effectively this kind of action could provide a suspenseful and compelling structural framework for a tale of political intrigue and espionage, the pattern of hurried journey across a distinctively structured landscape has been one of the most basic rhythms of the spy story. One need only think of Latimer's journey from Istanbul to Paris in Ambler's *A Coffin for Dimitrios,* the train trips in Hitchcock's *The Lady Vanishes* and Greene's *Orient Express,* James Bond's stalking pursuit of and desperate flights from his multifarious antagonists, and Alec Leamas' clandestine journey into and out of East Germany in *The Spy Who Came in from the Cold* to realize how important Buchan's example was for this formulaic tradition.

Only one of Buchan's spy stories has a completely coherent structure because it is almost completely organized around a single, sustained, hurried journey. This was the first, and best, of the Richard Hannay stories, *The Thirty-Nine Steps.* By looking at this novel in greater detail we can see both the reasons for the effectiveness of this kind of structure and the special and unique characteristics which Buchan was able to give to it.

The story begins on the eve of World War I in London and is narrated by the central figure, Richard Hannay, who introduces himself as a mature man who has made his fortune in South Africa. Now, returned to the comfort of London, he finds himself at loose ends:

> Here was I, thirty-seven years old, sound in wind and limb, with enough money to have a good time, yawning my head off all day. I had just about settled to clear out and get back to the veld, for I was the best-bored man in the United Kingdom.

Fortunately for his peace of mind, if not his physical comfort and safety, Hannay is soon plunged into an adventure as exciting as he might have wished. Returning to his lodging one evening, Hannay meets another tenant of the building on the stairs. Though they are not acquainted, this man, acting strangely and furtively, begs to be let into Hannay's apartment. Bolting the door, he announces suddenly:

> "Pardon . . . I'm a bit rattled tonight. You see, I happen at
> this moment to be dead."

This curious gentleman reveals to Hannay that he is one Franklin
P. Scudder, an American newspaper correspondent who has become a sort of amateur secret agent. He explains to Hannay that
"behind all the governments and the armies there was a big
subterranean movement going on, engineered by very dangerous
people." In a typically Buchanesque passage he reveals how he
has come upon their secret, and how he has since scurried about
Europe in disguise to avoid the enemy's agents:

> I got the first hint in an inn on the Achensee in Tyrol. That
> set me inquiring, and I collected my other clues in a fur-shop
> in the Galician quarter of Buda, in a Strangers' Club in
> Vienna, and in a little book-shop off the Racknitzstrasse in
> Leipsic. I completed my evidence ten days ago in Paris. I
> can't tell you the details now, for it's something of a history.
> When I was quite sure in my own mind I judged it my busi-
> ness to disappear, and I reached this city by a mighty queer
> circuit. I left Paris a dandified young French-American,
> and I sailed from Hamburg a Jew diamond merchant. In
> Norway I was an English student of Ibsen, collecting ma-
> terials for lectures, but when I left Bergen I was a cinema-
> man with special ski-films. And I came here from Leith with
> a lot of pulp-wood propositions in my pocket to put before
> the London newspapers. Till yesterday I thought I had
> muddied my trail some, and was feeling pretty happy.
> Then . . ."

The three motifs announced here—unravelling a mystery, the
dangerous lone journey, and the series of disguises—become the
basis of the development of *The Thirty-Nine Steps*. Scudder
explains to Hannay that a plot is afoot to assassinate an important
European politician when he visits London, and gives him
tantalizing hints about the secret organization. He refers to a
Black Stone, to a man who lisps, and to "an old man with a

young voice who could hood his eyes like a hawk." But before he can get any further information, Hannay discovers Scudder with a knife in his heart.

After this brisk opening, which Buchan accomplishes in a single chapter, Hannay's hurried journey begins. He realizes that if he waits for the police to arrive, he will certainly be arrested and probably convicted of Scudder's murder. Since he will not be able to do anything about the enemy plot if he is locked up in jail, he decides to elude the police by going to Scotland, where his Scots background will enable him to blend into the country and he can try to unravel the mystery of Scudder's death and the assassination plot. Disguised as a milkman he leaves his apartment and boards a train for the North.

Hannay's arrival in Scotland marks the beginning of a series of narrow escapes from capture by either the police or the forces of the enemy conspiracy. The combination of these adventures is ineffably Buchanesque, a synthesis of moral allegory, fantastic scrapes and social comedy which has never quite been duplicated by any other writer of spy adventures including, alas, Buchan himself. The chapter titles with their flavor reminiscent of Sherlock Holmes' adventures, give a pretty good idea of the distinctive ambience of this major section of *The Thirty-Nine Steps*: "The Adventure of the Literary Innkeeper; The Adventure of the Radical Candidate; The Adventure of the Spectacled Roadman; The Adventure of the Bald Archaeologist; and The Dry-Fly Fisherman." Each "adventure" is actually a sequence of incidents which elaborate in a different way the same basic pattern: Hannay, isolated and alone, pursued by both police and enemy agents, must find someone he can trust in order to communicate his knowledge to the higher authorities. To find such a person and to elude his pursuers, he disguises himself in various ways, but his disguise is finally given away by some unforeseen flaw. Moreover, many of the persons he meets turn out to be enemy agents. This patterning of the situation enables Buchan to generate a variety of suspense effects and sudden twists: Will Hannay's disguise be penetrated this time or will he get away?

Will the friendly gentleman turn out to be a real friend or an enemy agent in disguise? Will the police capture Hannay before he locates the enemy? In addition, this complex of situation and setting leads Buchan to imagine a rather marvelous sequence of contrasting and paradoxical incidents which take on a special force because of their connection with the underlying moral allegory. Hannay passes through a striking series of disguises, from South African mining magnate in trouble with the diamond association, to a "trusted leader of Australian thought" addressing a local political rally on colonialism and free trade, to a dirty and drunken Scottish road mender. Despite their fantastic diversity, Buchan manages to make each of these impersonations a plausible thing for Hannay to do in the light of his background and ability. Each situation of disguise is managed with a quality of humorous incongruity as well as danger and peril and Buchan is thereby able to take advantage of the emotional effectiveness of our uncertainty whether a given moment will move toward fear or laughter. Alfred Hitchcock would later display an even greater mastery of this kind of suspense effect, but Buchan certainly showed the way to make this kind of incident an important part of the spy thriller.

The overall structure of these adventures also embodies Buchan's flair for paradox and allegory. Each character Hannay meets has a Bunyanesque flavor in that he tends to be more a symbolic representative of some moral or social characteristic than a unique individual character. Hannay's own disguises and the perils he encounters are also the embodiment of temptations and obstacles to the accomplishment of the mission which, it becomes increasingly clear, is basic to the security of England. Even coincidence, which Buchan depends on to an inordinate extent, takes on something of a moral quality in the allegorical world of Buchan's fantasy. Throughout his adventures in Scotland, Hannay's flight leads him closer and closer to the heart of the enemy's power. Finally, with his pursuers close behind, Hannay comes to the isolated country house of a "benevolent old gentleman," an amateur historian and archaeologist of the local countryside. Certain that such a distinguished gentleman can be trusted, Hannay quickly blurts out his plight and the old gentleman turns away the pursuers with a misleading story. Then . . .

> I emerged into the sunlight to find the master of the house sitting in a deep armchair in the room he called his study, and regarding me with curious eyes.
> "Have they gone?" I asked.
> "They have gone. I convinced them that you had crossed the hill. I do not choose that the police should come between me and one whom I am delighted to honour. This is a lucky morning for you, Mr. Richard Hannay."
> As he spoke his eyelids seemed to tremble and to fall a little over his keen gray eyes. In a flash the phrase of Scudder's came back to me when he had described the man he most dreaded in the world. He had said that he "could hood his eyes like a hawk." Then I saw that I had walked straight into the enemy's headquarters.

The way in which Hannay's seemingly random flight leads him unerringly to a direct confrontation with the enemy is a sign of Hannay's instrumentality as the agent of some higher moral power. In Buchan's world, there is really no coincidence or accident. What appears to be chance is actually the mysterious and enigmatic working of providence. As Hannay puts it in *The Three Hostages,* "then suddenly there happened one of those trivial things which look like accidents but I believe are part of the rational government of the universe."

By his tenacity, his willingness to embark on a moral quest without assistance, his ability to disguise himself to elude both police and enemy agents, his courage in facing the technology of airplanes and motor cars which his pursuers send after him, and the skills in wilderness living with which he escapes alone across the desolate moor of Scotland, Hannay has demonstrated his worthiness to serve the cause of goodness. Thus, providential action leads him to the heart of the evil conspiracy and then puts him in touch with what might be called the good underground, the only political force capable of overcoming the threats of the evil conspiracy. Though captured by the enemy agents, Hannay manages to escape and find his way to the cottage of Sir Walter Bullivant of the foreign office. Bullivent has already received a letter from the late Mr. Scudder outlining the plot to assassinate the foreign politician Karolides. When the assassination occurs, Sir Walter knows that Hannay has stumbled onto a dangerous plot. But this time, Hannay has managed to solve the mystery of Scudder's mysterious hints about the Black Stone and he realizes that the enemy agents have more important plans. As Hannay characteristically puts it, "the fifteenth day of June was going to be a day of destiny, a bigger destiny than the killing of a Dago." It turns out that the final plot is to steal Britain's secret naval plans from the Admiralty and then to employ these in a surprise attack which would cripple the British navy. The remainder of *The Thirty-Nine Steps* deals with Hannay's tracking down of the Black Stone, the secret group of German agents, capturing their leaders just as they are about to turn over the stolen plans to an enemy submarine waiting off the British coast. The thirty-nine steps are finally revealed as the number of steps down to the sea from the coast villa where the group of enemy agents are finally captured. This final section of the story, though marred by the kind of implausibilities that Buchan often could not resist—for example, the naval plans are stolen by an enemy agent disguised as the First Sea Lord, who takes them from a meeting with a group of military leaders who have been in intimate contact with the real First Sea Lord for years—is on the whole an effective continuation of the suspenseful chase initiated in the first chapter.

None of the later Hannay books are as completely successful as *The Thirty-Nine Steps*. Works like *Greenmantle, Mr. Standfast,* and *The Three Hostages* come alive when Buchan deals with the hurried journey motif, but are generally more rambling and digressive narrative structures with too many subplots and different phases of action. Though these later novels have many striking incidents and characters, they seem increasingly clotted

by an attempt at seriousness and moralism, as if Buchan had
begun to take his fantasy creations too seriously as a vehicle for
social and political opinions. This trend reached a peak in later
novels of international intrigue like *A Prince of the Captivity*
which is far too full of apocalyptic ideological warnings about
the vast conspiracies threatening Western civilization to be a
very effective tale of secret adventure. Political ideologies inevitably play an important role in the spy story because the
agent's mission must be related to larger political conflicts in order
to increase our sense of its importance and to heighten our feeling
of suspense about its outcome. However, the presence of
political or moral attitudes which later audiences find outdated
or noxious invariably leads to a fairly rapid decline in the
appeal of the stories which contain them. We cannot respond
emotionally to the story's suspense without taking its worldview
with some degree of seriousness. Buchan's popularity has thus
declined rather precipitously since the 1930's. In fact, his work
seems most likely to continue to appeal to wider audiences
mainly in the form of the superb film which Alfred Hitchcock
based on *The Thirty-Nine Steps*. In his film version, Hitchcock
retained Buchan's excellent suspense structure, but eliminated
most of his ideological moralizing. At the same time he strength-
ened the comic and satirical aspects of Buchan's original by
inventing a witty and sophisticated romance which he made one
of the main lines of plot development.

Yet Buchan's fantasy vision of the world retains a considerable
degree of historical interest because of the degree to which it was
shared by other popular writers of the time, men like Dornford
Yates, "Sapper," E. Phillips Oppenheim and Saxe Rohmer. In
addition, it is this vision, which a later generation of writers,
men like Eric Ambler and Graham Greene, would inherit and
have to struggle with. These writers would face the problem of
maintaining the effective structures of suspense and action which
Buchan's generation had created, but of expressing these structures in terms of a very different vision of the world. Thus,
Buchan's view of the world both provides us with some clues

about dominant moral and political fantasies in the first part of the twentieth century and gives us a position from which to measure the extent to which a later generation departed from these fantasies.

Richard Usborne, in a fascinating study of the heroes of Buchan, Sapper and Yates, coined the rather nice term "clubland heroes" to describe Hannay and his compatriots Bulldog Drummond and Jonah Mansel. This characterization of the hero is an important aspect of Buchan's fantasy. Hannay is a clubman, which means that he is above all a gentleman and an amateur, a member of the upper middle classes with an independent income, and one who lives by a very strong moral and social code in which the ideals of honor, duty, and country play a primary role. He is not a professional agent, nor does he belong even temporarily to any formal governmental secret service. Even during the height of the war, he does his spying while on brief leave from his main occupation, the traditional gentlemanly one of military officer. After the war, his great dream is to settle down in a lovely country house in the Cotswolds and serve happily as the local squire. In these respects, Hannay symbolizes the continuity of British social tradition, the vision of an ordered and hierarchical social world which has lasted from time immemorial. The search for reassurance that this tradition can go on is one basic impetus of Buchan's fantasy:

> Many of my pre-War interests revived, but, so to speak, on sufferance, for I felt that they had become terribly fragile. Would anything remain of the innocencies of the old life? I was reassured by two short holidays. One was a tramp in the Cotswolds from which I returned with the conviction that the essential England could not perish. This field had sent bowmen to Agincourt; down that hill Rupert's men, swaying in their saddles, had fled after Naseby; this village had given Wellington a general; and from another the parson's son had helped to turn the tide in the Indian Mutiny. To-day the land was as quiet as in the beginning, and mowers were busy in the hay. A second holiday took me to

Tweedside hills. There, far up in the glens, I found a shepherd's wife who had four sons serving. Jock, she told me cheerfully, was in France with the Royal Scots; Jamie was in "a bit ca'd Sammythrace"; Tam was somewhere on the Arctic shore and "sair troubled wi' his teeth"; and Davie was outside the walls of Jerusalem. Her kind old eyes were infinitely comforting. I felt that Jock and Jamie and Tam and Davie would return and would take up their shepherd's trade as dutifully as their father. Samothrace and Murmansk and Palestine would be absorbed, as Otterburn and Flodden had been, into the ageless world of pastoral.

Though this statement would sound right at home in Richard Hannay's mouth, it was actually made by Buchan, himself, in his autobiography.

But if the clubman's image of the world as a place of unchanging and stable social tradition is the ideal, Buchan is well aware of its fragility. It is significant that his hero is not only a clubman, but a colonial and a self-made man, accustomed to scenes of violence and at home in the wilderness, for only such a hero might be capable of coping with the manifold dangers which threaten "the innocencies of the old life." For the traditional world is threatened both by external and internal enemies. New forces of barbarism have arisen on the periphery of civilized society (i.e. the British empire). In addition, there are threats from within as the average man's civilized restraints and his committment to traditional social values are subverted by the increasing moral chaos of modern life:

> The barriers between the conscious and the subconscious have always been pretty stiff in the average man. But now with the general loosening of screws they are growing shaky and the two worlds are getting mixed—That is why I say you can't any longer take the clear psychology of most civilized human beings for granted. Something is welling up from primeval deeps to muddy it. . . . The civilized is far simpler than the primeval. All history has been an effort to

> make definitions, clear rules of thought, clear rules of con-
> duct, social sanctions, by which we can conduct our life.
> These are the work of the conscious self. The subconscious
> is an elementary and lawless thing. If it intrudes on life, two
> results must follow. There will be a weakening of the power
> of reasoning, which after all is the thing that brings men
> nearest to the Almighty. And there will be a failure of nerve.

The external threats are most strikingly dramatized in the
fantasy of a great racial drama which is being played out on the
world stage. Buchan was by no means a virulent racist. As a man
and a colonial administrator he appears to have been unshake-
ably convinced of the superior virtues of the Anglo-Saxon. But
there is little evidence that he was hostile to other races and
cultures. Even in his stories he is no direct manipulator of the
popular paranoia surrounding the "yellow peril" like Saxe
Rohmer. Nevertheless, the adventures of Richard Hannay have
an unmistakably racist flavor, as if in fantasy Buchan was able to
give vent to feelings about racial good and evil which he would
never have made the basis of calculated political action or statement. Hannay's continual and automatic use of racial epithets
like "dago," "nigger," "wog" while doubtless a real enough
characteristic of a colonial gentleman of his era, is one of those
aspects of Buchan's work that most embarrassingly grates on the
contemporary reader's ear, preventing us from accepting Hannay
as a hero without serious reservations.

But, on a deeper level than that of racial epithet and the instinctive superiority of the Anglo-Saxon gentleman, Buchan's
treatment of the drama of racial conflict reflects his sense that the
English Christian tradition is no longer able to cope with the
larger social forces which the twentieth century has unleashed
in the world. Buchan presents these forces as spiritual and racial,
rather than political and economic and in a number of ways he
seems rather ambiguously attracted by the enemy, though
ostensibly his stories represent heroic victories over the enemy's
conspiracy. Indeed, the Buchan hero is often strongly attracted

by the racial or spiritual force represented by the opposing supervillain.

> There would be no mercy from Stumm. That large man was beginning to fascinate me, even though I hated him. Gaudian [another German agent] was clearly a good fellow, a white man and a gentleman. I could have worked with him, for he belonged to my own totem. But the other was an incarnation of all that makes Germany detestable, and yet he wasn't altogether the ordinary German and I couldn't help admiring him. I noticed he neither smoked nor drank. His grossness was apparently not in the way of fleshy appetites. Cruelty . . . was his hobby, but there were other things in him, some of them good, and he had that kind of crazy patriotism which becomes a religion.

In *The Three Hostages,* Hannay must use all his spiritual resources to overcome the psychological spell of supervillain Dominick Medina, one of whose powers involves the almost hypnotic control of others, the capacity to bring both followers and opponents under his complete spiritual domination.

On the surface these supervillains and the forces they represent are evil because they pose a basic threat to the good tradition of the clubland world. Yet, in Buchan's fantasy, the new forces have a way of seeming far more compelling and attractive than the ordered life for which the hero officially yearns. After all, who would actually fritter away his life in the routine pastoral joys of the Cotswolds when he might be dashing about the world unmasking secret conspiracies which are, fortunately, everywhere. We recall that at the very beginning of the Hannay saga our hero had become so bored with civilized life in London that he was about to return to the African veld. The murderous intervention of a German conspiracy saves him just in time. Later, in pursuit of the Islamic prophet Greenmantle, one of Hannay's friends regrets that the prophet's attractive message of primitive fanaticism should have become perverted to the evil ends of German imperialism:

Well, Greenmantle is the prophet of this great simplicity.
He speaks straight to the heart of Islam, and it's an honorable message. But for our sins it's been twisted into part of
this damned German propaganda. His unworldliness has
been used for a cunning political move, and his creed of
space and simplicity for the furtherance of the last word in
human degeneracy. My God, Dick, it's like seeing St. Francis
run by Messalina.

A similar ambivalence reveals itself in Hannay's romantic life.
In the course of his adventures he meets and falls in love with the
lovely Mary Lamington, who is in most respects the very epitome
of English womanhood. Hannay dreams of retiring to a country
place in the Cotswolds with his beloved Mary, yet the real intensity to their romance results from the fact that Mary is also
a secret agent, one of the most daring members of the informal
espionage group Hannay himself works with. Not surprisingly,
the supervillain Graf von Schwabing also falls in love with her
and ruins his conspiracy through an attempt to take Mary back
to Germany with him. Even before his first encounter with Mary,
Hannay's own feelings about the opposite sex had been most
strongly aroused by the German agent Hilda von Einem:

I see I have written that I know nothing about women. But
every man has in his bones a consciousness of sex. I was shy
and perturbed, but horribly fascinated. This slim woman,
poised and exquisitely like some statue between the pillared
lights, with her fair cloud of hair, her long delicate face,
and her pale bright eyes, had the glamor of a wild dream. I
hated her instinctively, hated her intensely, but I longed to
arouse her interest.

When Hannay finally marries his perfect English lady spy and
settles down to the life of a country squire in the Cotswolds, it is
not long before he is drawn back into the fascinating world of
new racial and spiritual forces. The comforts of the traditional

life quickly pale when a visitor brings news of new forces at
work in the East:

> That took him to Central Asia, and he observed that if he
> ever left England again he would make for those parts, since
> they were the refuge of all the superior rascality of creation.
> He had a notion that something very odd might happen
> there in the long run. "Think of it!" he cried. "All the places
> with names like spells Bokhara, Samarkand—run by seedy
> little gangs of Communist Jews. It won't go on forever.
> Some day a new Genghis Khan or a Timour will be thrown
> up out of the maelstrom. Europe is confused enough, but
> Asia is ancient Chaos."

The way in which the basic spy themes of conspiracies and
disguises are treated in Buchan's works also illustrate a curious
ambivalence. Though the British countryside is explicitly presented as an ideal world with the values of the British social
tradition as the apogee of the civilized world, this way of life
is also shown to be riddled with weakness and conspiracy.
Significantly, the arch conspirators typically wear the garb of
symbolic representatives of the tradition. The evil German
agent with eyes hooded like a hawk is disguised as a Scottish
country gentleman and amateur historian. The Graf von Schwabing has passed for many years as Morgan Ivery, liberal politician
and philanthropist. And their agents seem to be average British
citizens. English country life thus seems at once the epitome
of human civilization and a base deception, riddled with enemy
agents. Buchan's treatment of disguise is even more curious. His
supervillains are above all men of many faces, and their skill at
disguises is implicitly condemned by contrast with the honesty,
openness and direct integrity of the British character. Though
Hannay's missions frequently force him to dissemble his identity,
he usually feels extremely uncomfortable when he must pretend
to act in a way contrary to his nature. Yet this moral contrast
between honest pilgrim Hannay and the enemy agents who
delight in their deceptions and disguises is undercut on numerous

occasions by characters who reflect a fascination with the idea of the British identity swallowed up in some alien way of life. The most striking of these characters, Sandy Arbuthnot, was evidently based on the historical figure of T. E. Lawrence. The way in which Buchan develops this character suggests the profound ambivalence which his generation felt toward the character and exploits of Lawrence. Sandy is as British as they come, the off-spring of an aristocratic Scottish family with a long and brilliant tradition of political and social leadership. Yet he has the capacity to become so totally identified with an alien way of life that he ends up not merely as an effective agent, but a leader of some bizarre tribe or sect:

> Billy Arbuthnot's boys? His father was at Harrow with me. I know the fellow—Harry used to bring him down to fish— tallish, with a lean, high-boned face and a pair of brown eyes like a pretty girl's. I know his record, too. There's a good deal about him in this office. He rode through Yemen, which no white man ever did before. The Arabs let him pass, for they thought him stark mad and argued that the hand of Allah was heavy enough on him without their efforts. He's blood-brother to every kind of Albanian bandit. Also he used to take a hand in Turkish politics, and got a huge repu-tation.

Sandy's extraordinary conduct seems to be the same kind of dis-sembling for which the villains are condemned, yet for Buchan, there is clearly an important difference. Here we encounter one of the prime virtues of the race:

> Lean brown men from the ends of the earth may be seen on the London pavements now and then in creased clothes, walking with the light outland step, slinking into clubs as if they could not remember whether or not they belonged to them. From them you may get news of Sandy. Better still, you will hear of him at little forgotten fishing ports where the Albanian mountains dip to the Adriatic. If you struck a Mecca pilgrimage the odds are you would meet a dozen of

Sandy's friends in it. In shepherd's huts in the Caucasus you will find bits of his cast-off clothing, for he had a knack of shedding garments as he goes. In the caravanserais of Bokhara and Samarkand he is known, and there are Shikaris in the Pamirs who still speak of him around their fires. If you were going to visit Petrograd or Rome or Cairo it would be no use asking him for introductions; if he gave them, they would lead you into strange haunts. But if Fate compelled you to go to Lhasa or Yarkand or Seistan he could map out the road for you and pass the word to potent friends. We call ourselves insular, but the truth is that we are the only race on earth that can produce men capable of getting inside the skin of remote peoples. Perhaps the Scotch are better than the English, but we're all a thousand per cent better than anybody else. Sandy was the wandering Scot carried to the pitch of genius. In old days he would have led a crusade or discovered a new road to the Indies. To-day he merely roamed as the spirit moved him, till the war swept him up and dumped him down in my batallion.

Richard Hannay, the muscular Christian squire who fights to protect the old stabilities of British social tradition from the dangerous forces which threaten it, represents one side of Buchan's fantasy. But there is an equally important side encapsulated in this description of Sandy: the lure of the exotic, the dream of casting off the burden of identity like a suit of old clothes and letting oneself be swallowed up in the mysterious spiritual worlds of alien peoples, the desire to escape from the dull routines of civilized life into a more primitive and daring world, the search for a crusade to deepen and intensify the sense of life, to get away from the orderly and civilized patterns of the Cotswolds which seem so constrained and restrictive. In this area of his fantasy, Buchan reflected the same tensions that have been so characteristic of a whole stream of modern Western European feeling and literature. The quest for the exotic, the urge to cast aside the constraining roles of civilized man, the ambivalent fascination with colonial peoples; these are the same urges which were articulated more powerfully and tragically in the life of a *poète maudit* like Rimbaud or in later works of Joseph Conrad like *Heart of Darkness,* or in both life and paintings of Paul Gauguin. The social-psychological causes of these curious urges in modern European culture have been often explored from many different perspectives. Freud argued in his *Civilization and its Discontents* that the development of civilized society inevitably brought with it a neurotic desire to escape and to destroy. His explanation seems compelling in many ways, though it does not completely account for one central feature of this cultural phenomenon, its relation to colonialism and imperialism. It would appear that at a certain point in the development of democratic imperialistic societies, there emerges a fascination with the idea of entering into the identity of the colonial peoples. One of the key features of this fascination is a lurking fear that these peoples' traditional cultures which have been destroyed or transformed by imperialistic power, possessed some deeper insight into the meaning of life. While this feeling has been an important theme in the culture of Britain and France since the end of the nineteenth century, it has only recently become widespread in America, where it has particularly taken the form of a fascination with traditional American Indian cultures.

Important cultural themes or ambivalences like this are often explored on a conscious and articulate level in the work of philosophers, artists and novelists. In contemporary English literature, for example, the theme of fascination with the traditional culture of colonial peoples was explored with great subtlety and insight in Forster's *A Passage to India.* Popular literature, however, tends, as we have seen, to work toward a resolution of value conflicts and a reaffirmation of conventional beliefs or perspectives. With this in view, we are in a better position to see why Buchan's fantasy world was widely enough shared by his generation to make his stories highly successful, and also why more recent generations have found that they cannot become easily identified with the network of assumptions and attitudes that rules this landscape of the imagination.

Buchan's work represents a world in which the "Anglo-Saxon" Christian social tradition is under attack, but is still strong enough in the minds of men to be not only victorious in defeating its enemies, but to be revealed as an expression of the underlying truth of the universe. This latter characteristic is especially important in defining the spy stories of Buchan and most of his contemporaries in comparison with more contemporary works, like those of Ian Fleming. There are, as we will see, many fundamental similarities between the epics of James Bond and Richard Hannay, but one of the most striking differences is the almost complete absence in Bond's world of the sense of providential governance which still plays such an important part in Buchan. We have seen how the sense of Bunyanesque moral allegory pervades the Hannay stories and how coincidence takes on the meaning of an illustration of higher powers taking a hand in human affairs. While there is certainly enough moral melodrama and coincidence in the works of Ian Fleming, there is never a hint that the confrontation between our hero and his enemies is being shaped by the decrees of providence, or that Bond and his allies are being tested by transcendent forces. It is probably the association which Buchan makes between Hannay's beliefs and actions and the symbols of religious tradition that makes it most difficult for contemporary readers to enter imaginatively into his stories. While Hannay's casual racist slurs might be accepted as no more than tics of character, or melodramatic artifices, the way they are in Fleming, when we are asked to associate Hannay's obvious ideological limitations with the views of heaven, the delicate tissue of plausibility and emotional identification breaks down and we become too conscious of dated moral attitudes to temporarily suspend our own committments and attitudes.

If Richard Hannay were only the clubland hero defending British social tradition with the help of higher powers, Buchan's work would doubtless have faded into the oblivion that has swallowed up most of his contemporaries and followers like Dornford Yates and "Sapper." However, Buchan also responded in his fantasies to a more contemporary sense of ambivalence about the social and religious tradition. While he worked to resolve this ambivalence through characters like Sandy Arbuthnot who remains a solid British aristocrat despite his total involvement in Eastern ways of life, the fascination with the new forces unleashed in the world remains an important undercurrent of Buchan's fantasy. Though his works of adventure are optimistic on the surface and he imagines a revitalized Christian social tradition able to overcome the threats of the twentieth century, his stories also reflect on a deeper level a sense of the critical failure of modern civilization and a yearning for a more glorious, simpler and more mystical way of life. On this level, he still speaks to some of the major currents in the fantasy life of men in the twentieth century. The modern spy story, even in the cynical and despairing intrigues of John Le Carre and Len Deighton, has come to express this kind of feeling still more strongly. Thus, Buchan was instrumental in giving both a model of form and an inner spirit to the story of espionage, giving it through his vision of the world a capacity to express in terms of contemporary international politics and intrigue, the yearning for a lost world of fullness and heroism. In this respect, it might be said of Buchan's fantasy vision what he himself said of one of his contemporaries:

> He was not quite of this world; or, rather, he was of an earlier, fairer world that our civilization has overlaid. He lived close to the kindly earth, and then he discovered the kindlier air, and that pure exultant joy of living which he had always sought.

Henry James's
The American
As a Centennial Novel

ROBERT FALK

Novels celebrating political anniversaries, births of nations, or important historical events belong to a rare and special class of fiction. In America Kenneth Roberts, Gore Vidal, James Michener and others have written novels about past history, sometimes patriotic and sometimes revisionist. Michener's *Centennial* belongs to the type more by its title than its content. It reads more like a documentary account of a Colorado region, than a "novel," as he himself terms it. In 1876, America's first anniversary of the nation's founding, very little interest was shown by the new generation of novelists, Howells, James, and Mark Twain. John DeForest alone sensed the epic significance of the Civil War and slavery as themes for fiction. During and after the publication of *Miss Ravenel's Conversion* (1868) there was much speculation about "the Great American Novel" and who would write it and what it would be like. Cooper and Mrs. Stowe were cited as possible precedents for handling broad social conditions in an epic vein. The West was ripe for a Mark Twain, but he did not or could not handle it in terms of conventional fiction as it was then understood. And in 1876 there was no suitable precedent in English fiction for a nationalistic novel or for a centennial one.

Henry James, taking up his residence in Paris in 1875 and committed to a long stay in Europe, was a most unlikely candidate to write "the American novel" of the centennial year. At thirty-five and the author of two novels and a number of short stories with European settings, he was just beginning to be known on both sides of the Atlantic. He had already decided that the materials his own country offered the novelist were thin and unpromising, and the American scene was not his dish of tea. In *Hawthorne* (1879) he was to describe the American background as "crude and simple," lacking the richness, complexity, and accumulated tradition necessary to the lifeblood of the novelist. His famous list of "items of high civilization" absent from the American scene brought him into debate with Howells in which James insisted that it takes "an old civilization" to set a novelist in motion. America, he felt, lacked "paraphernalia"— manners, customs, usages, habits on which the novelist must depend.

Despite his indifference to the native scene as literary inspiration, James was well aware of the legends, fables, and tall tales which had flourished during the early nineteenth century as a part of the national folklore. Constance Rourke was the first to point out in 1931 that as a small boy James frequented Barnum's "where the whole American legend was racily sketched," and he was also familiar with the "color of the California adventure, with its outline of the composite American character." Christopher Newman was James's version of the western innocent abroad, and his portrait is colored by what he referred to in *Hawthorne* as "that American humour of which of late years we have heard so much." But in addition to his western origins, Newman's character was shaped by other aspects of the American myth. He was a business man, an innocent, a Ben Franklin, a Yankee of sorts, even a Lincolnesque figure. And he was both a subject of satire and a representative of the kind of romantic philosophy of the 18th century emanating from France and given expression in Crevecoeur's idealistic essay, "What is an American?" In the winter of 1875-1876 when James began the first serial chapters of *The American* he did not suggest in personal letters or elsewhere that he intended to seize the occasion to portray the generic American as he conceived of his development in a century of democratic political experiment. Still, the self-conscious nationalism of the title and the intellectual stimulation of the centennial hopes and aspirations of that year must have been primary considerations to the young novelist.

Almost 30 years later, when James re-read and revised the text for the Preface to his collected edition, he made no mention of the centennial year of its original composition. Instead, James concentrated on the way in which the idea for the *donnée* came into his mind in a Boston horse-car, and he also enumerated the weaknesses he found in the plot. His self-deprecations and criticisms of the novel probably derived from the frustrations which followed his unhappy experience with the stage version of the novel which ran for three months in 1891 in the British provinces and in London. His effort to appeal to the popular demand for sentiment and melodrama (Claire marries Newman, the Bellegardes are defeated, Valentin is resurrected and reconciled to Lord Deepmere by Noémie) required revisions which were difficult and reprehensible to James. The theme of the American-European contrast was reduced to a stagey intrigue and comedy which failed to add to his literary stature and paid him small royalties. It is not surprising that he saw the original novel through a screen of disappointment when he revised it for the Preface in 1905-7.

James's summary of the plot for the novel is that of a "compatriot" who, in another country and in an aristocratic society, would be betrayed and suffer "at the hands of persons pretending to represent the highest possible civilization and to be of an order in every way superior to his own." This American would then find himself accidentally in possession of the means of revenge against his aristocratic adversaries. He would hold and cherish it, but in the end he would throw it away in disgust, "a strong man indifferent to his strength," and too strong within himself to resort to the assertion of his "rights." James emphasizes that it is not a Christlike forgiveness of his enemies so much as an "aversion" to react and a natural magnanimity of mind which would "deeply appeal to our sympathy." The Bellegardes, on the other hand, would be shown as cruel and arrogant. It occurred to James that he had been "plotting arch-romance without knowing it."

The remainder of the Preface discusses this and other faults of the novel. James recalled that, after making some progress, his ship had "a hole in its side more than sufficient to have sunk it." He spoke of his "affront to verisimilitude," and confessed that the Bellegardes, instead of rejecting Newman as too "commercial," would positively have jumped at him for a son-in-law. He was concerned about keeping Newman "consistent"—a point I will discuss later in this chapter—and he further acknowledged that Claire was never fully realized as a flesh and blood heroine. James's account of the plot of the novel applies only to the final third of the story from the point where Newman discovers he has been betrayed, and Urbain and his mother have withdrawn their support of his suit of Claire. This occurs in Chapter 18 of a total of 26 chapters. The question was what would he "do" in such a predicament? But, proportionately, nearly the first two-thirds of the novel are devoted to Newman's native origins, the national legends and American "humour" which were part of American folklore, and the witty international contrasts between Newman and Valentin, the dialogues with his confidante, Mrs. Tristram, and the subplot of the Nioches. The reason for the novel's title, the obvious symbolism of Newman's name, and the centennial occasion of its writing all went unmentioned in the late Preface. I believe these elements were strongly present in James's mind when he began to write, and they play a larger role in the finished work than has been acknowledged by critics of the novel.

Why the Boston horse-car? In a recent unpublished dissertation on *The American* Judith Collas has shown that the "horse-car" became an important symbol for Henry James, Sr. and the frequent subject of table conversations in the James family. In *Society, the Redeemed Form of Man* (1879) H.J., Sr. described the horse-car as evidence of "God's visible presence . . . dwelling among men." At the dinner table the talk often turned to the horse-car as a symbol of the relative spiritual states of America and Europe. In comparison to manners produced by "an authoritative church and a consecrated state" as in the Old World, the Boston horse-car was an emblem to H.J., Sr. of mankind in a state of freedom where mutual forbearance and the right of one's neighbor were pursued with such unselfishness and deference as to make it "our true Schechinah at this day." Thus, it was his father's Americanism and idealism which first shaped James's philosophic theme of the contrast between the New World and the Old, a theme which he refined upon in most of his best fiction.

In the late Prefaces James liked to use dramatic metaphors for the art of fiction. The novel could be divided into two halves, approximately equal, in which the first half was the preparation or theatre for the second half, or the resolution in dramatic terms of the situation developed in the earlier part. Often he found the preparatory half became disproportionately long, leaving his two halves "unequal." His language is not precise on this, but sometimes he referred to the two aspects of the novel as "picture" (i.e. preparation) and "scene" (i.e. dramatic conflict or resolution). In his Preface to *The American* James does not use this image. However, the account of the *donnée* is devoted entirely to the "betrayal" of Newman, his revenge, the intrigue, the final decision to forfeit his revenge—in short dramatic resolution of the story. This was also the briefer half, whereas the beginning and longer half was taken up with Newman's origins in the West and the international contrast in terms of H.J., Sr.'s "horse-car" philosophy. Like Cooper writing about the prairie amid the gilded butterflies of Paris salons, James was remote from the materials he needed to build Newman into a convincing and composite American in his native setting. It was a bold stroke to attempt to bring together the myths and legends which had become part of the national folklore, and blend them into a romantic love-plot in a European setting.

Constance Rourke noted that Newman's local origin was never given, though the Pacific coast was the scene of his first financial successes. We are introduced to him in Chapter I where he is lounging with outstretched legs in the Salon Carré in the Louvre in Paris. He is described as healthy, tall, lean, and muscular with a well-formed head. His legs, a detail possibly suggested by the angular figure of Lincoln, or by the cartoons of Uncle Sam which were appearing in *Harper's Weekly* in the post-Appomattox years, are often in an extended position which James says "was always a sort of symbol of his taking mental possession of a scene." He has "the flat jaw and sinewy neck which are frequent in the American type." His other features are described in a series of paradoxes: "that typical vagueness which is not vacuity, that blankness which is not simplicity." His eye expressed a blend of innocence and experience. It was "both frigid yet friendly, frank yet cautious, shrewd yet credulous, positive yet sceptical." Good nature, ease and informal in manner (in contrast to the stiff formality of the Bellegardes), naive about art and artists, but receptive of new experiences—such are the characteristics of this "new" man as he lounges in the exotic setting of the Louvre.

In the omniscient narrative manner of his earlier fiction James summarizes Newman's early life. He was a Californian who had served in the war and come out of it penniless. At fourteen he had had to earn his own supper and had known how to go without it. Like Ragged Dick of Horatio Alger (except for the western setting) Newman went to the big city where his luck turned. He came to San Francisco (James compares him to Ben Franklin coming to Philadelphia), but Newman even lacked the penny Franklin used to buy a loaf of bread. His determination to succeed and "to make money" gradually bore fruit. He became a success in the classic American way, as much through Algeresque luck and pluck as Ben Franklin industry.

Newman describes to Tristram an experience which occurred in Wall Street, a psychic transformation or "vastation" beyond his will which changed his life and sent him to Europe. He was sitting in a drab and greasy hack contemplating a $60,000 deal he was bent on at the expense of a rival when he experienced a sudden disgust for his business life. He decided to throw away his chance, become a new man inside his "old skin," and he sailed for Europe. The episode seems to prepare for his later decision to renounce his revenge against the Bellegardes. It may also be a transposition of James's own effort to exorcise the American life he might have led, like Spencer Brydon in "The Jolly Corner," and to live in Europe. Newman's experience prepares him for the role of gentleman-hero of a romantic tragedy, or semi-tragedy. Newman breaks from his past, and like his creator, is living in Europe ready for a new experience. "I have come to Europe to get the best out of it I can. I want to see all the great things," he says, "and do what the clever people do." The episode breaks sharply from the native elements of Newman's history, and it may have concerned James in revising the novel for the Preface that he was not "consistent."

Newman's character develops through dialogue and action, talks with his confidante, Mrs. Tristram, scenes with the Nioches, and with his friend Valentin. The international contrast grows steadily in his favor, with occasional drops into satire and recollections of his American limitations. He confesses to know nothing about history or art or foreign tongues, but is determined "to know something about Europe before I have done with it." Mrs. Tristram replies with a "Bravo! . . . . You are the great Western Barbarian, stepping forth in his innocence and might, gazing awhile at this poor effete Old World, and then swooping down on it." Here James points with irony to the exaggerations of 18th century French *philosophes,* like Rousseau or Voltaire, who imposed their own romantic primitivism on the American character. But Newman protests: "I am not a barbarian. . . . I am a highly civilized man."

Although he has renounced the money-game and the success dream, Newman's conception of marriage has a preponderance of the commercialism attributed to him by the Bellegarde family. He tells his confidante,

> What else have I toiled and struggled for all these years? I have succeeded, and now what am I to do with my success? To make it perfect, as I see it, there must be a beautiful woman perched on the pile, like a statue on a monument. . . . I want to possess, in a word, the best article in the market.

In an essay by Henry James's father, "Property as a Symbol," H. J. Sr. wrote: "You cannot set your life's happiness upon any outward possession, be it a wife or a child, or riches, without an incessant shuddering or dread." Philosophically Newman is the source of his own defeat, but the narrative attributes the villainy to the Bellegarde's opposition to the marriage—another inconsistency in his portrayal. James's handling of the trans-Atlantic contrast between Newman and Valentin has some of the best writing of the novel and is most revealing of Newman's "American" traits. Under the surface of these exchanges is the serious theme of democrat versus aristocrat which occupied Cooper and others before James. But the talks between the two friends belong to James's youthful, comic manner and to the history of American humor. Both sides of the contrast are treated with indulgent exaggeration. Bellegarde envies Newman his self-made wealth and his "air of being thoroughly at home in the world." Valentin tells Newman that he has lacked the American's freedom to do what he wanted because his place in life had been predetermined by his station. He asks his friend what it is he has missed. "It is the proud consciousness of honest toil," is Newman's reply, "of having manufactured a few washtubs." And when Bellegarde protests that this alone does not explain him, Newman soars away in a patriotic strain which the reader must accept as James's dig at the tendency to make the eagle scream. "Then it's the privilege of being an American citizen," said Newman. "That sets a man up."

In telling Bellegrade of his earlier life, Newman finds it amusing to color episodes in the manner of western tale-tellers. He had learned the trick from "sitting with western humorists, in knots, around cast-iron stoves and had seen 'tall' stories grow taller without toppling over." Valentin is sceptical, but he too enjoys a good story. Entering into this spirit he gives his own version of Newman's life:

> You have spent some deadly dull hours, and you have done some extremely disagreeable things: you have shovelled sand, as a boy, for supper, and you have eaten roast dog in a gold-diggers' camp. You have stood casting up figures for ten hours at a time, and you have sat through Methodist sermons for the sake of looking at a pretty girl in another pew.

Contrarily, Newman saw Valentin as "the ideal Frenchman, the Frenchman of tradition and romance." In short, each saw the other through a screen of romantic convention and each was aware that the stereotype was a part of the joke. In their attitudes toward two crucial subjects—women and honour—the two friends diverged. Valentin was at once sentimental, chivalric, and rakish toward women, attitudes which led to his affair with Noémie Nioche and his death in a duel with his rival lover. Newman's attempts to teach Valentin common sense fails. He considers the Frenchman's constant talk about women and honour "analogous to the cooing of pigeons and the chattering of monkeys, and even inconsistent with a fully-developed human character." Toward Noémie he is quite aware of her true motives and at the same time indulgent toward her and her shabby-genteel father.

The "Puritan conscience," an over-serious view of life, and the tendency to suspect beauty and art as somehow immoral—these were American qualities which preoccupied James in his fiction. The Babcock episode in *The American* yields an added dimension to the portrait of Newman. The Reverend Babcock is a foil for Newman. He is a prude, a prig, suspicious of Europe and its "impure" art. He regards Newman as "cynical" and too much devoted to his own amusement. Newman replies: "You worry too much; that's what's the matter with you." They have a disagreement over the paintings of Luini, which Babcock considers immoral. In writing of this experience to Mrs. Tristram, Newman is puzzled as to just what all this means. He tells her that after parting with Babcock he had met a worldly Englishman who was precisely Babcock's opposite number. The Englishman tells Newman that he is too "virtuous."

> He told me in a friendly way that I was cursed with a conscience; that I judged things like a Methodist and talked about them like an old lady. This was rather bewildering. Which of my two critics was I to believe? I didn't worry about it and soon made up my mind they were both idiots.

Thus James says that the American represents the ideal balance between two opposed extremes.

The portrait of Christopher Newman is a highly complex assimilation of national legends and autobiographical elements. On close analysis it is full of contradictions and inconsistencies, but the final effect is satisfying to readers of the novel. Insofar as he was a centennial hero, Newman's character is a composite of many traits. It can be read in terms of James Sr.'s philosophical idealism about the "New World." And it can be read as a part of the American "joke" whereby the international contrast is carried out by a witty exaggeration of both sides of the proposition. James uses, but only deftly and lightly, certain of the American myths: the western adventure and tall-tale, the Horatio Alger boyhood and Franklin story of success. There are hints of the innocent American countryman in his views of art and Europe, and in his accounts of business dealings are touches of the "shrewd" Yankee trader and the business tycoon. Newman is also Henry James whose "complex fate" involved balancing off the values of America and Europe. But as the romantic plot of the betrayed compatriot becomes dominant, Newman changes. He becomes increasingly a Jamesian spokesman, a youthful Strether, and the "reflector" of the experience of the novel.

Despite his own reservations as expressed in the late Preface and despite the objections raised by Victorian readers at the time it appeared, including Howells, who were disappointed at the tragic ending without a wedding and a happy couple, James was nevertheless content with his early "international" novel. It has remained one of the most popular among readers of James. Some critics who prefer the later and impressionistic style of *The Ambassadors* or *The Golden Bowl* regard *The American* as early and unsophisticated, perhaps influenced by James's own strictures as to its excessive romance. Yet he himself included it in a list of his "advanced" novels to a young man who asked advice on reading his books. Included with it on this list were *The Wings of the Dove, The Ambassadors,* and *The Golden Bowl.* Even the fine *Portrait of a Lady* was not on this list. In comparison with the later novels, Christopher Newman's history was written with more verve and humor than James's later style contained. James felt that his "affront to verisimilitude" and his over-romantic juxtaposition of the American hero with his cruel adversaries were faults of his youth and inexperience. But readers today may be less concerned with the plot elements of the latter third of the novel, with the cloak-and-dagger revenge story and secret rendezvous and the skeleton in the Bellegarde's closet. They may reread it today with more interest in the fact that this portrait of an American came closer to a "centennial" novel than any of James's contemporary writers of fiction. The first two-thirds, or what James sometimes called "picture," remains as a convincing blend of diverse materials to produce in Christopher Newman an idealized yet authentic "American" type in the year 1876.

Consensus: How Academics Keep From Murdering Each Other At Professional Meetings

LOUIS FILLER

General Robert E. Lee, viewing battle movements and the dispersal of armed forces, remarked that it was fortunate that war was so terrible, for otherwise one could learn to love it. The outlooks of Confederate Lee and his Union antagonists in battle, however, were relatively simple, compared with those they were afterwards required to develop. Earlier, means for survival came before anything else, and battle-lines were distinct. Later, there was commerce between North and South. Society's needs created new alliances, so that friends and enemies became intermixed. Relationships, goals, the very words passed between former foes were subtly changed, so that protagonists could hardly themselves have known just what they meant or intended.

Both North and South were relatively clear in purposes when they threw their hundreds of thousands of young men into fighting formations along Virginia, Kentucky, and Missouri fronts. But the subsequent accounts of these actions by their historians took shapes which could not have been foreseen. As good a metaphor for their complexities as could be found would have been the career of Woodrow Wilson. It starts with his chaotic fancies as a young, post-war southerner who aspired to national consequence. It widens into a stream of ideas and interpretations which in time becomes a Niagara of eloquence and prophecy. Finally—following World War I—it ends in all but total silence as he retreats into himself, once his matured vision of a League of Nations has been rejected. The rest, however, is very far from silence.

Not only young southerners, but young northerners, struggled to develop new formulas which would, from their separate viewpoints, satisfactorily explain the national crisis for the new time. It is remarkable that not a little related northerners and southerners despite sectional differences. In the South, Sidney Lanier in conventional poetic measures expressed his contempt for industry. Sang Lanier:

O Trade! O Trade! Would thou wert dead!
The Time needs heart— 'tis tired of head. . . .[1]

Meanwhile in the North what the drama historian Arthur Hobson Quinn called "an Indian summer of romance" emerged. In effect, there was in the nation as a whole an emotional and cultural revulsion against "the new industry" which in post-War decades produced little of enduring cultural value; the future was with a new fictional realism and an irregular poetic rhythm. However, the anti-industry feeling did serve southern traditions better than it did northern. The South, after all, was the country's old agricultural section, with a long history of suspicion of northern mill-owners and money-changers. Northern poetasters who agreed with them, even when they sentimentalized the boys in blue and the boys in grey,[2] were in essence conceding that the war from the southern side was at least partly in protest against heartless, anti-humanistic, machine-like social forces.

Woodrow Wilson quoted Sidney Lanier, and throughout his career emphasized what he thought of as heart-truths. Indeed, one of Wilson's favorite words in essays and oratory was "heart." Wilson's major achievement was not that. It was to persuade leaders of society that he was also practical, and scholars that his views of sectional differences were based on facts. "Dr. Wilson's" first major publishing success, *Congressional Government* (1885), was hailed by northern as well as southern reviewers as a thoughtful critique of what Wilson called "government by committee," government which had drained the presidency of strength and hurt democratic processes. Hidden in Wilson's charges and inaccuracies was his bitterness toward Federal post-War reconstruction policy. It was a policy which had punished the old South and its leaders by depriving them of the suffrage and giving it to the freed slaves.

What Wilson had discovered was that others besides dedicated southerners like himself had tired of congressional rule, though all in the North were not so committed—they did not have to be—to white supremacy as was Wilson.

Wilson's campaign to find a national forum for his views was remarkable. In the South, he honored Robert E. Lee. But addressing more national audiences he was vigorous in expressing reverence for the martyred Abraham Lincoln. His book, *Division and Reunion, 1829-1889* (1893), was prepared more soberly than was his wont. He had used such romantic words as " 'twas" in his book-long essay on George Washington, which did not contain a single original fact or idea. Aside from his use of Lincoln, Wilson would not concede anything to the northern point of view on the war. It had been fought, he declared, on constitutional differences. It had been a tragedy which had brought honor to both sides.

Supposed to be concerned for history and scholarship, Wilson did not hesitate to challenge his betters in the field. In an unsigned book review—Wilson was extraordinarily keen on when to express himself publicly and when to lie low—he dared to criticize James Ford Rhodes's *History of the United States,* which included what was to be recognized as a standard examination of the workings of slavery. Wilson dismissed Rhodes's long labors as lacking "insight." As in other instances, it was Rhodes who was apologetic, not Wilson. Rhodes wrote the editor of the periodical, offering to correct any errors his anonymous critic would point out.[3] Wilson had no information; but he could maneuver with a resourcefulness beyond Rhodes.

This is not to suggest that Rhodes was putty in the hands of a Machiavellian southerner, nor were others who expressed awareness of Wilson's bold attacks in fields which they had themselves worked intensively. There were critics who in professional journals and elsewhere freely expressed their views of Wilson's scholarship and who were conscious of his southern background while doing so. The point was that they agreed with him that history was culture as well as data, and that a factual statement might fail because it did not reveal understanding. In Wilson's graduate school days at Johns Hopkins University, the "German" method of research was producing theses firm with data. But they were not memorable except to the specialist interested in footnotes and references and other doctoral details. Wilson gained his first teaching job at the new Bryn Mawr College near Philadelphia with his long and dubious essay in congressional rule, after having been beaten out for another academic job by a much more soundly-trained historian, one Frank H. Hodder, who went on to a long-term professorship at the University of Kansas and to the writing of several worthy papers not warranting mention here.

At Johns Hopkins with Wilson was young Frederick Jackson Turner of Wisconsin, with good connections which would enable him to obtain a professorship at the University of Wisconsin at an early age and with little achievement. He and Wilson enjoyed each other's company, agreed on the need for an attractive writing style, and on democratic tenets. Wilson, like other southern writers in history—and southerners were almost compulsively historical no matter what their esthetics—was enchanted by Turner's frontier thesis—a thesis which saw the frontier as a creator of democratic institutions, both in struggle and strife, but with the best man winning. Wilson was moral. He became a symbol of morality. But his emphasis upon the "indomitable" nature of the Anglo-Saxon people in effect created a higher morality than law, borne out by good works and superior genes.

In time, numerous southerners came or passed through particular northern institutions. One of them was the University of Wisconsin, where a complex tradition was born. On the one hand it passionately affirmed democratic ideals—ideals which Robert M. La Follette would classically typify. This tradition praised the people, and the voice of the people, free enterprise, liberty, even socialism. On the other hand it welcomed a succession of academic southerners who would find ways to express views which could be identified as southern in origin but, as will be seen, without being tainted with the colors of slavery and secession.

No similar phenomenon occurred in the South. A northern historian who went South became southern in his phraseology, or he ignored sectional questions, at least as they pertained to the late war between the sections.

As interesting a figure as any the South produced during its struggles to fight back from military and constitutional defeat and reestablish a humanistic education was William E. Dodd. A son of North Carolina farmers, Dodd had to strain to obtain a higher education in history in Virginia's Randolph-Macon College. The novelty in Dodd's views was that he repudiated the Sidney Lanier approach and asserted the need for a hard realism. No deity to him was Jefferson Davis, but a representative of "property, of the 'interests' not of the struggling masses of common mankind who had adored Jefferson."[4] Such "realism," which in fact romanticized the "struggling masses," made Dodd in his generation more a candidate for service in northern universities than southern. In 1909, he received an offer from Professor Andrew C. McLaughlin, head of the history department at the University of Chicago, to join its staff in order to develop substantive studies in southern history. McLaughlin was a constitutional historian wedded to the rule of reason. While at the University of Michigan he had published a biography of Lewis Cass (1891), Michigan "doughface," in which he had vigorously denied that Cass was a "doughface," that is, a northerner with southern principles. McLaughlin's protests in defense of Cass's "popular sovereignty" program—which could in practice have extended slavery into northern territory—underscored his academic conviction that more light, more data would make men free. The University of Chicago was a pioneer in bringing the study of southern history to the North, and continued the tradition in following years.

What was significant was Dodd's economic emphasis, at the expense of the old moralities which had once seen slavery as a sin, and which had resulted in an antislavery enterprise which had sustained the North through an all but intolerable civil war among brothers. Dodd turned away from such explosive material to discuss the interests behind the battles. As such, he became a southern exponent of a "new history" of which Charles A. Beard, originally from Indiana, now at Columbia University, was to become the supreme example.

Beard's *An Economic Interpretation of the Constitution* (1913) deserves an esthetic analysis such as it may never receive in a historical profession which prides itself on its hard-headedness. Beard in his time assumed a stance which in a later time would be taken as offering thoughtful, rather than definitive, hypotheses. In other words historians would stop grubbing for facts. They would claim to be stimulating, evocative, interesting, and thus inspiring to their readers, rather than merely informative. Readers would then be free to go off on a search for further knowledge themselves. In practice, however, this meant that one could propose as fact what he scarcely knew as theory, and go on, if necessary, in the face of facts. In due course there would be thinly researched hypotheses which would suggest that abolitionists were not motivated by idealistic considerations; it only appeared that they were on the surface. Deep down they harbored class attitudes, bigotries, sexual frustrations, and economic greed or envy.

All such developments are improperly imputed to Beard himself. He offered an economic interpretation of the Constitution, true. But it was presumably not the only possible interpretation. Beard protested, while he suggested, that George Washington and others of the Founding Fathers had not been merely mercenary after the Revolution. They had not transgressed the Articles of Confederation merely because it was impotent to pay them back the money they were owed by the new nation. Beard then went on to provide evidence that a number of the Constitution-makers had been owed money—or "personalty," as he more delicately phrased it—by a revolutionary junta which had, after all, repudiated its own debts to the British Crown and merchants.

Beard's evidence of a movement for economic gain was quite incomplete, as competent historians jealous of revolutionary traditions bitterly proved. Beard's presentation was almost cunning in its innocence. He offered short statements sometimes almost of a memo character, as though he was jotting them down. His examples were presumably indicative of other examples which might be made or could be discovered. We could all join Beard in developing the economic interpretation of history. Beard's purposes are not presently relevant. He was probably speaking for an older Jeffersonian ideal which had been offended by the powerful actions of the latest capitalists, those of the John D. Rockefeller and J. P. Morgan stripe. Beard was a northern Progressive, as William E. Dodd was a southern Progressive. Both had something to gain for the new realism; but of the two, the southerner had much more to gain for his impugned Confederate cause.

Actually, neither Beard nor Dodd invented the new realism. For instance, there was E. L. Godkin, a transplanted young Englishman, editor of the *Nation,* which had been founded to help the freed Negroes of the South to adjust to their new conditions. The *Nation* had quickly forgotten its mission, and had instead become a brilliant forum for a New England intellectual elite which included the historian Francis Parkman, the Adamses, the Jameses: all the proud latter-day scions of gentility. Godkin was a peculiarly bloodless man with but one cause: Free Trade. This spelled out to him international peace, plenty, and social control. Godkin cared little for anyone, and somewhat less for humble folk. Yet he was quite capable of romanticizing anybody—Chinese, Negroes, the farther away the better—in his hatred of commerce and commercial warfare. As to the South, which he visited in 1877, he saw there not treason, or tradition, but what might be called "green power." In his own phraseology: northern politicians "would have us believe . . . that Southerners are a peculiar breed of men, on whom time produces no effect whatever." Godkin saw no signs of interest in a new rebellion. "Their minds are really occupied with making money, and the farms show it, and their designs on the negro [*sic*] are confined to getting him to work for low wages."[5]

The historians, North and South, with their new realism, were no more than reflecting this social compulsion and attitude toward a new expanded industry indifferent to old moral and religious beliefs.

Once again, it would be the grossest inaccuracy to see in such developments anything like a conspiracy. Dodd was, to be sure, excited by Woodrow Wilson's ascendency to national stature. He made close contact with his fellow-southerner and Democrat, and in time served him, as he would later serve another Democrat, Franklin D. Roosevelt, as his Ambassador to Nazi Germany. But the choices in life which Dodd and others made were freely made. Dodd, for instance, had also made contact with Theodore Roosevelt, a Republican, and sent him his study of Jefferson Davis (1907). Dodd had received an invitation to visit the White House, and he had enjoyed conversation with its lively occupant. Dodd also engaged in civic reform in Chicago, as he had, or had attempted to have while he was still in the South. Like Wilson, Dodd had been impressed by Turner's thesis on democracy. Both

Dodd and Wilson in their historical writing and social attitudes responded to North-South relations of individual and group complexity.

For instance, Wilson, who had been critical of the northerner Rhodes, was also critical of the Tennessean John W. Burgess, though both Wilson and Burgess had been interested in history, German educational ideals, and constitutional law. Burgess was author of the two-volume *Political Science and Comparative Constitutional Law* (1891), which Wilson reviewed. He criticized Burgess for not writing "in the language of literature [though Burgess had once taught literature] but in the language of science." Wilson, employing his curious critical apparatus, swept aside Burgress's research as being "simply the ordered pieces of statements," and he concluded: "A book thus constituted may be read much and consulted often, but can itself never live: it is not made of living tissue. It may suggest life, but it cannot impart it."[6]

Burgess and Wilson were both southerners, though Burgess as a Border State southerner had actually served in the Union army. They did not contribute to a junta determined to bend northern intellectuals to their will. If any bending was done, it would be done voluntarily, by northerners themselves, and because they chose to do so.

There was no conspiracy. There were only attempts by individuals drawn from sectional circumstances to assert their personalities and ambitions. Such circumstances affected Wilson, Dodd, and Burgess. They would affect later permutations of the New Immigration, when time would enable them to disport themselves on the national scene.

At the turn of the century a young man of energy and somewhat obscure purpose came to Columbia University to do work in the department of history. Ulrich B. Phillips had spent seven years at the University of Georgia, taking his undergraduate and graduate work, acting as a tutor in history, and as assistant librarian. There, he had become fascinated by Georgia lore, and, given ephemeral materials about his state to catalogue, had become so absorbed in deciphering them that he had all but ruined his eyesight. Something Phillips knew he wanted to write of was Georgia and of his native South.

In 1898, he had attended a summer session at the University of Chicago, which had been addressed by Frederick Jackson Turner. Phillips had been sufficiently excited by Turner's views of sections and democracy to feel some crystallization of his ambitions. Nevertheless he entered Columbia University, rather than the University of Wisconsin, possibly because of the reputation of William H. Dunning, an expert in political systems. Phillips, too, was uninterested in Burgess. Dunning was no Doughface or southern partisan. He was simply not interested in the moral statement of politics. His book on *Reconstruction* (1907), for instance, had emphasized politics and economics, and seemed refreshing after excesses of patriotism and emotion. As the *American Historical Review* later had it, in assessing Dunning's career, he had maintained a "humorous detachment from the ancient prejudices with which that portion of our history [Civil War and Reconstruction] had been environed, [and] . . . was able to view it with a wholesome freshness."[7]

There continued to be in the North many old-fashioned pundits who kept the eternal lights aflame for the boys in blue. As Beard himself complained in 1914, he "constantly [met] large numbers of students who have no knowledge of the most elementary facts of American history since the Civil War."[8] This fact served him, and also southern historians in devising fresh formulas for ridding the events preceding the War of their boring content, in the interests of a new, apparently more objective interpretation which saw neither devils nor angels, but self-interested people of varied qualities, North and South.

Ulrich B. Phillips undertook to study at Columbia not the slavery system, not secession, but developments in Georgia statehood which, as he said, finally included the entire antebellum period. His approach, he said, had not been to use "the historical imagination." "The method is that of the investigator rather than the literary historian." This was interesting, in view of the fact that Phillips became famous for his literary grace and insight. In effect, like William E. Dodd, like Beard, like others who will be mentioned, Phillips protected himself from charges of southern bias by emphasis on his dedication to the facts.

Georgia and States Rights (1902), which inaugurated Phillips's distinguished career in history and won him an American Historical Association prize, presented an image of his beloved homeland not normally available to northerners.[9] It was a state, Phillips explained, which had been founded by idealists who had given new opportunity to ruined and jailed Englishmen. It had resisted South Carolina's effort to absorb Georgia into her state borders. Georgians had been in the forefront of the liberation war against Great Britain, and they had helped win the Constitution for the new nation.

The crisis with the Georgia Indians, the Cherokees, gave Phillips his great opportunity to show the indomitable nature of Georgians, the inevitability of Indian removal west from their ancient hunting grounds. As to Negroes, Phillips's section-heading gave some of the tone of his eight-page summary in a volume of 218 pages: "The Whigs and the Democrats: Slavery." Phillips reported his findings with austere conscientiousness, though some of his one-line generalizations hardly covered the various subjects, even though they were implemented by bibliography. An example might help: "The cabins of the negroes [sic] were frequently as good as those of the poorer whites. The fact that they were not always clean was due to the habits of their occupants."[10]

That such peremptory treatment of a whole people was not challenged suggested not necessarily agreement with its principles on the part of Phillips's fellow-historians, but recognition of the indubitable talent and research Phillips had poured into his labor of love. He had done the work, and had the right to his opinions. No one before him had done such careful and detailed digging in Georgia history. The information which he had drawn from newspapers, compilations of laws, and plantation records was fresh and new. It reflected the lives and activities of the dominant class in Georgia, a fact which seemed appropriate to realistic students of the era. And if this was at the expense of the detailed stories and eloquent accounts which had once been highlighted by abolitionists, there seemed a gain in the more balanced, the more realistic, and the more intensively researched version which Phillips offered.

On receiving his Ph.D. from Columbia, Phillips became an instructor at the University of Wisconsin, where he enjoyed the company and ideas of Frederick Jackson Turner. In 1908, he joined Tulane University in Louisiana for a stay of three years. Phillips's absorption in economic history was sincere; it resulted in his *History of Transportation in the Eastern Cotton Belt* (1908). His two-volume documentary history, *Plantation and Frontier* (1909) contained many social items, including those engrossing the life of the slave and free Negro. Phillips was totally committed to finding new and representative materials in a field which had received inadequate attention, and he did not shrink from indicating, in one selection, what he termed "the barbarism of slavery." The problem was to compare Phillips's overall selections, in which the Negro residents of the South were all but buried, with those, for instance, which Theodore D. Weld, abolitionist of the 1830's, had selected in his *American Slavery As It Is* (1839). Weld's materials had been plucked by the thousands from southern periodicals to depict slavery as an unmitigated evil.

In effect, a pendulum had swung from extreme empathy with the Negro cause based on moral grounds, to a materialistic awareness of the limitations life offered its different social groups, an awareness from which Phillips, a loyal Georgian, gained.

Phillips went on to the University of Michigan in 1911, and gathered distinctions there until 1929, when he transferred to Yale University. In 1928, he published his most controversial essay in the *American Historical Review*. "The Central Theme of Southern History." He defined that theme as, not slavery, but white domination. The next year he won a $2,500 prize offered by the Boston publishers Little, Brown for his *Life and Labor in the Old South*. In it, in rich, evocative prose, Phillips portrayed a

generally happy land despite inevitable sorrows and regrettable
side-lights which could also have been found in the North.
Southerners tended to suggest that such sorrows existed in greater
number in the North. Phillips had come a long way since he had
first stated his case in terms of cold fact. A Yale scholar and
gentleman whose seminar attracted able scholars naturally affected
by his views, he was one of the outstanding members of the
American Historical Association: a national collegiate figure,
rather than a sectional one.

In 1933 a book appeared which made little impression on the
historical profession and none beyond. It is doubtful that more
than perhaps 750 copies of the book were actually distributed.
Yet those few volumes dug a niche in the sectional debate far
beyond their own reach. Their author was a Gilbert H. Barnes,
originally from Nebraska, a Methodist who entered the University
of Michigan in 1912, and there was interested in economics and
sectional perspectives by Ulrich B. Phillips. Barnes went on to
teach economics at Ohio Wesleyan University. Early in the 1930's
he came upon an historical find: the abolitionist Theodore D.
Weld's private papers. The result was Barnes's book, *The Antislavery Impulse, 1830-1844,* which was dedicated to Phillips.

Barnes stated that the revelations in the Weld papers, and
in other historical materials he had examined, had been so
dramatic that the body of his footnotes would be necessarily
extensive. The footnotes were indeed many, but the drama lay
in the thesis, which was nothing else than that William Lloyd
Garrison, the Boston abolitionist firebrand, had been no help at
all in the struggle against slavery. His actions had been harmful
in affronting northerners who might otherwise have been willing
to cooperate with a less intense version of antislavery. Garrison
himself had been sly, greedy, egotistical, and dishonest. The true
hero of the antislavery struggle was Theodore Weld, whose
passionate religious rhetoric in the 1830's had raised up legions of
antislavery fighters, mainly religious, who were able over the

next period to persuade a conservative North of the need for change.

In a separate article on Weld, published in the first edition of the *Dictionary of American Biography,* Barnes went much further, calling Weld one of the greatest statesmen of his time. This article, and indeed the book, made no mark on general history. It did signal the end of Garrison's apotheosis, which had once united the general northern public and the northern academic profession. Nevertheless, Garrison's name and that of John Brown were to remain oddly conspicuous together among the naive and uneducated, though one was totally opposed to the use of arms, "carnal weapons," and the other made his fame by insisting upon their use. The Barnes book, in addition, opened new avenues for the antislavery argument which even southerners could accept, who agreed that slavery was an outmoded labor system which had probably worked as well as or better than harsh free enterprise, but which had outlived its time.

The Antislavery Impulse, 1830-1844, diminished the entire abolitionist crusade. It asserted that the moral issue had been necessary only to enlighten the North on slavery's evils. Once that was accomplished, political abolition could take over, fighting wars with the South over constitutional questions, western land, and congressional majorities—everything but the status of the slave and the Free Negro. What Barnes did not underscore was that by 1844, Weld had entirely left the antislavery cause for a private life, that there were hundreds of nationally-known antislavery figures—including John Greenleaf Whittier, John Quincy Adams, James Russell Lowell, Frederick Douglass, William H. Seward, and others, some of whose names would extend into the twentieth century—who had yet to fill the years from 1844 to 1860 with antislavery sentiments before they could see a North committed to union and Free Soil.

In 1934, Barnes issued a two-volume compendium of the letters of Weld, his wife Angelina Grimké, and her sister Sarah which reinforced Barnes's authority in the field. Along with

Barnes in this enterprise was his young associate at Ohio Wesleyan University, Dwight L. Dumond, who had taught in ordinary Ohio schools, taken his degree at the University of Michigan, and then returned to it as a long-term professor. Dumond then issued his own two-volume compilation of the letters of James Gillespie Birney. Birney was a southerner who believed that he had been driven from his homeland because of his antislavery convictions. Dumond, who wrote better than Barnes, had to endure his mentor's view that Birney had been "an admirable but not a great man," as Barnes thought Weld had been. But Barnes's aggressiveness could not hide the basic conservatism of their common opinion, which Dumond more clearly enunciated in his view that Abraham Lincoln had been an abolitionist: a view which Lincoln himself had earnestly repudiated all his life.

In effect, an intellectual trade-off had been achieved between northern and southern academics. It condemned abolitionism as excessive, eccentric, removed from the public will: all they had been accused of being before the battle for Free Soil and the War had made the abolitionist arguments useful and relevant to northerners fighting for the life of the Union. In return for vilifying the abolitionists, southern loyalists acknowledged that slavery had outlived its function.

The implications for the modern world varied with individuals. Barnes himself, for example, seems to have fancied that he was striking a blow for institutional religion as against the blasphemies of the Garrisonians. Merle Curti, however, a younger historian, began as an advocate of peace and liberalism. He appears to have been anti-religious, yet he accepted the Barnes "thesis," as it came to be called, because, he said, without having investigated the matter, he assumed Barnes's argument was sufficiently documented for credibility. It is likely that Curti's distaste for Garrisonian piety, its scorn of liquor drinking and materialism generally, also encouraged the acceptance of Barnes's thinking by such historians as himself. Barnes gave aid to their view that there was less sincerity in the abolitionist crusade than offense by rural and conservative elements who had been shunted aside by new capitalist types, and whose sole means for obtaining public attention was to reaffirm their "moral" authority.[11]

Such modern skepticism about the sincerity or effectiveness of abolitionism made easier the road for those who were bored or annoyed by the old crusaders. However, this is not to say that the new analysts approved of slavery, or depreciated Negroes either in the past or the present. On the contrary, they not infrequently professed the most intense unity with Negro hopes and concerns. To the University of Wisconsin, for example, came a William B. Hesseltine, a Virginian who had attended Washington and Lee and the University of Virginia, had taught in Alabama and Missouri, and acquired his Ph.D. at Ohio State University. His study of *Civil War Prisons* (1930) while he was professor of history at the University of Chattanooga was interesting as being set forth as a "Study in War Psychology," an approach which could make possible ingenious interpretation of historic areas other than prisons.[12]

At the University of Wisconsin, Hesseltine sponsored a number of theses which contributed to the bad name of abolitionists. One of them essentially concluded, in the face of a hundred years of literature on the subject, that there had been no underground railroad to aid Negro runaways from slavery. The thesis expressed skepticism of all accounts by white abolitionists, including Thomas Garrett of Delaware, who may have helped some 2,500 slaves to escape from Maryland into Pennsylvania, and who was himself financially ruined in court by a vengeful judge. This thesis, however, accepted all Negro accounts of having helped escapees to freedom.

Most effective of the Hesseltine theses was that by Hazel C. Wolf, *The Martyr Complex in the Abolitionist Movement* (1952), which held that the abolitionists had been essentially neurotics with compulsions toward being punished or killed, a thesis which impugned their rational and direct hatred of slavery.[13] This thesis aided the views of such others as Richard Hofstadter, who sought not only a better world, but a best world, not subject to the vagaries of religion or puritanic ethics, but based on full equality and materialism.

Hesseltine was a southerner, but he was also somewhat social-istic as well, and this distaste for an old radicalism was not in-frequently a byproduct of a new radicalism, curiously born out of what had been touted as another and more legitimate crusade for democracy. The Woodrow Wilson campaign against Junker Germany had in the 1920's degenerated into satire and bitterness. The subsequent Franklin D. Roosevelt-led battle in the Depres-sion Era, first against poverty, then against Adolf Hitler and the Nazis was presumably justifiable on grounds of international justice and humanity. It was followed by a wave of economic prosperity in the 1940's: an era of full employment in shipyards, government offices, and industrial services, born in the midst of horrible bombings and battles abroad on land and sea; a prosperity destined to continue unabated for twenty-five years. It did not bring with it a spiritual or cultural awakening. The faceless surburbs were born, lawns were watered, television was followed reverently. A generation of youth was raised glutted with affluence and asking the uniquely American question: "What have you done for me lately?"

Beats, rebels without a cause, libertarians who made much of drug and sex freedoms were able to lace their discontents with socialist slogans and ideals in ways which disrupted some campuses, but more severely shook the academic disciplines which were presumably the reason for the campuses in the first place. With such high utopian goals as the era sponsored, who needed sanctimonious, water-drinking, pious, monogamous abolitionists, proud of their Ameircan heritage?

By 1950, the battle to depreciate the white abolitionists among the academics, as having done too little, of having been insincere, status-ridden, neurotic, intrinsically conservative was all but over. Lipservice there always was and would always be. But in the centers of opinion-making, decisions had been rendered. As a new Yale professor, David M. Potter, a native of Augusta, Georgia, a graduate of Emory University in Atlanta, and a sensitive student of Civil War history, put it: "What could be the justification for a war to hold the South to an alliance that was essentially unreal and ill-founded?" Potter held the abolitionists responsible for having caused the war, but he was not complimentary in this judgment: "Peace, no matter how makeshift, would have been of immeasurable value to the men who were killed between Sumter and Appomattox."[14]

The implications, if there were any, were that the Civil War had been futile, the passage of the Thirteenth Amendment, ending slavery, and of the Fourteenth and Fifteenth Amendments guaranteeing civil rights to all people and the suffrage to Negro men, not worth dying for. Thus, a new war for independence needed to be waged: one which would put the abolitionist crusade still further back in the shadows. Potter himself was a conservative gentleman and scholar uninterested in libertarian battles, but his views did not transgress those of radicals. While storms of controversy shook campuses and public places, academics adjusted their intellectual bifocals still further. Two books on William Lloyd Garrison, totaling some one thousand pages, proved that he was not worth writing about. The thesis denying honor to the white workers of the underground railroad was endorsed as true, for example by Professor Benjamin Quarles, a highly talented historian of Morgan State University. Another development of the 1960's featured a Martin Duberman, whose edited volume *The Antislavery Vanguard* (1965) highlighted a psychological interpretation of antislavery sentiment which underscored the neurotic component in their crusade. A noted southern historian, David Donald, utilized the findings of two psychiatrists to conclude that Charles Sumner's prolonged sickness, after having been beaten by a hot-tempered southerner with a heavy walking stick while Sumner was seated at his desk in the United States Senate, was "largely psychogenic." Why, asked one pro-abolitionist, who had himself contributed to the neurotic theory of white abolitionism, why hadn't Donald investigated the sanity of Sumner's assailant?[15]

All such questions failed to turn back the argument to the simpler question of historical accuracy. Those who in the 1960's felt that abolitionists had done too little were, whether they intended this or not, at one with those who despised abolitionists and abolitionism in the first place. The fact that some of the critics of abolition dreamed of a higher freedom and a nobler social equality did not negate the fact that their immediate target was not an Ulrich B. Phillips—Phillips flourished more than ever among academics, secure in his strong, relatively unchallenged research—but those whose vision had favored abolition. The now aged Dwight L. Dumond capped his anti-Garrison career with a volume, *Antislavery* (1961), which passionately denounced slavery, rather than documented its decline under abolitionist auspices. For this he was gratefully honored by the N.A.A.C.P.

A true curiosity of the time was the appearance of two biographies of the firebrand John Brown, both carefully researched, which saw him not as irresponsible—as Garrison had been seen —but as a profound Puritan whose actions could be justified by the intolerable nature of the slavery system. The books did not inspire general debate. Once more there can be discerned here a type of trade-off between southern and northern academics. The southern partisan could say: We have our crackpots who still yearn for the good old slavery days, and you have yours who believe John Brown accomplished something by his insane and worthless assault at little Harpers Ferry. Indulge yourself as you please. Only let us agree that the moral element in abolition— the element which accused our forebears of sin and crime—may be buried as unrealistic, if not worse.

A distinguished successor of Potter at Yale, C. Vann Woodward, a native of Arkansas and graduate of Emory University, and an admirer of Ulrich B. Phillips, summed the matter nicely in his article "The Antislavery Myth" (*American Scholar*, Spring 1962, 312 ff.), expressing approval of the underground-legend thesis, and depreciating the white abolitionists with the now usual charges. The N.A.A.C.P. honored him also as a friend of freedom and a humanistic voice in history. Realism made a living arrangement with radicalism. At the University of Wisconsin, even while irate students agitated in opposition to the Vietnam War and American life and morals generally, the head of the history department explained to his graduate students that he intended to teach them history the way a carpenter taught his apprentices carpentry.

Paul H. Buck, a Harvard historian, had, in his *The Road to Reunion 1865-1900* (1947), traced the many ways, social, economic, cultural, which North and South had taken to accommodate one another. The final solvent of differences had been patriotism, enabling ex-Confederates and ex-Union troops to fight together during the Spanish-American War. Patriotism in the 1970's was in a low state. If anything, anti-patriotism enabled southern and northern academics to drink together at conventions and exchange scholarly hypotheses about other people's neuroses.

A Russian proverb has it that in the house of the hangman you do not mention rope; and a certain caution and evasiveness, laced with courtesy, helped relegate the question of slavery and abolition to the background. But while Jim Crow died patently on many campuses, the question of latent attitudes and loyalties continued to disturb corners of the academic scene. In 1974, the scholarly world, and parts of the general reading public, were shocked by the appearance of Robert W. Fogel and Stanley L. Engerman's *Time on the Cross*, a two-volume work employing computers, but also clear, disturbing prose. There was no questioning the liberal credentials of the authors; one was married to a Negro. Yet their book seemed to prove that there was little difference overall between the lot of the Negro under slavery and under freedom, and that the lot had been far from dire.

Roused liberals took consolation in the appearance in 1975, of Herbert G. Gutman's *Slavery and the Numbers Game*, which quarreled severely with Fogel and Engerman's methods, findings, and results. Gutman argued that slavery had been cruel, and that slaves had been far from satisfied with the "Protestant ethic" of their masters. Gutman worked over the statistics, but he also found himself resorting to the moral argument, as did some others in the history profession who found *Time on the Cross* distasteful. But in a world in which rip-offs had been defended as a direct means for getting one's own back from society, and even arson and murder more or less justified in particular cases, it was difficult to sort out justice from injustice, morals from immorality. There were differences, but differences within a consensus. It kept would-be partisans frustrated by ideas controlling their moralistic impulses. But at least kept them talking and amiable at professional meetings, luncheons, and cocktail parties.

There is no known way by which the social impulse toward consensus can be overcome. The sections and levels of American life are too many and too irreconcilable to generate peace of themselves. Only an effort at paying off contestants through compromise can prevent them from flashing intellectual knives to their common disgrace.

How well a particular consensus serves the general establishment is best judged during crises, in which new dissidents pour satire and criticism on the establishment while hinting that they, when they are in power, will produce a social formula of intrinsic beauty and truth. Should the consensus prove vulnerable, it will break, possibly by falling momentarily into the hands of the dissidents themselves. Then, a period of rant and idealistic promises may be expected, during which the major antagonists will reorganize, once more seeking a formula viable to different people for different purposes.

None of this need interfere even for a moment with the general effort to make more secure the major fighters in their strongholds, salaries, and illusions. A sophisticated nation has a sophisticated consensus. To the extent that it doesn't, it courts trouble.

NOTES

1. *Poems of Sidney Lanier* (New York, 1893), 60.
2. See Bronson Howard's "Shenandoah," and William Gillette's "Secret Service" in Arthur Hobson Quinn, *Representative American Plays* (New York, 1917), 533 ff.
3. Arthur Link *et al.*, eds., *The Papers of Woodrow Wilson* (Princeton, 1970), 8: 301.
4. William E. Dodd, *Statesmen of the Old South* (New York, 1911), 209. Dodd got his "interests" from the revelations of big business chicanery being revealed by David Graham Phillips in the "Treason of the Senate" articles he had recently prepared for *Cosmopolitan Magazine*.
5. Louis Filler, "The Early Godkin," *The Historian*, XVII (Autumn, 1954), 61.
6. Link *et al.*, eds., *The Papers of Woodrow Wilson* (Princeton, 1969), 7: 202.
7. *American Historical Review*, vol. 28, (Washington, 1922-1923), 174.
8. Charles A. Beard, *Contemporary American History 1877-1913* (New York, 1914).
9. See introduction by Louis Filler to *Georgia and States Rights* (Yellow Springs, O., 1968), by Ulrich B. Phillips.
10. *Ibid.*, 154.
11. Merle Curti, *The Growth of American Thought* (New York, 1951), 376 ff.
12. The idea of a southern junta penetrating northern universities was aggressively suggested by Louis M. Hacker in "Some Sons of Dixie," *Fortune*, July 1947, 6, 9, in reviewing James G. Randall's *Abraham Lincoln: Liberal Statesman*. Hacker also noted Hesseltine, and Avery O. Craven of the University of Chicago. Hacker deserted a "consensus" of his own to give up an anti-capitalist viewpoint and embrace one which saw capitalism as giving us "the physical means of achieving abundance"; for details, John F. Gerstung, "Louis M. Hacker's Reappraisal of Recent American History," *The Historian*, Spring, 1950, 140-166.
13. This thesis finally reached the hands of a highly learned and competent student of religious wars, and enabled him to justify indirectly nothing more nor less than the Massacre of St. Barthol-

omew. It enabled him to conclude almost jocundly: " 'The blood of the martyrs is the seed of the church': it has also been fuel for the labors of generations of historians, and by now more ink than blood has flowed as a result of the events of that weekend in Paris four hundred years ago" (Donald R. Kelley, "Martyrs, Myths, and the Massacre: the Background of St. Bartholomew," *American Historical Review*, [vol. 77] December 1972, 1342.) Professor Kelley argued that the Protestants aggravated the authorities with their importunities, and thus pulled the public vengeance upon themselves. After all, the French were a nation, as well as a Catholic nation.

14. *New York Herald Tribune*, April 16, 1961.
15. Lewis Perry, "Psychology and the Abolitionists," *Reviews in American History* (Westport, Conn., September 1974), vol. 2, 312.

The Thingness Of Things

M.W. FISHWICK

"Things are in the saddle and ride mankind."
Ralph Waldo Emerson

"I am collecting the history of our people," Henry Ford wrote forty years ago, "as written into *things* their hands made and used. A piece of machinery or anything that is made is like a book—if you can read it."

Let's learn to read objects—especially those that are icons—as a basic need in the area of popular culture. If and when we do it, we may find that we have discovered a new base on which we—and many of our word-centered colleagues—can stand, expand, and explain.

Alice discovered in Wonderland that the world was made up of cabbages and kings and a number of things. We also live in a wonder land in which (said Walt Whitman) a mouse is miracle enough to stagger sextillions of infidels. All around us are an infinity of things, filling the space-time continuum. They determine not only our lives, but our ideas and thinking. Man the tool-maker wrestles with the raw stuff of life—stone, wood, metal. As he increases in skill and fortitude, he develops a technology. And as man has a technology, so does he have a history. And the most vital, subversive, explosive segment of that history we call popular culture.

Objects are the building blocks of reality. They are sensitive indicators of who we are, where we come from, where we intend to go. Long after an individual has died, and even his language and culture have disappeared, artifacts remain. By digging into the earth, archaeologists uncover the story of the past. Things form the solid basis of our understanding and concern for millions of human beings who preceded us. Archaeology plus imagination equals historical insight.

Dynamos, telephones, cameras, film, printing presses, plastic discs, picture tubes: are these not the essence of popular culture? Have they not literally shaped the mass media which carries the message?

The thingness of things has fascinated the liveliest intellects since Aristotle's time. A conscious interest in what Lewis Mumford calls (in *Art and Technics*) "the go of things" has been such an obvious major factor in history that one posits and predicates it in every period, event, sequence. Yet how few people in the academy know how to deal with—even to describe or classify— the artifacts that make things go. Having given the standard definition of artifact—"a thing made by man purposefully, so that he transforms materials already existing"—he goes back to his notes and his lecture.

There is ample evidence to support a fine article by Professor Harold Skramstad called "American Things: A Neglected Material Culture."[1] Some of his readers must have been surprised to find him single out "New Journalist" Tom Wolfe for special praise, since Wolfe "demonstrates how insights from a study of new artifact forms are able to increase our understanding of present day American civilization."

More frequently and traditionally praised is Professor James Harvey Robinson, whose "New History" (now fifty years old) insisted that we study "not only the written records, but the remains of buildings, pictures, clothing, tools, and ornaments."[2] A promising start was made in the midtwenties in the twelve-volume *History of American Life* series edited by Arthur M. Schlesinger and Dixon Ryan Fox in which some attention was paid to "non-literary remains" and "physical survivals." T. J. Wertenbaker's volumes on *The Middle Colonies* and *The Puritan Oligarchy* made use of material culture. But when Caroline F. Ware edited *The Cultural Approach to History* for the American Historical Association in 1940, neither her introduction nor the thirty-six essays describing the so-called new tools of the cultural historian had a word to say about the historic artifact.

Research Opportunities in American Cultural History edited by Frances McDermontt in 1961 calls attention to many important possibilities but none of them involve a study of artifacts. A look at the volumes that have appeared in *Documents in American Civilization* suggest how an idea of the historian can be illustrated by an artist, rather than how the work of an artist or artisan can lead the historian to a new idea. Meanwhile the American Historical Association, having in 1934 created a Conference on Historic Sites and Monuments, and in 1939 added a Special Committee on the Preservation and Restoration of Historic Objects to its standing committee on Historical Source Materials, discontinued both in 1947. In 1962 the AHA tabled a motion made in the Council to create a new committee on historic sites. As far as I can tell, the first and only session devoted to material culture as such by the AHA was at its 1964 annual meeting, and by the Organzation of American Historians at its 1972 annual meeting. Meanwhile, the 1955 edition of the *Harvard Guide to American History* gave more enthusiastic and specific support to what it called non-documentary sources—although only two and one-half pages—than did the 1974 edition. That same edition also pointed to this incredible state of affairs in our highly-organized computerized time:

> There are no systematic state or national surveys of museum holdings. Thus the individual wishing to locate and use artifacts will be obliged to search them out on a museum-by-museum basis.

Happily, the teacher of popular culture may not have to institute such a search for objects that will serve his needs. *Vox populi* not only puts what Everyman wants on the TV screen, radio network, movie marquee, and billboard, but in the kitchen, garage, pool hall, and the supermarket as well. The more prevalent (or popular) the object, the more certain its importance as a cultural cipher. As Richard Latham points out in *Who Designs America?* to de-cipher is to find the key to the culture in which people actually live. Observe this simple event, and ponder the questions Latham raises: a hundred-pound woman drives a two-ton car two blocks to the grocery store. Circling ten minutes to find a parking space, she goes in, buys a loaf of bread, and drives home. Does she know that:

1. the cost of the bread now includes factors like gas consumption and car depreciation?
2. that she has added to problems (such as energy shortage and air pollution) that may bring down our whole nation?
3. that she has missed a chance to walk in the winter air—one of the few natural exercises left to her by which her body can maintain chemical balance?
4. that she is grossly inefficient, since she could have walked to the store and back in half the time?

This simple episode—which any student could both understand and analyze—in effect raises the whole question of idea-object relationship. Does an object require more time, expense, and attention than it is worth in terms of work or enjoyment? How do cause-and-effect measure the merit of a civilization?

Take another example which might well entice any teacher of popular culture—toys, the oldest and most wide-spread artifacts. "Toys," Suzanne K. Langer writes, "are the most important products of popular art, because they impinge on a completely receptive being." And what of adult toy-play, which we like to call hobbies? There are pathetically few clues. Ruel Denney's analysis of hot-rodders in *The Astonished Muse,* and Faulkner's account of the American's love affair for his auto at the close of *Intruder in the Dust,* come quickly to mind. So does Professor Luther Gore's study of the decline in interest in model airplanes.

A generation ago, experience with model airplanes provided a significant part of the motivation for youth's interest in technology, and so was a factor in the rapid development of the aircraft industry. In contrast, America's first successful space ventures brought no significant upsurge in hobbies related to aerospace technology. The plight of engineers and designers who lead the army of the unemployed is part of the popular understanding. Is the famous "Yankee know-how" in disarray? And does this changing image correlate to the declining youth interest in model airplane building and flying?

Again: what does furniture tell us about the style-revolution through which we have lived? Even today's furniture made by hand, and of traditional material, is devoid of ornament or symbolism. On every level there is a conscious effort to break away from historical styles of the nineteenth century—along with a huge wave of nostalgia. What can this paradox mean?

"Things are in the saddle," Emerson complained, "and ride mankind." If they are in fact in the saddle, one could never guess it from most courses in American history and culture. Objects cry out not only for description, but also for identification, authentication, evaluation, and interpretation. The real work has not even begun.

To study artifacts, the artist Paul Klee pointed out, is to shatter them. We must dissect them to reveal their component parts. Once dissected, Henry Glassie notes, we may be able to view artifacts as the product and source of meaning:

> The thing is only a thing until a man wanders into the
> picture and begins relating the thing to other things. Then
> the thing becomes an icon. The conceptualization of associa-
> tions, relations, and meaning is the recognition of the
> thing's functions and of the icon's power.

ICONS: for most of us, the word rings Byzantine bells making us turn our minds eastward and our hearts heavenward. Derived from the Greek eikōn, "objects of uncritical devotion," the concept offers a whole new realm of penetration for the teacher of popular culture. Leslie Fiedler has helped us see how certain popular characters in American literature (Natty Bumppo, Huck Finn, Flem Snopes) are "mythopoeic." Can it be that the same quality, applied not to fictional characters but to objects, results in icons? Science has "gone iconic" since Heisenberg and Bohr. What Marshall McLuhan calls the "War of Icons" ranges all around us, reaching epic proportions in sports, politics, and advertising. Icons thrive because they function: warm for devotion, cool for companionship. They can gain, or lose, meaning. The swastika which thrilled in the 1940's repulses in the 1970's. The image precedes the idea in the development of human consciousness. When they work together, we get an icon.

"Thinking in pictures" is the first stage of icon-making. All cultures invent icons. Freud spoke of "optical memory-residues . . ." things as opposed to words. We look with our eyes, see with our minds, make with our hands. Form and formula fuse. The word becomes flesh, and dwells among us. The time is ripe to revitalize the word and relate it to a world where men walk on the moon and young people stage folk-wanderings to hear electric guitars. Not in crypts or cathedrals, but on billboards and magazine covers will we find our evidence. Manna may still come from heaven, but our vital information flows through the Big Tube. Icons go pop.

Speaking to the flux and impermanence of contemporary Protean Man, the key is simultaneity. He lives for and by images of a more fragmentary nature than those of the past. Faddish and fleeting, these images set the tone of his psychological life. Yet the old process continues: events create history, history becomes mythology, mythology begets ritual, ritual demands icons. Today's hard rock folk festival points towards tomorrow's creeds and icons.

Note the number of generic nouns which can be made specific merely by using an article: the pill, the bomb, the scene, the new look, the sound. Another is the merging of brand names with lifestyles: Pepsi (generation), IBM, Xerox, Coke, Sears. We are all married to the mechanical bride.

Icons seek out a spot of veneration. "All sacred things must have their place," writes Claude Levi-Strauss. "Being in their place is what makes them sacred" Men still want to make sense out of the universe, their post-Watergate government. They want to integrate official, elite, and popular culture into a single way-of-being. To help them do this is the major task of teachers of popular culture.

Help wanted: pop iconology. Instead of indiscriminate praise or damnation of popstyle (two current postures) why not devise new categories for intrinsic meanings? Profiting from Erwin Panofsky's *Studies in Iconology* (1938), we should apply the same serious analysis to the current American Renaissance as was used for the older Italian and French. This would involve not only surface data (identification, description, authentication) but interior qualities (evaluation, interpretation, significance). It would also require an openness to popular culture which is notably absent in the academic community.

A hundred years ago Baudelaire invited fugitives from the world of memory to come aboard to seek the new. Subsequently there developed what Harold Rosenberg calls *The Tradition of the New*. There have been few scholarly studies of it.

We must seek a point of significant beginning. This involves not only comparative study between elite, popular, and folk, but also configurational or structural analysis of the total *gestalt*. Scholarship and criticism must catch up with performance. If today's poets and artists are (as they have always been) joint bearers of a central pattern of sensibility, let's find out what that pattern is.

The main channel of iconology in our time—because of dissemination through mass media—is the popular stratum. The mechanized trivialized standardized world of which elitists complain provides the raw material for a new lifestyle. That pop artists have singled out objects for extensive use is an iconic clue. Ever since Robert Rauschenberg's 1958 "Coco-Cola Plan" that famous container, the most widely recognized commercial product in the world, has been featured. Long before 1958, the high and low met at the Coke machine, and history stopped for the Coke break. For generations of Americans brought up in gasoline stations, boot camps, and drug stores, Coke *was* America.

Coke bottles are apt motifs not because they are unique, but because they are omnipresent. In the traditional sense, they are anti-icons. The nature of icons has changed between the Age of Faith and the Age of Atoms. Not the unique, but the omnipresent, triumphs. The Coca Cola company jealously protects its trade mark and 1915 bottle design while putting those marks and bottles in every hamlet of the world. Pop icons are not only accessible; they are unavoidable.

Does it offend you to think that a TV tube, a Coke bottle, and a VW are icons? Are they not building blocks of the cultural realities of the 1970s? This is what is new about teaching history and touching reality today.

For the anthropologist, reality dwells in acculturation, diffusion, ethos, role and function; for the art historian, in style, form, symbol, influence, and uniqueness. Just where is it for the pop culturist?

Traditionalists need not reject such a notion out of hand. As any historian ought to know, putting the adjective "new" in front of a noun doesn't sever old connections. It may even end up exalting the old. The popularity of Camp in the 1960's put Victoria back on the throne, even as Bonnie and Clyde resurrected pint-sized gangsters from a suddenly-glamorous Depression. Simultaneously a reprint of the 1897 Sears-Roebuck catalog became a best-seller. Since the bully days of T.R., Americans' perception of reality has changed. For example, the camera has become Everyman's Third Eye. Is the camera itself an icon of our age? As an instrument it *transmits* rather than symbolizes images. Not even photographers keep old cameras. The camera reaches its symbolic peak swinging from the necks of tourists around the world. But then it is an amulet rather than an icon—a charm which gives the wearer magic power.

But surely the canvas or assemblage featuring the coke bottle, as well as the bottle itself, is an icon: an image converted into plastic form. Ideas like mass production, distribution, and taste become real in the three dimensional coke bottle or canvas on which it appears. Only in music has the validity of popstyle won wider recognition than in art. Pop icons have been both identified and enshrined (if we can borrow that sacred word for our secular culture) by artists like Andy Warhol, Robert Rauschenberg, George Segal, Robert Indiana, Claes Oldenburg, and Roy Lichtenstein. Theirs is not the world of forests and wheat fields, but of automobiles, comic strips, junk yards, and go-go girls. The whole apparatus of retail emotions, gadgetry, and packaging is material for their art. They exalt the thingness of things.

"I am for art you can sit on," Claes Oldenburg writes. "I am for the art of fat truck-tires and black eyes. I am for *7-Up Art*, Pepsi Art, Sunkist Art . . . the art of tambourines and plastic phonographs and abandoned boxes tied like pharaohs."

In such statements as this, I contend, is a whole new educational theory for those who will seek and seize it. The artifacts and icons which engulf us offer not only new material for teachers of popular culture or social history. They offer a new approach to education, for they are the basis of a new reality.

In the Middle Ages all experience found philosophical unity and visual form in a single metaphorical system. Such unity and meaning may be found again, in our time. Those seeking it might well take the advice of the famous epitaph written for Christopher Wren: SI HISTORIAM REQUIRIS, CIRCUM-SPICE. (If you seek history, look around you.)

NOTES

1. The article, which appeared in the Spring 1973 issue of *American Quarterly*, contains a helpful bibliography for this whole subject.
2. I am endebted to research and conversation with Dr. E. McClung Fleming, of Winterthur Museum, for the comments that follow about courses on material culture.

Colonial American Theology: Holiness and the Lyric Impulse

NORMAN GRABO

In the beginning of American literature was indeed the Word. For preaching and writing it, English ministers were examined, silenced, and banished. To preach and write the truth to make men free, they followed the sun westward. And to assure posterity that the darksome blot of ignorance should never stop the conduits of God's grace to right believers, they promptly established in the wilderness of the New World a printing press, schools, libraries, and a civil polity designed to combine might with right thought. Behind early American action lay grace-full words; behind the words, sinewy thought; and behind thought, the designs and decrees of God. To relate act, thought, and divine will was the work of colonial theologians, and they brought to it a sense of language essentially poetic. That a literature of power could be something other than a literature of knowledge would have been meaningless to them. In fact, the joining of knowledge and power in the mystery whereby grace passed from God to his elect through the words of men not only dignified language and hallowed its uses, but hints at the special importance of theology for American literature from its beginnings.

For frontier Puritans God-lore occupied no unobtrusive corner of the mind, but towered over all intellectual activities as the science of sciences. The possibility, then, that all early American writing was properly theological is supportable, if not entirely useful, and numerous studies of the relationship of America's Puritan experience to its literary development seem to credit that possibility. Perry Miller has exposed the marrow of Puritan divinity—the covenant theology and its views of God, sin, and soul—brilliantly in his books and articles, anatomizing the intellectual system basic to all American expression before 1740. Clarence Faust has shown that system harden into a brittle legalism increasingly divorced from American destiny by the middle of the eighteenth century, and Herbert Schneider has demonstrated that despite the sclerosis of its vital parts Puritan theology persisted in forming both an American conscience and habits of mind continuously significant to American literature. Josephine Piercy has traced the nineteenth-century essay to its roots in the seventeenth-century sermon, and Kenneth Murdock, whose *Theology & Literature in Colonial New England* most amply treats "the Puritan legacy," thoroughly explores the "ways of thought and feeling, fundamental intellectual and emotional points of view, which have the power to stimulate new attempts to map the changing current of life."[1]

Subterranean as that current so often is, Professor Murdock has nonetheless erected very useful signposts to the Puritan heritage of Hawthorne, Melville, Longfellow, Emerson, Thoreau, and James. Between them and their colonial forebears run a number of common qualities or concerns: a pointed, direct, plain style—brief and perspicuous; the abiding interest in the interior dimensions of human character; the sense of historical place and, concomitantly, of the American's election to fulfill some manifest destiny in the West; a pervading respect for nonconformity, idealism, and individualism; the view of life as a drama of cosmic significance; and an overriding moral seriousness. These are, of course, merely convenient, though striking, parallels, and they might be extended to include determinism as it passes from providential to scientific in Emerson, the pull of blood that Faulkner obsessively traces, and the lamentations of the early T. S. Eliot. For these were also the conscious concerns of colonial writers, not only the theologians, but historians like Edward Johnson and William Bradford who consciously inflated their plain and simple truth to epic and scriptural proportions, adventure writers like Mary Rowlandson, whose Indian captivity she transmutes to illustrate *The Sovereignty and Goodness of God,* or poets like Mistress Bradstreet, for whom the path between the "black clad cricket" and the name "graved in the white stone" was both inevitable and indelible. Precisely here may exist the crucial difference between modern and colonial interest in these and other subjects, the point at which the tempting parallels begin to diverge. For, as Murdock suggests, colonial writers knew what they meant by religion, "centering it on a consistent and reasoned theology . . ." (p. 207).

It is in the relationship of literature not to isolated or separate ideas, then, but to systems of ideas, that one finds the literary character of colonial theology and its peculiar place in American literary history. Colonial theology enjoyed its own rage for order as it sought to explicate the reasons and principles underlying religious experience. The faith it explicated was the faith of John Calvin, based on a literalistic reading of the Bible and on the example of the Christian churches of the first three centuries (John Foxe's age of primitive purity), but modified first by the codifications of the Synod of Dort (1618-19) and even more by the federal or covenant theories of William Ames, William Perkins, and John Preston. In short, it was a borrowed system, old cloveboards sawn and shaped in Geneva, baled in England, and clapped upon the new temple in the American wilderness. The job of the American ministry was to explain the system and put it to use. Use, application, experience—these were the primary aims of colonial theology, and they often dictated the character of theological writing.

Ironically, the most obvious feature of colonial theology is its disorder, largely the result of its mundane, practical, divisive, and occasional nature. That is, speculative curiosity regarding the philosophical bases of belief was a much less immediate motive for writing than was some specific occasion—the sudden appearance of a troublesome or heretical notion, unexpected criticism, the formation of a new church, the need for a catechism, the administration of the sacraments, funerals, thanksgivings, fasts, elections, and so on. Matters of basic faith had been hammered out by European protestants in a series of "confessions of faith," often assembled for publication in Europe and England in convenient "harmonies of confessions" like John Legatt's *Harmony of the Confession of the Faith of the Christian . . . Churches* (1643), and summed up satisfactorily by the English Westminster Assembly's *Confession* of 1646. Doctrine settled, the ministry's main task was to interpret the *Confession*'s significance for current events and to apply its truths to daily problems. Consequently, until Jonathan Edwards' proposed "Rational Account of the Main Doctrines of the Christian Religion" began to appear in the 1740's, there was no fully developed speculative theology worthy of systematic examination.

Moreover, the first care of the ministry in the wilderness was the organization of men rather than of ideas, which also contributed to the fragmentary and partial treatment of theological problems. Attention turned especially to pastoral affairs, spelling out ecclesiastical structures, the Congregational system, its relations to civil polity, the duties of officers and members to the church and to one another. Viewed most broadly, this pastoral literature was political and impersonal, a literature of platforms and policies, consisting largely of committee reports like Richard Mather's *Cambridge Platform* of 1649, which established ecclesiastical polity in New England, or like his son's *The Necessity of Reformation* (1680), recording a Boston synod's worries with the spiritual deadness of the times. The ecclesiastical polity itself acted against the production of any single great theological work. Just as in the eighteenth century men of parts would be deflected from belles-lettres by faction and political party, so in the seventeenth, an ecclesiastical system advocating small, independent, autonomous, "particular" churches; rejecting the stabilizing centrality of Presbyteries or episcopacy; cooperating only through consociation, not association—such a system, whose synods could only advise, admonish, and recommend, was not congenial to unified thought. Subject to difference and adaptation, it promoted a literature of dialectic, permitting change and hoping for progress, nurturing the ironic possibility that from the very pulpit that once proffered God's grace from the lips of Increase and Cotton Mather, young Ralph Waldo Emerson would renounce the system and its theology.

This divisive potentiality was realized in a series of open controversies. Five major ones prompted the bulk of theological writing in the first century of American settlement: first, the construction and defense of the Congregational or New England way, from 1630 to the Cambridge Platform of 1649; second, the antinomian controversy with Roger Williams and Anne Hutchinson in the 1630's and with the Quakers in the 1650's; third, the issue of infant baptism, settled very insecurely by the half-way covenant of 1662; fourth, the consequent debate regarding the nature and proper administration of the Lord's Supper, especially from 1680 to 1710; and finally, the furor that accompanied and largely defined the evangelism of the Great Awakening between 1740 and 1746. That such controversies, pricking fundamental assumptions of religious faith and practice, should find voice in a literature of anger, protest, and denunciation would not be surprising. But more important is the strategy of this literature, a strategy of indirectness that commonly set each issue in relation to a body of fundamental dogma, and addressed it from that ground. The purpose may have been polemic; the tone was only so in part.

The surprising result of this strategy of indirectness is that differences of practice and policy are transmuted into theoretical considerations. And these, in turn, revolve around one persistent, central, speculative question: what is the nature of true holiness and how can truth be distinguished from illusion? What, in short, evidences true sanctity?

One way or another, each controversy turns upon that question, which, when faced squarely, significantly influenced the tone and style of theological literature in this period. First, its answers lay outside pastoral discipline, beyond both history and nature, and in the realm of transcendent, even mystical, verities. Samuel E. Morison has contended that mystical theology was in effect outlawed for colonials,[2] but in fact, when tracing not effects but nature and cause, colonial theologians moved inevitably from pastoral to mystical considerations. What is more, in so moving, they responded to their philosophical discoveries excitedly, pouring forth their conclusions in an ecstatic, rhapsodic, sometimes lyric prose. Reason pursued to an *O Altitudo* marks a continuing and important tradition in early theological writing, a tradition that attempts to define the point at which external and objective signs truly designate spiritual essence and value.

"The reason why the Children of God are so little regarded here in the World," wrote Samuel Willard in 1684, "is because the World knows not who they are, nor what they are born unto. . . ."[3] To correct that unfortunate ignorance was the primary attempt of Thomas Shepard's *The Sincere Convert* (Boston, 1641). English born, educated at Emmanuel College, Cambridge, and one of the early arrivals in the Bay Colony (1635), Shepard's reputation for eloquence and spirituality exceeded even that of John Cotton and Thomas Hooker. Nowhere can one see the reason for that reputation to handsomer advantage than in *The Sincere Convert,* whose twenty editions bespeaks a ready audience until at least 1821. The book's central problem is to reveal the small number of true believers and the difficulty of knowing whether one has been savingly converted, but it does not address that problem singly or simply. Instead, Shepard sets it in the whole system of New England's faith by plainly opening six "choice and Divine Principles"—that there is a God most glorious, that God made man in "a blessed estate," that man's misery followed his fall through Adam, that only Christ can pay the price of redemption, that "few are saved, and that with difficulty," and that man's damnation is his own responsibility.

The system is complete and familiar, nothing new at all, and its very familiarity might easily have earned the book oblivion were it not that Shepard, whom Moses Coit Tyler calls a preacher's preacher, is incapable of dullness.

His aim is to break his readers' hearts and to awaken their consciences, to jostle them from the security of intellectual belief without "experimental" knowledge. But the job is not easy, as Shepard fully realizes: "people are so Sermon-trodden, that their hearts, like foot-paths, grow hard by the Word"; they would "rather burn than turn. . . ." Their lethargy results from false values that either blind men to evidences of true grace when present or foist off general and common grace as truly saving. "Let a man have false weights he is cheated grievously with light Gold; why? because his weights are too light; so these men have too light weights to judge of the Weight of true grace; therefore light, clipt, crackt-pieces cheat them. Hence you shall have those men commend pithless, sapless men, for very honest men as ever brake bread; why? they are just answerable to their weights." Clearly, Shepard thinks it possible to correct such spiritual myopia, to distinguish true grace from seeming grace, and much of *The Sincere Convert* is an attempt to identify where the distinctions lie.

The distinctions themselves Shepard had worked out elaborately during the antinomian controversy in a series of sermons preached from 1636 to 1640. These sermons are a word-by-word analysis and commentary on the parable of the ten virgins (Matth. XXV:1-13), designed to prove the "Erronist" Anne Hutchinson and her followers a wrong-headed set who, like "devout Monks," let visions, dreams, and supposed immediate revelations stand in the way of a proper hearing of gospel preaching. To prove their error rather than denounce the heretics, these sermons (not published from Shepard's notes until 1695 under the title *The Parable of the Ten Virgins* [Boston])[4] mainly address the questions of "the Difference between the Sincere Christian and the most Refined Hypocrite, [and] the Nature & Characters of Saving and Common Grace. . . ." How, Shepard asks essentially, may one know that all his religion is not merely dry, empty, legalistic "Church-craft"? His answer is to "try it therefore by this Rule, does it come from a principle of life or no? Your lamp burns, but look what is in your vessel that feeds this flame. . . . In this case we are not to look so much to what is done, as from what power and principle it is done: for therein the best Hypocrite ever fails. We shall ever observe in some Beasts there are *umbrae rationis*, yet there is no rational soul, nor any wise Man will believe their acts proceed from such a Principle: so there are shadows of the power of grace in a carnal heart, and yet no Judicious Christian will say they come from an inward soul, or principle of life. Consider therefore whether there is this principle or no. . . ." And to find this principle of life which is also a principle of love, one must attend whole-heartedly to the gospel: "Oh therefore if you would have the Spirit dispensed to you, wait here upon the Ministry of the Gospel for it; neglect not private helps, books, and meditations, &c., but know, if ever you have it dispensed, here it is chiefly to be had; buy at this shop."

Private helps, even books (which Shepard calls "but a Carkass of the living Word"), cannot substitute for hearing the gospel preached, yet his own *Sincere Convert,* penned very shortly after his exposition of the parable, does everything it can to breathe life into such a "Carkass." First, its general organization constantly moves from general gospel principles to specific judgments, pungent diction, and lively imagery. By virtue of false values, "men *sinning* take *Christ* for a *dish-clout,* to wipe them clean again"; any good in man "is but as a drop of Rose-water in a bowl of poyson"; everywhere "God's Justice is questioned; men think God to be all Mercy, and no Justice, all Honey, and no Sting"; "Great Politicians are like Children, always standing on their heads, and shaking their heels against Heaven"; and "the never-dying worm of a guilty Conscience shall torment thee, as if thou hadst swallowed down a living poysonful snake, which shall lie gnawing and biting thine heart for sin past, day and night." Such a style is metaphysical it is true, or quaint, homely, and fantastic, but it is also appealingly vigorous and imaginative.

Sometimes its excellence relies upon conventional tropes and schemes to effect predictable ends. Thus Shepard heartily urges his reader: "Oh labour to see and behold this God. Is there a God, and wilt not give him a good look? Oh pass by all the Rivers, till thou come to the spring-head; wade through all Creatures, until thou art drowned, plunged, and swallowed up with God." Or, in a contrary mood, exposing the fate of the natural man: "God is a consuming fire against thee, and there is but one paper-wall of thy body between thy Soul and eternal flames. How soon may God stop thy breath? There is nothing but that between thee and Hell; if that were gone, then farewell all. Thou art condemned, and the muffler is before thine eyes; God knows how soon the ladder may be turned: thou hangst but by one rotton twined thread of thy life over the flames of Hell every hour." At other times, and even more energetically, Shepard writes extended passages of equal rhetorical skill, but infused with his private sense of urgency, commitment, wonder and delight. His excitement fuses cadence and diction into lyric passages combining principles with specifics, system with details, and reason with heartfelt emotion: "When we see a stately House, although *we* see not the man that built it, although also we know not the time when it was built, yet will we conclude thus, sure some wise Artificer hath been working here: can we, when we behold the stately Theatre of Heaven and Earth, conclude other, but that the finger, arms, and wisdom of God have been here, although we see not him that is invisible, and although we know not the time when he began to build? Every Creature in Heaven and Earth, is a loud Preacher of this truth. Who set those Candles, those Torches of Heaven on the Table? Who hung out those Lanthorns in Heaven, to enlighten a dark World? Who can make the statue of a man, but one wiser and greater than man? Who taught the Birds to build their Nests, and the Bees to set up and Order their Common-wealth? Who sends the Sun post, from one end of Heaven to the other, carrying so many thousand blessings to so many thousands of People and Kingdoms? What Power of Men or Angels can make the least pile of

Grass, or put life into the least Flie, if once dead?" And one inevitably anticipates Edward Taylor's response,

> Who? who did this? or who is he? Why, know
> It's Onely Might Almighty this did doe.[5]

To introduce Edward Taylor into the company of Thomas Shepard as a theologian in place of Samuel Willard or Increase and Cotton Mather may seem eccentric, for Taylor's prose was never published in his lifetime, and whatever claim he makes on our attention today is by his poetry, not his preaching. But Taylor's connection with Shepard extends far beyond the similarity of phrasing in the two (which is, however, ample). Shepard's distinction between true and seeming Christians, sincere converts and hypocrites, is in the last analysis more ardent than precise. There was room and need for more helpful directions, but like Shepard's, they would have to proceed from an examination of God's essence, attributes, persons, and works, which were tough meat even for the first generations of American Puritans. In his *Magnalia Christi Americana* (1702), Cotton Mather could single out only very few preachers whose doctrine was so basic. But after 1680 there seems to have been a concentrated effort to examine such problems anew. One way to do so was to republish earlier examples of basic theological writing, especially when its tone and style exemplified the devotional ardor wanting at the end of the seventeenth century. The London editor of Shepard's *Sincere Convert* (1680) exulted in the publishing phenomenon: "What infinite cause hath this Age to acknowledge the unspeakable mercy of God in affording us such plenty of spiritual Tractates, full of Divine, necessary, and conscience-searching truths, yea precious, soul-comforting, and soul-improving truths? Such whereby Head, Heart, and Soul-cheating errours are discovered, and prevented; such as soundly difference true grace from all seemings and paintings." In America that cause was unintentionally abetted by the "liberal" reforms of Solomon Stoddard, whose most tenacious opponent was Edward Taylor.

In 1693, having reached a point of utter exasperation with
Stoddard's refusal to distinguish between true grace and all seemings and paintings, Taylor entered the controversy. Stoddard had
in effect surrendered Shepard's attempt to distinguish sincere
converts from hypocrites, and signified the futility of such efforts
by opening the Lord's Supper to all persons of nonscandalous
behavior. Such apostasy so close to his own congregation at
Westfield brought from Taylor limited but pointed epithets—
Arminian, Pelagian, Popish, and perhaps worst of all, pre-
sumptuous! To show these errors budding and blossoming in the
very heart of New England became Taylor's main purpose in the
eight sermons he structured into what may be called his "Treatise
Concerning the Lord's Supper."[6] Like Shepard, Taylor suggests
here that the want of evangelical righteousness is what locked the
five virgins of the parable out of the wedding feast. But Taylor's
"Treatise" explores another parable involving another wedding
feast, the wedding feast of the king's son at which appeared a guest
without a proper wedding garment (Matth. XXII: 2-14). Hereby
Taylor is led to a different body of images—primarily images of
spinning, weaving, and decorating holy robes for glory—while
maintaining the same central position that Shepard does.

Though Taylor uses clothing imagery profusely in all his
writing, here his robes are the wedding garments of the parable,
which symbolize evangelical righteousness or true holiness. "Holy
garments and a holy life Suite one another. Every third of this
garment is a twine of holiness, and hence the Web is holy and the
person that weares it, wares it onely in holy Wayes." The main
question for Taylor, after assembling testimony from scripture
and learned divines regarding the nature of true holiness, becomes this: how do you know that the robe you wear to the feast
(the Lord's Supper in Taylor's exposition of the parable) is
cloth of the Lord's weaving, and not a cheap imitation? How do
you know if you have true holiness? Taylor's answer is less
interesting than is his method. First, such knowledge requires
special faculties or powers—"A Discerning Eye to Discern
Spirituall things." "A Receiving hand," and a "Concoctive Power

or Faculty"—which are themselves evidence of holiness. Given these faculties, each man must make trial of his own soul-state, and to assist in the trial Taylor offers a series of "helps" by which to come to the probable and saving knowledge of one's spiritual state. First he presents a series of negative considerations, "Such as you must not draw your conclusion from": awareness of sin, the hankering after forbidden fruit, multitudes of carnal thoughts, doubts of the nature and presence of true grace or even of the existence of God. All these may be present and still not prove that a soul is not truly gracious. On the affirmative side, he advises, seek an unprejudiced will and affections, a clear spiritual sight, and with them examine yourself to find an invincible hatred for sin and an invincible love for spiritual things—holiness itself, the sacrament of the Lord's Supper, manifestations of grace in all private and public ways, and God and Christ as the source of all loveliness.

At this point Taylor's emphasis on the affections and the loveliness of holy things moves him to rapturous exclamation, much as Shepard was moved by his own considerations: "Oh! the Sweet heart ravishing Melodies, Musicks, and Songs of a Spirituall nature with which Christ entertains Souls hereat, what tongue of man, or Angell is able to relate?" And he proceeds to exhort his reader to experience the delights of this knowledge of true holiness in passages paralleling his logic, tone, and imagery both in *God's Determinations* and in the *Preparatory Meditations*. On one hand, then, in so bringing knowledge to poetical power, Taylor's work reveals colonial theology working as a source and motive for American poetry of no mean value. But on another, he manifests the lyric inclination of colonial theology itself, an inclination strong enough to have obviated the need for formal poetry through its contemplation of the source of all beauty. Certainly the evidence for this is strong in other documents that turn on this same issue. And Increase Mather's *Practical Truths* (1682) and *Meditations on the glory of the Lord Jesus Christ* (1705); his son Cotton's *Companion for Communicants* (1690); and especially Samuel Willard's posthumous *Brief Sacramental*

Meditations for Communion at the Great Ordinance of the Supper (1711) all show that Taylor's unpublished "Treatise" is not a unique or even eccentric work in subject or tone, and that within the confines of special purposes and controversial occasions there was often room in colonial theology for writing of beauty and excitement as well as close reasoning and tough thinking.

By 1710 the public debate over Stoddardism was subsiding. In fact, Stoddard's "easier" religion had pretty much its own way until nearly midcentury, supported by a literature rather social and evangelistic than either rapturous or analytic, and by the talents of Stoddard's grandson and successor at Northampton, Jonathan Edwards. Beginning in 1734, Edwards' preaching began to enjoy a success beyond accounting, and his entrance onto the American and international literary scene would come as a description of that success in his *Faithful Narrative of Surprising Conversions* (1737). Within two years, this collection of case studies of experimental religion went through twenty printings in three editions, finding both German and Dutch translations.[7] But after the 1740 Boston arrival of George Whitefield, the anti-intellectualism, anti-institutionalism, simple antinomianism, and general hysteria that accompanied the rich harvest of souls in New England began to draw criticism, especially for its unabashed emotionalism.

Edwards, too, acknowledged the excesses of the Great Awakening, but sought to salvage what of real value there was in the experience. The same analytic and objective spirit that prompted the *Faithful Narrative* now turned to explore the arguments against the validity of wholesale conversions in general, and against religious emotionalism in particular. In his *Distinguishing Marks of the Works of the Spirit of God* (1741) and *Some Thoughts on the Revival of Religion in New England* (1743), two important emphases developed in Edwards' thought. First, like Shepard and Taylor, he found himself insisting (quite against grandfather Stoddard's teaching) on the possibility of distinguishing the workings of true grace from hypocritical paintings and seemings; and secondly, he refused to disallow the affective or emotional significance of religious experience. To these he brought his own splendid talent for close and insistent thought, and a speculative concern with the grounds and reasons of all things unmatched in earlier American writing.

Some time between these two publications, Edwards sought to work out his distinguishing signs of true holiness more precisely than he had heretofore, probably in a series of sermons. His conclusions appeared in 1746 under the title, *A Treatise Concerning Religious Affections,* devoting 343 pages to the doctrine that *"True Religion, in great Part, consists in holy Affections."* Of the importance of his subject he entertains no doubts: "There is no Question whatsoever, that is of greater Importance to Mankind, and that it more concerns every individual Person to be well resolved in, than this, *What are the distinguishing Qualifications of those that are in Favour with God, and entitled to his eternal Rewards?* Or, which comes to the same Thing, *What is the Nature of true Religion? and wherein do lie the distinguishing Notes of that Vertue and Holiness, that is acceptable in the Sight of God."*[8] And what is more, he argues, differences over this fundamental theological question lie behind all religious controversies; his treatment, therefore, socially or historically conditioned as Shepard's and Taylor's were not, achieves a degree of sophistication beyond theirs.

Like Shepard, as Edwards' editor John E. Smith points out, Edwards' first concern is to maintain the necessity of the affections in religious experience. The similarity is emphasized by frequent citation of Shepard in his footnotes, especially of *The Parable of the Ten Virgins* and *The Sincere Convert.* Both Shepard and Edwards insist that affections, will, and understanding act intimately together in the regenerate, sanctified soul, and both maintain the supernatural nature of the principle from which holy characteristics proceed, though Shepard (like Taylor) calls it a principle of life, while Edwards treats it as a divine sense. Of course Edwards is much more detailed, emphatic, and complex in *Religious Affections,* but even allowing for his willingness to take support wherever he finds it (he quotes or cites Stoddard almost as frequently as Shepard), it is clear that he found Shepard's thought congenial. But there is nowhere in the *Religious Affections* the rapture and excitement of either Shepard or Taylor. What there is, nonetheless, is Taylor's method—first a series of twelve inconclusive signs such as Taylor advised "you must not draw your conclusion from"; and then twelve "Distinguishing Signs of Truly Gracious and Holy Affections." Each of the signs—supernatural origins, disinterested appreciation, the loveliness of divine things, the rectified mind, the "reasonable and spiritual conviction" of the reality of divine things, evangelical humiliation, a change of nature, the Christ-like spirit, tenderness, symmetrical and beautiful dispositions, insatiable longing, and their display in Christian practice—each is readily matched in Taylor's "Treatise," though Edwards' terms and images will cluster around words of taste, while Taylor's, like Shepard's, more traditionally evoke concepts of insight and illumination. By virtue of his more insistent and elaborate exploration, Edwards, far beyond either Shepard or Taylor, makes clear the complexities of man's moral nature that would fascinate Hawthorne, Melville, and James. For he acknowledges even in the midst of hope for a purer time to come that "there never will, in this World, be an entire Purity; either in particular Saints, in a perfect Freedom from Mixtures of Corruption; or in the Church of God, without any Mixture of Hypocrites with Saints, and counterfeit Religion, and false Appearances of Grace, with true Religion and real Holiness."[9]

For later American writers, this would be the concern of serious narrative. But for Edwards, in spite of his earlier narrative inclination in the *Faithful Narrative,* its results were song, as he indicates not in his *Treatise* but in the "Personal Narrative" written about the time his thoughts on these matters were foremost. There he shows us that thinking on holiness led him not only to visionary gales of ardent longing to be "wrapt and swallowed up in God" and to songs and chanted meditations, but also to the very imagery of Taylor's *Preparatory Meditations,* where the soul so frequently appears as Edwards describes it: "like such a little white flower as we see in the spring of the year; low and humble on the ground, opening its bosom to receive the pleasant beams of the sun's glory; rejoicing as it were in a calm rapture; diffusing around a sweet fragrancy; standing peacefully and lovingly, in the midst of other flowers round about; all in like manner opening their bosoms, to drink in the light of the sun . . . and there was nothing that I so earnestly longed for."[10]

With his curious and penetrating intellect, Jonathan Edwards could never rest content with the relatively facile conclusions of Thomas Shepard, much as he felt their rightness. Nor could he, except in an even more private and personal way than Edward Taylor, give lyric form and voice to the moving truths of his theology. But in spirit he was one with them, and his exceptional talent may be said to prepare the way for later American literature in several ways. First, he established questions about the complexity of human character and urged that they be addressed while disallowing simple dogma to stand in the place of honesty and logic in answering them. Second, he gave native theological sanction to the sentimental, even sensational, appeal to the emotions that would mark the fiction of sensibility as it developed in the magazines during and after the Revolution—at least one strand of which derives from his own case studies of religious sensibility. And third, he elaborately probed the dominant problem of nineteenth-century literature, the difficulty of distinguishing appearance from reality in the world of moral judgment.

In a very real sense, then, Edwards brought to realization the major implication of colonial theology for American literature. It was not simply the accident of time and circumstance making theology the dominant interest of early American writing that makes it important; it is the fundamental problems of human as well as divine nature with which theology itself was concerned and with which aesthetic sensibilities had to catch up before a significant American literature could develop. Edwards' intuitive and solid grasp of the possible relationships between beauty and

truth, even uncomely truth, belongs at the head of the in-
dividualistic and psychological interests that would wither before
the social and political interests of the end of the century, but
come to brilliant fruition in the work of the early Emerson
and Hawthorne.[11] But as an historical event himself, Edwards
would be the first to demand that he be accounted for by some
cause. And that cause lies in the mystical theology represented
best by the meditative and devotional writing of Edward Taylor,
itself rooted in the temperament and work of Thomas Shepard.
Perhaps too much has been made of the Hooker-Stoddard-
Mayhew-Franklin tradition of the first two centuries of American
history. Its importance for American institutional and political
development cannot be denied, but it has unnecessarily clouded
another tradition of even greater importance for American art
and literature. When Jonathan Edwards said that the nature of
the truly gracious affections was inseparable from the question,
"What is the Nature of true Religion?" he signified that the
search for and creation of beauty in human forms is at least
above the political and ethical sphere of much American writing,
and not unrelated to true godliness. Thomas Shepard as much
as anyone first established the tradition; Edward Taylor showed
that it could be not only the source but indeed the substance
of real lyric poetry; and Jonathan Edwards enunciated its psychological and aesthetic potential for greater artists to follow.

NOTES

1. The works referred to here are the following: Perry Miller, *The
New England Mind: The Seventeenth Century* (Cambridge, Mass.,
1939) and *Errand into the Wilderness* (Cambridge, Mass., 1956); C. H.
Faust, "The Decline of Puritanism," in *Transitions in American
Literary History*, ed. H. H. Clark (Durham, N.C., 1954); Herbert W.
Schneider, *The Puritan Mind* (New York, 1930); Josephine K.
Piercy, *Studies in Literary Types in Seventeenth Century America*

(1607-1710), Yale Studies in English 91 (New Haven, 1939); and Kenneth B. Murdock, *Theology & Literature in Colonial New England* (Cambridge, Mass., 1949).

2. *The Intellectual Life of Colonial New England* (New York: Cornell University Press, 1956), p. 170.

3. Samuel Willard, *The Child's Portion* (Boston, 1684), p. 66; cited in Perry Miller and Thomas H. Johnson, eds., *The Puritans*, rev. ed. (New York: Harper & Row, 1963), I, 369.

4. Shepard's incomplete notes were prepared for publication by his son Thomas and Jonathan Mitchell, whose "Epistle to the Reader" apologizes for the roughness of style: "It may also easily be observed, that not curiosity of words, but weight of things was here studied by, and flowed from the heart and pen of the Author, which yet produceth the best and truest, *i.e.* a real Rhetorick" (Sig. A3).

5. "The Preface" to "Gods Determinations touching his Elect," ed. Donald E. Stanford, *The Poems of Edward Taylor* (New Haven: Yale University Press, 1960), p. 387, lines 19-20.

6. All quotations are from the Taylor holograph in the Prince Collection of the Boston Public Library. A fuller description of the sermons and their possible influence appears in my introduction to *Edward Taylor's Treatise Concerning the Lord's Supper* (East Lansing, Mich., 1965) and in my *Edward Taylor* (New York, 1961), pp. 34-38.

7. See Thomas H. Johnson, *The Printed Writings of Jonathan Edwards, 1703-1758: A Bibliography* (Princeton, 1940), pp. 4-15; and Clarence H. Faust and Thomas H. Johnson, eds., *Jonathan Edwards: Representative Selections*, rev. ed. (New York: Hill and Wang, 1962), p. 420.

8. Jonathan Edwards, *A Treatise Concerning Religious Affections* (Boston, 1746), Sig. A2. Cf. vol. II of *The Works of Jonathan Edwards*, ed. John E. Smith (New Haven: Yale University Press, 1959), p. 84.

9. Edwards, p. iii; Smith, p. 86.

10. From "Memoirs of the Late Jonathan Edwards, A.M.," in *Works*, ed. Samuel Austin, 8 vols. (Worcester, 1808), I, 38.

11. The most comprehensive treatment of later literary uses of "the Puritan legacy" is Kenneth Murdock's excellent *Literature & Theology*, cited above.

The Canadian Crank

VICTOR M. HOWARD

The calamitous tendency of Canadians to self-abasement verging on self-abuse has long been the acceptable 'central cedar pole' of American foreign policy with respect to Canada. A more appropriate metaphor: Canada, until quite recently, has occupied the third drawer on the left of the U.S. State Department's Western Europe desk. So confident have American displomats and politicians been of Canada's 'good form' that no Canadian Prime Minister, as of the Bi-centennial summer, had ever addressed the two houses of Congress. The State Department's explanation that 'it just forgot' seems, until recently, to have satisfied Ottawa.

What has happened to alter this reasonably happy situation and thus to prompt the creation of Canada-Watchers is the unexpected shift of Canada to the role of 'crank'. One remembers with some admiration that country's late achievements as 'peace-keeper', as arbitrator and negotiator, diffident, politic. Now without a doubt, that disposition has been set aside to be replaced by a countenance that is surly, tight-lipped, even, one hesitates to propose, stern. The Crank.

The approach of Canada to this new identity over the past five years might have been noted by Americans had they not, during the early 1970's, been absorbed in the final solution to the national dream of a greater south Asian co-prosperity sphere. A brief and fleeting anxiety about political morality also took its toll in public opinion. By the time Americans had collected their wits and looked north, the Canadian Crank had come into being. What Americans had not seen during those lost years:

1. The Brantford Raids. On seven occasions, from April 1 to April 17, 1970, platoons of the Second Battalion of the Duke of Durham's Canadian Light Infantry made incursions across the Detroit River into Michigan at points ranging south from Port Huron to Detroit itself. Disguised variously as delegates to an International Rotary convention and as pollsters representing a Windsor, Ontario, commercial radio station, WCKL, the troopers entered the United States, moved quickly to staging points where they armed themselves from munitions caches first established in reprisal for the Fenian Raids into Canada during the 19th Century. Denounced eventually by the Canadian government as "an isolated incident not at all in consonance with Canada's good neighbour policy", the raids none-the-less sharpened that nation's appetite for confrontation. Although little damage was done by the raiders and no casualties were suffered on either side, in part because the raiders came and departed without being discovered by any Americans, their commanding officer, Major Dundas Brantford, declared the mission "an unqualified success": for, as Major Branford put it over WCKL, on April 19, "my young eagles have been blooded".

2. Bill 42. Acceded to on November 12, 1971 by the Legislative Assembly of Manitoba, this legislation required the dismissal from any Canadian language spoken or written or otherwise employed by a living person within the legal boundaries of Manitoba of: "words, phrases or sentences known to be American in origin". Again, the Canadian government disassociated itself from this action. Its spokesperson, Lillian Contretemps, an information officer in the Canadian Consulate Office, Minot, North Dakota, asserted: "Regrettable."

3. The Colorado River Controversy. Residents along the 1500 mile Colorado River were alarmed on the morning of May 6, 1972, to discover that the river had reversed its course so that it flowed from north to south instead of the other way. A fourteen month study by the U.S. Department of the Interior concluded that apparently the reversal was man-made, that the perpetrators were Canadians living in Denver but that "no malice seems apparent". Shortly after that, the Colorado River dried up.

4. The Louisiana Purchase. The most provocative development occurred on December 7, 1972, when the Government of Canada, by Order in Council, declared that it had bought the State of Louisiana. Conceding a long-standing interest in francophone nations or states, the Order insisted, however, that the sale had been initiated by "Americans for Ethnic Rehabilitation," a middle-of-the-road lobby. Citizens of Louisiana were given a choice between taking out Canadian papers or moving to Texas or Mississippi or Arkansas.

This sequence of events, scarcely attended to by Americans, as has been noticed, can now be placed in perspective. They are nothing more than an elaborately planned subversion of American interests. The reaction of the Government of the United States in the last days has been understandable. Confronted by evidence of this Canadian scenario, the President of the United States moved to create The "Legion of Canada-Watchers." Simultaneously, the Chief Executive named the Legion's first chairman: Professor Creighton Lipset MacDougal, Distinguished Professor of History, University of West Florida. Sworn in on June 12, 1975, Professor MacDougal immediately called a press conference during which he outlined his credentials (a visit to Expo 67 and 'friends in Canadian university circles') and described his concern over the appearance of the Canadian Crank. Said Professor MacDougal:

> Such phenomenan as the Brantford Raids and Bill 42 have no place in the North American Way. But they have taken

place and there is little that we can do about them now. But I will call your attention to an insidious penetration of our country's culture by Canadians who, under the guise of dis-affected entertainers, intellectuals, writers and military authorities, have slipped below the border and have, over the years, infiltrated those most crucial processes whereby we form national and public values. "Canadianization" is taking place to a degree and at a pace that, knowing I speak on record, I can only label 'startling'.

I refer you to that mild-mannered, consummately fair patriarch, Ben Cartwright, who is really from Montreal, but who has interpreted our early history as though he were actually an American. His three sons, Joseph, Horse and What's-His-Name, were all born in New Brunswick, and the Cartwright family home is demonstrably a poor but de-liberate copy of Kingsmere!

I refer you to James Kirk, also from Montreal. That eminently skilled technician, that paragon of absolute au-thority, is a Canadian. Heroes to millions of American youths, Kirk and his assistants, one of whom is a Scot from Mississauga, Ontario, bear responsibility for organizing our children into blind, hapless, followers.

I refer you to John Canaday, an Eastern establishment art critic who has cleverly concealed his Canadian birthright (born in Newfoundland) by declining over a thirty-five year career ever to comment on Canadian art.

I refer you to one, G. Trudeau, a satirist and folk-artist well known to our youth, who is by his own confession, the natural son of the scion of the prominent Montreal service station empire.

I refer you to the balladeer and aptly named, Hank Snow.

Slowly but surely, such rascals are taking over our life-styles, Canadianizing, Canadianizing.

Professor MacDougal's address, ranked by many as being as crucial a document as the Turner Thesis, next outlined the *apparat* by which his Legion would proceed on its assignment. MacDougal ingeniously opted for the 'Kleindienst' Gambit, a tactic used previously during the Siege of Paris and the Occupation of Mexico City. Briefly, the K. G. [so-called by F.S.O. (abbreviation for Foreign Service Officers)] calls for the black-mailing of natives of the country-under-surveillance who have some extraordinary relationship to the United States. In the case of Canada, that relationship was immediately seen to be through the presence of several thousand American traitors euphemistically named "United Empire Loyalists." Descendants of Americans who refused to fight against the British during the late war for independence and who had sneaked abroad, into Canada, seeking refuge and a place in the sun, these Canadians now clung by their very fingertips to a precarious existence. Ostracized by the French, scorned by the Ukrainians, humiliated by the Italians, the U.E.L. (short for United Empire Loyalists or, colloquially, Uncommonly Elegant Loungers) had languished in the backwash of Modern Canada. Relegated in Ontario to living on prescrbed tracts of land described by one occupant as "not fit for Five Nations injuns," the U.E.L. had further been deprived of their civil rights, their 13th grade education and their tots of rum.

In accord with the K.G. (short for Kleindienst 'Gambit'), the U.E.L. would be approached by a representative of the Public Broadcasting System who would seek their assistance in preparing a documentary (complete with sound) fil-em of displaced and misplaced tribes, half-grown societies, marginal incomes, incestuous families and scoff-laws. Acknowledging as net income per capita of 48¢ per annum, the U.E.L. was quick to respond to the P.B.S. officer's appeal which promised $84 down, 1% of the gross and final cut. In return, he asked only that the U.E.L. smile, appear natural, wear native costumes and identify other non-U.E.L. Canadians who might be watched.

The actual watching would be done in three towns along the 49th Parallel: Cleveland, Ohio; Minot, S.D. (the home of Lillian Contretemps) and LaTouche, Michigan. Each of these towns was linked by Metro-Cable, a top-secret radar/hi-fi/fil-em scanner which, properly coded and indexed, would focus on a "Canadian" once that figure had been so designated. Now came the crucial part. The actual designation to be carried out by the ostracized, scorned and humiliated U.E.L. was, quite simply, a large "M" painted discretely on the back of the Canadian. Chalk seems to be the most reliable substance for maximum and durable imprint. So it was that chalk, 147,000 pounds of it, slipped across the 1000 Island Bridge on the evening of August 15, 1975, hidden in bauble earrings worn by the girl friends of draft-dodgers living in Gananawuary, Ontario. Dodgers and dodgees, themselves scorned by everyone, dispersed the chalk to U.E.L. Kleindienst Gambit was underway.

By the end of August, the Legion of Canada Watchers had begun to carry out its assignment. In Minot, in LaTouche and in Cleveland, discreet young GS-12's and GS-13's gathered about the hi/fi fil-em scanners and watched as the 'M' 's came into focus. The first to be spied appeared on the back of Mrs. Lola Brane, an American, from Buffalo who was found standing on the corner of Bloor and Yonge in DOWNTOWN Toronto. Her resemblance to a native Canadian was striking, so claimed Professor Fisher Wing, a U.S. Federal Government analyst and real Navaho. Thus, a U.E.L. had mistakenly chalked her. The next 'fix' as GS-14 Herbert Harbert put it, came moments later, actually at 16:50, (Nautical Time), September 2, 1975. "There's one!" cried Harbert. And no doubt about it. There was, after all, a Canadian.

So it went that summer and into the autumn, as Canadian after Canadian was identified, M and all, registered in a central directory after confirmation by Professor Wing and a file, an individual file, opened for cross reference. Gradually, the excitement and challenge of the search swept all three stations so that, comically, the staffs at Minot, LaTouche and Cleveland actually vied for successful achievement of daily quotas. Cleveland took the month of August with 55 actual Canadians identified, though Minot came through in September with 140. Think of that. By Christmas, naturally enough, the work had become somewhat humdrum although the young GS officers assigned appreciated that this work would figure prominently in their Civil Service dossiers. So it would. In fact, GS-14, Quinn Morow, as a direct consequence of his 47 hour record at the scanner during which he positively identified 14 Canadians, shortly after the first of the year, 1976, became our new Ambassador to San Salvador! No doubt well deserving, Ambassador Morow must be perplexed and chargrined to know of the next assignment in the Legion of Canada-Watchers: the identification and abduction of an actual Canadian Crank!

Code-named Operation Blossomseeley, the identification and abduction of an actual Canadian Crank demanded careful planning, utmost secrecy and permission from the Oval Office. Seeking to assuage the President's doubts as to the legality of Operation Blossomseeley, Professor MacDougal, head of the Legion of Canada-Watchers, personally briefed the Chief. Actually, the President, always quick off the mark, raised the first question: "MacDougal, what in hell *does* a Canadian look like?" Drawing on his visit to Expo 67 and more recent reports from Minot, LaTouche and Cleveland, MacDougal ingeniously sketched a profile: Mostly Anglo-Saxon in skin tone, mostly slight of stature, inclined (the men anyway) toward knickers, dark stockings, double-breasted blazers and Hush Puppies. The women tend to dress somewhat more severely, most of them being Anglican and staying at home a lot. Blouses without bosoms, sensible shoes, hair in a bun, that sort of thing. The trend-setter in fashion, it seemed, was the Queen of Canada and India, Elizabeth II. The Canadian child, added MacDougal, blushing, is usually allowed to run naked in the yard.

"And what in hell language *do* these Canadians speak?" asked the President. MacDougal replied that the most common language was 'lingua-anglica' or 'ling' a corruption of the very handsome hybrid French/English language which had emerged during the so-called Golden Era in Canada after 1800. Thus, "How about coming over for a drink?" became, in the original Frenglish, "Comment-allez booze a mi casa." In 'ling', unfortunately, this became simply "Coboozoca."

Apparently satisfied, the President motioned for MacDougal

to proceed with the briefing. The head of the Legion of Canada-Watchers explained that Blossomseeley would involve the kidnapping of the Canadian Prime Minister, without a doubt the biggest crank of them all. "Are there precedents?" queried the President. MacDougal explained that the arrest of the President of San Salvador, the kidnapping of the Premier of France and the Leslie Fiedler drug bust were all legally established precedents. He added that the kidnapping was obviously in the national interest, in any case. The caper, as he put it, would take place next week on Friday, February 21, as the Prime Minister drove from his home to his office in the basement of Simpson-Sears Department Store in Ottaway, the capitol city of all of Canada. Though heavily guarded by units of the Duke of Durham's Canadian Light Infantry (the same regiment involved in the Brantford Raids) these troopers were notoriously pacific, not having been in a war in 47 years. It was assumed by MacDougal and his young military attache, Corporal Winston Churchill Mott, that a surprise move would baffle the Canadian soldiers.

The President signed the order of attack, turned his tape recorder back on, and said, "Good talking with you, MacDougal old man. Interesting project this," and walked out.

Blossomseeley proved more than successful. Without shedding blood and only frightening the P.M.'s guards a little, a cadre of 1500 ex-C.I.A. officers and former football greats, gathered gradually in an apartment in downtown Ottaway days later and when the P.M.'s caravan passed beneath their window, one leaned out and yelled, "Pee on you, P.M.," a cry of defiance which so angered the P.M.'s escort that they turned away from the limousine, rushed the apartment and thus distracted, did not see Corporal W. C. Mott, MacDougal's military attache, whisk across the street, pull the chauffeur from the car, slip behind the wheel and drive off in the bright daylight, his destination, LaTouche, Michigan. A potentially grim moment came at the Windsor, Ontario, tunnel when Canadian customs people came over to investigate, but since none of them recognized the P.M., the car swept through.

Victor M. Howard

The actual text of the debriefing of the Prime Minister is classified. However, the abstract that is set down here is known to be accurate. The Canadian P.M. and his interrogators were lodged in a Holiday Inn in downtown LaTouche where, over the following four days, the interview continued.

P.M. Call me Ti-Pi. My story is long, yes, but true, yes? Whenever I feel the chill of circumspection wrapping me in its ghostly. . . .

Q. Ti-Pi?

P.M. It is 'ling' for Ti-Pierre or Little Pierre. . . . . wrapping me in its ghostly. . . .

Q. What are you talking about?

P.M. Effervescence and efflorescence and federalism.
[The remainder of the interrogation on Day One thereafter subsided into vague philosophical rhetoric. Likewise Day Two through Three. On Day Four. . . .]

P.M. Federalistique, federalisme, federast. The North, the North . . .

Q. Mr. Ti-Pi?

P.M. Yes?

Q. Could we ask you some questions?

P.M. Have you put them on the order paper?

Q. Yes sir.

P.M. Very well. May I have an Orange Crush first?

Q. We will send for one. May we begin?

P.M. Why of course.

Q. Why have you Canadians become so cranky lately?

P.M. Being prime minister is not an easy job. You should try it sometime.

Q. The question. . . .

P.M. All right. Before I answer, will you guarantee me safe conduct, an airplane complete with provisions for me and my party to take us to haven in San Salvador?

Q. There is no one else in your party. You are all alone. And why San Salvador? What about Algiers or Havana?

P.M. One: I am the party. Two: I hiked across San Salvador

when I was 45, no 43. Took me 38 days without water and then I fell over the fence at that. I feel very, how do you say, sympathetic, to San Salvador.

Q. Why have you Canadians become so cranky lately?

P.M. No more Mr. Nice Guy for us! We are tired of being NICE. Do you know how debilitating and uncreative it is to be NICE? Always NICE. Where is my Orange Crush?

Q. But when you stopped being nice, you threw the whole infra-structure off balance. The Dow-Jones has dropped 145 points, the OAS has disintegrated. NATO is collapsing. Surely you know this?

P.M. Poo! No more jets, no more missiles—In your shorts you'll find some thistles! Good huh?! Thistles! Ha! Anyway, read my memoirs: *Ten Canadas*. Hurtig and Stewart, 1977.

Q. Why Ten?

P.M. Being prime minister is not an easy job.

Q. The crankiness; the crankiness. Let's get on with it.

P.M. We don't like you, you know. We deee-spize you! Big, tough, pushy gringos! So, we have decided to become big, tough, pushy too. Cranky! From ocean to ocean, from Arctic Circle to the 49th Parallel! Cranky. Fussbudget. Poo on you!

Q. And what do you hope to achieve?

P.M. Equal status. Equus, in 'ling'.

Q. And then? What will you have then?

P.M. A tirade in the UN, a filibuster in the OAS, an overflow in OPEC, a way out of NATO.

Q. How destructive.

P.M. Can you really ever hope to appreciate what it has meant all these years, all these years I say, to have been uniquely, singularly, absolutely the nicest bunch of people in the world. And with the second highest standard of living in the world, that same world! Even the Swedes went to bed with each other before they got married, if they did. Even the Swedes went skinny dipping with impunity. NICE. NICE. NICE. When the Mafia tried to take over Montreal, they withdrew

finally because the Quebecois were too NICE. When
Billy the Kid tried to escape into Canada, he turned
back because we were too infernally NICE. You know
why we were so long getting our soldier boys onto
the Western Front in WWI?

Q. Too nice?

P.M. Too nice.

Q. So now, you want to be a crank.

P.M. Yes. Yes. A crank. A mean, savage drooling, teeth-
gnashing, apoplectic crank. Vicious, biting, spastic,
UNAMERICAN!!

Q. Did you actually say UNAMERICAN!!???

P.M. Toute suite, mon ami. Okey dokey, now you com-
prenvous. I am a closet UNAMERICAN.
[The P.M. proceeded to describe himself as a closet
UNALABAMAN, UNALASKAN, UNARIZONAN,
UNARKANSAN. . . . . . UNWYOMINGAN not to
fail to mention all the territories]

Q. But we Americans don't want to be disliked. On the
contrary, we want to be well liked.

P.M. Who cares?

Q. Can we correct this unfortunate impression?

P.M. It is too late.

Q. You mean?

P.M. A wall is going up along the 49th Parallel. The lights
are going out in Minot.

And with that, the poor fellow darted out of the door, rushed
across the fields to his plane which gathered itself and soared
south to San Salvador.

Now comes the era in North American civilization which is
long to be lamented by observers. The era called "Entre Nous."
The catastrophe which marks this period was first sighted by
Mrs. Humbert Tell, a housekeeper from Vancouver, who had
crossed the border into Seattle on December 20, 1977, in order to
complete her shopping for Christmas. As Mrs. Tell puts it:
"Walking back to my bus which awaited me on the other side, I
crossed the actual line demarking the two nations, God Bless

'em. I happened to look between my legs and I saw a saw, one of those jaggedy edged saws, going up and down, up and down, along that very noble line, moving ever so slowly but carefully eastward toward the Atlantic. So shocked was I that when I came home, I could hardly put on the tea-kettle. Little did I know. . . ."

Yes, little did Mrs. Humbert Tell know that she was the first human person to witness the work of that master criminal-politician-QC, Lorne Morley, who had recruited a band of disillusioned Indians, Liberals, Korean War draft-dodgers and such riff-raff to assist him in: SAWING THE UNITED STATES FREE FROM CANADA!!!

Morley's Tomfoolery, as his colleagues in the Yukon Territory Legislative Assembly dubbed it, had been provided seed money by the Canada Council and the Canadian Booksellers League and with this sum, the arch-fiend had recruited his team, bought three handsaws and a compass and had proceeded, on November 16, previously to Mrs. Tell's trip, to SAW THE UNITED STATES FREE FROM CANADA. Not deterred by Mrs. Tell's discovery, Morley and his team of thugs sawed on, past Bellingham, across Glacier National Park, north beyond Minot—Eastward, ever Eastward.

Alerted now by the noises and the sawdust, the American government sought to counter-attack by depressing the muzzles of 476 Tital ICBM missles situated in the town of Minnow, Minnesota. Warned by the Russians against any unusual moves, the Americans hastily if reluctantly raised their muzzles, thus permitting Morley's fanatical band to saw on.

Troubled by this turn of events, the President of the United States called Professor C. L. MacDougal, head of the League of Canada-Watchers, to the Oval Office and there demonstrated his anxiety. "Do you know, MacDougal, that everything west of the Continental Divide has slid into the Pacific and that the east is teetering, literally teetering on the brink of the Atlantic? Do you have any insights?"

"I scarcely know what to say, Prime Minister."

"What," cried the President, "What did you call me?"

"Prime Minister! And now it can come out, for I have not sold my birthright for a mess o'Florida. My mother was a Canadian and my father, that proud, noble fellow, was a MacDougal and I, I must remain loyal to my country and queen. You, you savage, who dared to bully us, to heap opprobriums on the gentle Canadians, to mercilessly kidnap our leader and ship him to San Salvador. Your day is at an end. Ohhhh long I have waited for this moment."

And with that, the incredible MacDougal snapped his fingers, in rushed the President's aides, all Canadians smuggled in through the Harvard School of Business and Johns Hopkins School for Advanced International Studies, and these lads quickly fetched the President off in a helicopter to a cotton patch outside of Texarkana. MacDougal and his lads fled that same day to Ottaway where they were immediately assigned jobs in the Public Archives by a grateful, though leaderless, Parliament.

There now remains but to describe the indescribable: the drifting away of the United States. As Morley's mob came onto Vermont, their pace quickened and once into Maine, that tattered band positively accelerated until, with one final gasp swoop and gush of saw dust, they fell into the Atlantic at Robbinston. No sound at first, except for the far distant echoes off the Continental Divide, but then a great creaking there was heard unto and then a sigh, as if all the dead had smiled and then, slowly, ever so slowly, the United States edged away from Canada, edged slowly, then quickened until, until, it positively sailed into the sunset!

The United Nations, having heard what was happening, had long since hacked its way loose from Manhattan and from a perch in the mid-Atlantic, the General Assembly turned to its next order of business: what to do with the seat once held by the United States. San Salvador North, recently bereft of its connection with San Salvador 'propre,' had applied and there was every reason to believe that the United Nations would approve its admission.

Now thought the Canadians, lezznousdealavouswitKwabeck.

Roch Carrier's Trilogy:
A Second Look At
Quebec's Dark Years

GEORGES JOYAUX

Observers of the Canadian scene agree that Quebec has under-
gone more drastic changes in the course of the last few years than
in the previous three centuries. What Paul-Emile Borduas called
in 1948 *"le règne de la peur multiforme,"* has given way to the
reign of freedom, and the "will to survive"—which, in the long
run, was tantamount to death since it prevented all growth and
imprisoned Quebec in the inextricable links of a death-dealing
past— has given way to an earthy and boundless will to live:
"Maybe the dominant feature of the cultural transformation in
Quebec lies in the explosion of freedom, the need to break down
the constraints, to transgress the taboos."[1]
The voice which in 1914 urged Maria Chapdelaine "to stay
in the Province where our fathers remained and to live as they
had lived for in the Province nothing must die, nothing must
change,"[2] has been silenced at long last. Timidly at first, and
with increased vigor as Quebec belatedly entered the twentieth

century, new voices arose, insisting—and in the name of that same fidelity to its cherished past—that things had to change if the bare survival of the first French settlers within their garrison was not to lead to total annihilation through suffocation. Fixity, it was realized at long last, is not a choice offered to living organisms: either they grow, develop and adapt to changing conditions or they decay and eventually die.

The sixties and the *"Révolution tranquille"* gave the final touches to the metamorphosis. If, to some observers, especially outsiders, the Revolution appeared outward directed and thus somewhat associated with the pro-separatist violence which marked the sixties, one should keep in mind that the struggle was first and foremost a fratricidal one, pitting the old against the new, the past against the future, "the creative, rational, liberty-loving Quebec, against the parochial, obscurantist, spoils-tolerant society of the past."[3]

Furthermore, if the revolution was essentially a peaceful one, it was neither unexpected nor sudden. Though the events of the last fifty years—World Wars, economic crisis, urbanization, industrialization, rebirth of nationalisms—made the revolution unavoidable, it is also true that the evolutionary process had started long ago, and that the undermining of the old system had been continuous throughout the history of Quebec.

For a long time, however, Quebec refused, officially at least, to acknowledge the reality. A certain idyllic view of Quebec, created and nurtured by the Church, was superimposed on the real world and all that did not conform to this view of reality was refused *droit de cité*. As early as 1846, Patrice Lacombe had set the tone for this falsification of the Quebec scene. Addressing directly his readers in the last pages of his novel, *la terre paternelle,* he declared:

> We would like our readers to notice that we are writing in a country where mores are generally pure and simple, and that the sketch we made of it in the preceding pages would have been unbelievable and even utterly ridiculous had it ended

with murders, poisonings and suicides. Let the old countries, spoiled as they were by civilization, have their bloody novels and let us paint the son of the earth as he is and as he must remain, religious, sensitive, honest, peaceful in mores and temper.[4]

It remained for Abbé Casgrain to set the leitmotif for the literature of what was to be known as Quebec's Dark Ages, declaring "our literature should be chaste and pure like the virginal mantle of our winters."[5] Thus, for more than a century, Quebec produced a moralizing and edifying literature "whose sole purpose was to describe the native not as he was, but as his leaders, the elite group, would have liked him to be."[6]

The situation is quite different today: truth is not only no longer frightening, but it is passionately sought and expressed openly by writers who find it necessary to seek it in its entirety in an attempt to anchor the future on solid foundations. Such a writer is Roch Carrier: dissatisfied by the long-entrenched stereotypes propagated by the officially acceptable writings, he "has decided to descend into the darkness of Quebec and put into words its silent epic."[7] His trilogy, *la guerre, yes sir!* (1968), *Floralie, où es-tu?* (1969), and *Il est par là, le soleil* (1970), providing the readers with a second look at Quebec's Dark Ages, "constitutes a huge demystifying undertaking directed against all the false prophets and sorcerers who maintained a thick darkness over the country."[8]

Unlike the *roman-fleuve* of *l'entre-deux-guerres,* Carrier's trilogy does not present the reader with a huge social fresco, but rather with three moments in the history of Quebec in the first half of the twentieth century. *Floralie, où es-tu?*, the first novel from a chronological point of view, though published after *la guerre,* centers around the wedding of Anthyme Corriveau and his bride, Floralie. *La guerre,* which takes place some twenty years later, deals with the wake organized by the villagers for one of their sons, young Corriveau, killed in the war of *"les maudits Anglais."* The third panel of the triptych, *Il est par là, le soleil,* brings us still closer to the present and relates the confrontation of the *habitant*—in this case young Philibert, son of the grave-digger in *la guerre*—with the fast-moving and alien life of the metropolis, Montreal.

Yet, regardless of name, Anthyme, Floralie, Corriveau, Philibert, we are constantly dealing with the same character, the Quebec *habitant,* and what we are presented with in the three novels is his attitude at three specific moments of his life, each constituting the central image of one of the three panels of the triptych:

> The panels of the triptych are named Love, Death and Work. Love is presented in *Floralie, où es-tu?* Death is presented in *la guerre, yes sir!* and Work, that slavery which is mixed with the creation of a society, is the theme of the last shutter of the triptych.[9]

These images, as we will see, contrast singularly with the corresponding stereotypic images which *Maria Chapdelaine* (Maria's love, her mother's death and her father's clearing of the land) imprinted upon the general reader's retina.

Furthermore, the very movement in time of the three novels parallels the evolution of Quebec from an essentially pastoral, church-centered and contained society, to a more open one, no longer able to prevent the effect of events happening beyond the walls of the garrison and slowly, but ineluctably, accepting the urbanization and industrialization which is the fate of all modern societies.

La guerre, yes sir!, Carrier's first probe into Quebec's Dark Ages, is the account of a single night in the life of a small village. The activity centers around the wake organized for young Corriveau whose body is brought back home by an honor guard of British soldiers. Also returning to the village is another local boy, Bérubé, on leave from the Army, and, to a large extent, a duplicate of his dead countryman. The wake provides Carrier with an opportunity to present the villagers' reaction to death and to religion: "The relationship of the villagers to the Church is perhaps the novel's most important single theme."[10] At the same time, the concrete intrusion of the outside world (the British soldiers) into the close-knit and withdrawn Quebec world provides the villagers with an easily available scapegoat and thus a way to concretize the conflict which has always existed between them, *les petits,* and *les gros,* a hostile, all-powerful and protean force which victimizes them and prevents their full and free development.

All of the action centers around Corriveau's coffin and, in this sense, *la guerre* is in line with the traditional Quebec literature which has long been characterized by its obsession with death. But the similarity stops here: the lines of force are no longer centrifugal and death-oriented as was the case with earlier novels, but centripetal and life-asserting. The protagonists, the Quebec *habitants*—Corriveau's parents, Bérubé, Arsène (the grave digger), Henri and Joseph (who do not want to fight the war of *"les maudits Anglais"*)—are "the first Quebec revolutionaries,"[11] challenging in words and deeds a suffocating and death-dealing situation.

The book opens with two examples of self-mutilation which sets the tone for the rest of the novel and for the trilogy as well. Carrier leaves no doubt in the minds of his readers that this self-mutilation amounts to an emasculation deliberately chosen by the Quebec *habitant* in an attempt to insure its continuous existence behind the protective walls of the garrison.

Thus, after Joseph, one of the villagers, cuts off his own wrist with an ax to escape the cursed war of *"les maudits Anglais,"* his wife scornfuly complains to her friends: "Life is hard. . . . You marry a man and you find out you're sleeping with an invalid. . . . What's Joseph going to do with his stump in my bed?"[12] As for Henri, another villager and a deserter from the Army, he is forced to hide and live a clandestine, shameful and incomplete life in a cold and dark attic:

> . . . a man whose wife had been taken away from him and who was afraid that they would come to this black hole where he was scared, where he despised himself, and force him to go back to war.[13]

The themes of self-mutilation and emasculation are carried out relentlessly throughout the novels (critics have insisted on the many examples of unfulfilled sexual relationships—though lust and voyeurism are never lacking) and culminate in a haunting scene, whose central image, a coffin, is not uncommon in Quebec literature. Alone in his attic, where he longingly dreams of a warm and full sun, symbol of the life which is eluding him, Henri can only conjure up a vision of a silent and deserted world at the center of which Corriveau's ever-growing coffin inexorably attracts him, his fellowmen and the whole world, like a huge magnet:

> Henri noticed that, beneath this sun, something was arranging itself on the ground. It looked like a house, but as he observed more carefully, he saw that it was not a house, but a huge box, and, as he thought better, he realized that it was Corriveau's coffin. . . . Now people were arriving in crowds, whole villages at a time, huge numbers of people patiently awaiting their turn. . . . From four corners of the earth, people came running up, rushing into Corriveau's coffin which was swelling like a stomach. The sea, too, even the sea had become gentle as a river and was emptying into Corriveau's coffin. . . . The entire ocean had been drunk up and, in the whole world, nothing remained but Corriveau's coffin.[14]

Yet, unlike many of his predecessors (Rosa Anna, in *Bonheur d'occasion*; Grand mère Antoinette, in *une saison dans la vie d'Emmanuel*; and la famille Chapdelaine) who found solace and *la certitude* in such a vision, Henri will not follow meekly the path of resignation. Instead, like a trapped animal, he turns to violence and unleashes his blind and irrational rage against his "tormentors"—in this case, the British soldiers.

Henri's individual revolt coincides with the general revolt of the villagers against the same enemy: as the wake progresses, it turns more and more into "a wild and noisy celebration during which instinctive forces prevail over the forces of order,"[15] life and movement over death and fixity. Later on, the celebration further degenerates into a sadistic display of violence as Bérubé, powerless to direct his pent-up hatred at the British soldiers, finds release by turning against his very countrymen. Twice he will rush onto the scene, ready and eager "to knock down a few English faces and to show them what a French Canadian has at the end of his arm,"[16] (nothing but a stump, as we have seen earlier) and twice, reduced to "a ball of obedient muscles,"[17] he will obey his superiors and turn against his own kind: "such is the tragedy of powerlessness: it is self-destructive to the extent that it cannot make use of the violence and rage it engenders against the very dominating forces which caused it in the first place."[18]

These events, compounded further by the total ignorance of and the complete lack of understanding between the two forces in the presence of each other will eventually force the soldiers to intervene and drive the villagers out of the Corriveau's house, seat of the wake. Humiliated beyond control, the villagers in turn resort to violence to recapture their son, their home and their land from the foreign usurpers:

> When the villagers found themselves in front of Corriveau's house . . . , when they understood that they had been ex-pelled from Corriveau's house . . . , when they thought again that it was outsiders, *Anglais*, who had chased them out of Corriveau's house, a house that had come down through five generations of Corriveaus, all living in the village and in the same house on the same bit of land for more than a hundred years; when they reminded themselves that Corriveau, a little French-Canadian boy, a son of the village, had been killed in a war that the *Anglais* from England, the United States and Canada had declared on the Germans . . . ;

> when they realized that they had been sent out like dogs
> that had peed on the rug by the *Anglais* who weren't even
> Canadians but *maudits Anglais*, then the villagers knew the
> depth of their humiliation. . . . Joseph-with-the-hand-cut-off
> was the first to dash towards the house. The others fol-
> lowed. . . .[19]

The pitched battle comes to an end when Henri, who had left his cold attic "pursued by Corriveau's coffin which was following him through the night like a starving dog,"[20] shoots a British soldier thinking that he intended to arrest him and take him back to war forcefully. The death of the British soldier provides the needed release and makes possible a return to the original situation: The villagers recover their son, retake possession of their home and resume their life in the warmth of the garrison— though, as we are told in the last line of the novel, "the war had dirtied the snow."

If, as we have seen, the war and its concrete intrusion in the life of the village precipitates the conflict between the villagers and the *gros*, one should not conclude therefrom that the war and the British are the sole causes of the malaise which has long pervaded Quebec life:

> The war, in truth, has not profoundly altered the order of
> things in the village. . . . The war existed already in the vil-
> lage and amidst the villagers even before it started in
> Europe. All that happens in the course of the novel will, as
> far as the villagers are concerned, result from the war and
> they will try vainly to postpone indefinitely the moment
> when they will have to face the fact that death and violence
> are also present within them.[21]

The reader is made aware of this fact from the very beginning as he witnesses the many conflicts which pit man against woman, parents against their children and the villagers as a whole against a brutal and harsh land.

The British, it is suggested, are only an easily available personification of *les gros,* that obscure and all-powerful force which victimizes the villagers and leads them to alienation, self-mutilation and a state of permanent conflict. At the very moment when Corriveau's coffin reaches the station, "the first of our children which the war takes away from us," an unidentified character retorts:

> You mean Corriveau is the first child which the *gros* have grabbed away from us. Shit on the *gros.* They're all the same: Germans, *Anglais,* French, Russians, Chinese, Japs; they're all so much alike that they have to wear different uniforms to tell each other apart before they throw their grenades. I shit on all the *gros,* but not on the Good Lord, because he is even bigger than the *gros.* But he is a *gros* too. They are all *gros.* . . .[22]

Ironically, however, the excretory image applies most devastatingly to the victimized *habitants*: Corriveau, who spoke English "with a very heavy accent," was killed by stepping on a land mine while on his way to the latrines. As for Bérubé, he is responsible for the cleaning of the toilets in an Air Force Base, where he also learned English, which he spoke "as well as all the other toilet-cleaners, whether they be Poles, Hungarians, Italians, or Greeks."

Another episode, involving Bérubé, further enlightens the reader as to the deeper causes of the unhealthy state of affairs in Quebec: While in Gander, awaiting the plane which was to take him on leave, Bérubé is picked up by a prostitute, Molly, whom, as it turns out, he has to marry in order to regain the virility he could not achieve otherwise:

> The girl was in front of him, naked. . . . She held out her arms to Bérubé who was incapable of getting up. . . . Bérubé felt completely weak as if he had too much to drink. In his head, he heard a tick-tock, like a drumbeat. 'Always, never,'

> repeated the monstruous clock which marked the hours of
> his childhood, the clock of hell which throughout eternity
> would say 'Always, never'; The damned are in hell for ever,
> they never leave. . . . 'Always, never:' the clock of his child-
> hood beat out the measure, the clock of eternal damnation
> for those who go naked and those who touch naked women;
> 'Always, never,' sounded the clock and Bérubé had to beg:
> 'Do you want to marry me?'[23]

This scene, we should add, follows the scene during which
Joseph's wife mocks her husband's self-inflicted wound and thus
provides a fitting answer to the latter's retort, in which he points
out what seems to be the only available alternative to self-
mutilation: "And Corriveau? Is he a man, Corriveau?"[24]

There seems to be little doubt as to who is responsible for the
state of affairs in Quebtc. It would be hard indeed to ascribe
Bérubé's impotence to the British soldiers alone. A whole heritage
of constraints and death-oriented teachings have left their mark
on the Quebec *habitants* and conditioned them to resignation and
submissiveness, thus making them into an easy prey for future
tormentors:

> ForBérubé, sex is irremediably linked to evil and damnation.
> Sex brings to life all the satanic and obsessive images of the
> religious upbringing of his childhood. . . . He is dispossessed
> of his virility because the flesh itself has been dispossessed of
> its natural character. . . . Soiled by religious teachings, it can
> become good only through the mediation of certain rites of
> the same order. Once married, Bérubé recovers his virility.[25]

As we have seen earlier, the compensatory death of the British
soldier has brought a return to the status quo: the villagers, who
have retaken possession of their son, their home and their land,
are again behind the protective walls of the garrison. We should
not be surprised therefore to encounter, at this point in the novel,
the typical terror-sermon in which the curé admonishes his

parishioners and reminds them of their role and duty in the divine order of things: "My brothers, never forget that we live to die and we die to live. . . . You will submit to the flames of hell if you do not live like the angels who carry them."[26]

Still, if the Church and its teachings seem to have the last word, it is clear that the villagers cannot be equated with *Maria Chapdelaine*'s protagonists. Though they are unable and/or unwilling to verbalize its consequences, they are becoming aware of the contradiction in which they live. As Anthyme Corriveau puts it, "if it was necessary for coffins to go by, and for life to stop at a coffin, it was not fair for people to have such an evident love of life."[27]

If anything, Corriveau's death, and his ever-present coffin, leads them to place greater value on life as their instincts easily prevail over the doctrine:

> The villagers (unlike Corriveau) were alive. They prayed in order to remind themselves of this fact, to remember that they were not with Corriveau, that their lives were not ended, and, all the time thinking that they were praying for Corriveau, they were in fact shouting their joie de vivre in their sad prayers. The happier they were, the more they prayed.[28]

And, rather than the terror-sermon referred to above, it is Bérubé's *cri du coeur, "Au fond, tu m'abîmes, Seigneur,"*[29] (All in all, you crush me, Lord), which best sums up the first panel of Carrier's probe into the Quebec night. Thus acknowledging, though unconsciously, the crippling impact of a too demanding religious training, Bérubé prepares the ground for the final revolt of the *habitant*—in the person of Philibert, in the last volume of the trilogy—once he consciously confronts the issue and draws its logical consequences.

The first step in the final liberation is already taken in the last pages of *la guerre*, as Philibert, the grave-digger's son and assistant, now old enough to climb out of the holes by himself, turns his back on his father's activity and leaves the village: "Mon vieux Christ, if I'm a man, I'm getting the hell out. You can bury yourself all alone."[30] A step which, needless to say, contrasts singularly with the denouement of *Maria Chapdelaine* as Maria, who will marry a duplicate of her own father, chooses to remain in the garrison and to repeat the endless cycle while "a chorus of earth-spirit, ancestral and heavenly voices, backs her up."[31]

In *Floralie, où es-tu?*, which takes us a generation earlier to the wedding of young Corriveau's parents, Carrier further develops the theme of mutilation through an examination of the conflict which exists between man and woman—a conflict barely sketched in *la guerre*, as it was blurred by, if not totally transferred to, a more immediate and concrete issue, the intrusion of "*les maudits Anglais*." Again, Carrier chooses to set the action in the middle of the night, a time "when our inner life reveals itself best in dreams or nightmares,"[32] thus making it possible to voice "*l'amour si évident de la vie*,"[33] which the Quebecker carries deep within his heart, and to expose the depth of the scars which many years of official teachings have imprinted on his soul.

After the wedding, Anthyme and his wife, Floralie, are journeying back home on a beautiful spring evening which, instead of opening onto the expected beautiful dawn, will only usher them into a dim and frozen darkness, as the young bride and groom change overnight into the pathetic couple of *la guerre*, symbol of "a society where love has been assassinated, and where each and every joy has been soiled even before it comes into being."[34]

The first third of the novel deals with the journey through the Quebec forest, a harsh and inflexible opponent which the *habitant* must confront daily and which constantly requires of him that he call upon all his energies and physical strength—whereas he has been conditioned to resignation and submissiveness. The trek through the forest also provides the occasion for the consummation of the marriage by two partners equally gauche and ignorant concerning sexual matters and, what is more, mutilated psychologically from the start by the inhuman demands of their upbringing:

> Man must never delude himself into thinking that the sins of the flesh are in any way satisfying. To succumb to the fires of passion is understandable and even possibly excusable, but to enjoy it is the sure sign of different and everlasting fires to come.[35]

The misunderstanding which results from this first carnal encounter is made more bitter still when Anthyme discovers that Floralie does not match the image of womanhood with which he has been raised. Torn betwten the truth he has been taught and the reality with which he is confronted ("There wasn't a wall and there wasn't any blood"[36]), Anthyme will all the more easily become a victim of the alienation which has long characterized Quebec life and which produced a literature equally alienated from the real world of flesh and blood individuals.

Still, and despite these rather unpromising beginnings, it seems that the marriage could lead to a happy and rewarding relationship as both partners stand on the threshhold of a new life, impatiently awaiting its promises, willing to learn from and respond to their inner stirrings, and, in Anthyme's case, even willing to control if not discard the coarseness and brutality of his first assault. Unfortunately, "life will give way to crippling doctrine,"[37] and the two characters, unable to escape their conditioning, will deny the surge of life, resume their place in the order of things and thus accept the mutilation imposed upon them by the system.

Anthyme, compelled to fulfill the idea of manhood with which he grew up, damns his wife, beats her up—"though with much less force than he thought"[38]—and abandons her; at least temporarily. Floralie likewise, banishing all thoughts of love and happiness from her newly started married life, resigns herself to be the "animal-to-be-raped,"[39] and the breeder she is expected to be:

"Anthyme had hit her, but if he wasn't a brute, he wouldn't be a man."[40]

As for her damnation, it does not seem to affect her too deeply, as Carrier continues, in this novel, the celebration of life he had begun in *la guerre*:

> Floralie was damned, but she lived. She was young, beautiful; she was damned, but she smiled. . . . Floralie moved, to offer her face to the sun. She opened her arms and surrendered to the caress of the light. She was damned. The sun breathed so gently. And it did not know she was damned. . . . The forest was perfumed. Every tree had a good smell, like a flower that you bring up to your nose. The gentleness of the sun seemed eternal. Floralie was alive. . . .[41]

The physical separation which follows their first sexual encounter will give way to an unbridgeable psychological estrangement as the two partners, now alone in the night of the forest, engage in a fateful and crippling voyage into the darkness of the spirit, which occupies the remaining two-thirds of the novel. To dramatize the medieval character of Quebec's Dark Years, Carrier, in this part of the novel abandons his realistic approach and relies heavily on "the paraphernalia of medieval literature, including dream allegory, monologue debate, sorcerer of a sort, enchanted forest and the Seven Deadly Sins."[42]

At the end of this nightmarish journey into the depth of their tortured souls, a fantastic voyage where outwardly inspired images of God, demons, sin and damnation collide with an inner surge for a happy and fulfilled life in the here and now, Anthyme and Floralie will emerge into the static life of "*la résignation chrétienne*," and turn into the poignant and powerless figures of *la guerre*, for whom "nothing can be done," except obey—the constant drinking and cursing of the man and the meaningless praying of the woman providing them with the necessary safety valve to release their overbearing rage.

As was the case with *la guerre, Floralie* also includes the traditional terror-sermon in which Father Nombrillet—one of the awe-striking apparitions conjured up by the protagonists' subconscious—reiterates the Church's official teachings. It is significant, however, that a fire cuts short the Curé's sermon, engulfing the Chapel and a number of parishioners and thus creating an ambiguity which is not easily resolved. Yet, in view of the general tone of Carrier's trilogy, it seems possible to view this image as a burning away of the disease and its source. The Church (the essence of Quebec) and its teaching stood at the heart of Quebec like a gangrenous growth—concretized by the ever-present and enlarging coffin—which had to be removed to make a future possible. Thus, though the above episode ends with Floralie wishing "she had burned with the others," the last word remains with an unidentified passer-by who retorts: "Believe me, little girl, it's better to be a flesh and blood girl than a saint of smoke and ashes. I'm old enough to know."[43]

Nevertheless, the novel remains the account of a failure, a fact made clear from the outset as Carrier dedicated it to "those who calling for dawn have only known night." The weight of the Church's teachings proves too much for the two partners. Yet, if their hopes for dawn did not materialize, they were not thrown into the night without a struggle and their final defeat was not the meek and active acceptance of the Chapdelaines, but the enraged resignation of those who are powerless to escape their conditioning. Carrier's protagonists give the lie to the stereotypes and rehabilitate the Quebec *habitant*. It is this corrected picture— already presented in *la guerre*—which is again left on the reader's mind as the villagers, worried by the couple's failure to return home, successfully complete their search:

> Villagers, their shirts opened and their hair dishevelled from the night's watch, their suits wrinkled, their clothes stained with beer, swooped down on Floralie and Anthyme. They were jubilant. They danced around the couple, swearing to

> show how happy they really were, to express the beauty of
> a man a woman entwined in the grass. They flung out
> obscene cries. . . .[44]

As for the theme of mutilation, it is best summarized inadvertently by Anthyme as he echoes Bérubé's *cri du coeur* alluded to earlier, in the course of his nightmarish review of his life. The fear he is now experiencing, as dreams and the night assault him from all sides, recalls to his mind a childhood likewise marked by fear and leads him to confront God in a way not unlike Bérubé's:

> Where were you? Instead of sleeping all night like everybody else you were off chasing a boy who'd had some fun
> with a girl or you were knocking down some guy who'd
> had too much to drink. That's more fun than putting a
> child to sleep. Make a man suffer till he cracks up, then
> step on him.[45]

Whereas *Floralie* had turned back a generation from *la guerre, il est par là, le soleil,* takes us closer to contemporary Quebec. In the first pages of the novel, Carrier recalls, by means of a series of short but powerful vignettes, the reasons for Philibert's decision to leave his village and look for a new life. Philibert's case—as had been foreshadowed in the earlier novels (Corriveau's leaving home to enlist, Anthyme's recollections of his unhappy youth, Philibert's appearance in the last pages of *la guerre*)—is typical of the wretched childhood of most protagonists in Quebec's recent novels:

> Almost all significant Canadian French authors appear to
> see childhood with one dominant characteristic: misery. . . .
> Over and over, one encounters children who are unloved,
> frustrated, restricted and tormented. . . .[46]

Hence, the desire, so prevalent among the novel's protagonists to escape this claustrophobic, unhappy and threatening milieu—even, in some cases, to burn down the "Ancestral House"—so as to allow a rebirth and an unfettered growth.

Yet, as we have seen, leaving the garrison is no solution as it seems unavoidably to lead to death: young Corriveau, in the war: Bérubé, now a mindless machine used by *les gros* against his very own kind and equally rejected by both groups when he tries to pray for the dead soldiers; Philibert himself, as we will see later. On the other hand, staying in the garrison is equally fatal: the protagonists, mutilated physically or psychologically (Henri, Joseph, the Corriveaus), are reduced to living a stunted life in a death-dealing environment while awaiting—and at times not without anticipation—to be absorbed in the ever-growing coffin which always occupies center stage.

The theme of mutilation which pervades the trilogy finds its best illustration in this novel as Carrier depicts, in an unforgettable image, the annual procession of thanks of the LaLiberté family—whose very name, an ironic statement for the reality it represents, is a savage indictment of the responsible *gros*:

> Jonas LaLiberté and his wife walked behind the Curé, their eyes closed. Behind them, accompanied by their godfathers and godmothers, followed their twenty-one children. . . . The wheels of twenty-one wheelbarrows in which the twenty-one children were being transported turned with no sound from the axles, no noise of pebbles under the rims of the wheels. . . . The children were silent. Arms hung down from each wheelbarrow. Each one was filled not with a body, but with a sloppy, spreading formless paste, where a head with lifeless eyes and a blissfull smile floated. The big round heads would have tumbled outside the wheelbarrows and dragged the boneless bodies as they fell if they had not been held back by the godmothers' pious hands. . . .

Indeed, they owed much to all powerful God: not only had he not "withheld his blessings from their union by giving them only a few children," but "in the greatness of his divine wisdom . . . he had breathed a tenacious life in these little angels whom he had created crippled so that they would receive a greater love."[47]

One should not be surprised therefore to see Philibert—after Corriveau and Bérubé—run away from home as soon as he has reached the age of reason. He will discover, however, that a change of scenery is no solution if one carries with him the very conditioning to which he has long been subjected. Poorly prepared for the industrialized and fast-paced life of the city, Philibert, further hampered by his inability to speak English ("These immigrants should learn English before they set off for Canada"[48]), goes from failure to failure as he vainly attempts to find a niche in Montreal.

Philibert's fortune takes a turn for the better, however, when he meets the "Ninth Marvel of the World," a giant who makes his living by being the scapegoat—in this case, the punching bag —of all those, who, humilated beyond reason and yet powerless to change their situation, are in dire need of a safety valve to release their pentup anger. Not only does this episode again illustrate the theme of self-mutilation, but it reveals its eventual outcome, self-destruction, as Carrier carries it through to its logical conclusion.

The giant's different aliases, "Donato Ambrioso, alias Louis Durand, alias Agagad Aglagayan, alias Jean-Baptiste Turcotte, alias Boris Rataploffsky,"[49] suggests that he is the symbol of the little man in society, the "born loser, destined to suffer at the hands of *les gros*—who might comprise any one from 'le boss' (who might speak any one of a number of languages, including French), to God himself."[50] His very size, however, negates his long assumed role as a victim and suggests that the little men in society have the potential to chose a path other than self-mutilation and self-destruciton in answer to their apparent powerlessness.

For a while, Master Phil (he has now Americanized his name in another futile attempt to do away with his crippling past) will become the giant's impresario and partake of what seems to be the good life, though he is not completely unaware that despite his billing, "The Man with the Face of Steel," he is anything but human and that he suffers physically at the hands of his tormentors.

Tired of being constantly pummelled by others, the giant will eventually turn against them (his own kind) and in so doing travel a path which will lead to his own demise: the blood he has shed is his own and his ensuing suicide through drowning only confirms the real long-run consequences of the resort to self-mutilation.

As for Philibert, his picaresque adventures in the big city will eventually lead to his liberation—or at least show the way for a possible liberation for the *habitant*. As the successor to Bérubé, Anthyme, and other Carrier protagonists, he voices—and in practically the same terms—the contradictions inherent to his life. At the same time, he exposes, like them also, his anger against God, the *gros* par excellence: as we watch Philibert reading his mother's letter and resisting once more the urge to go back and resume the serene life of the garrison, the narrator comments:

> He was sorry that his childhood was so far away. He was sorry that he was so far away. Life back there was waiting for him with the fragrance of fresh bread. Tears came to his eyes. It was too sad, the life of the people he had left behind. It was like a quiet nightmare. Montreal weighed on his shoulders like a stone, but he was free. He was free, but the people in the village were crushed beneath the sky. . . .[51]

Later, as he faces the traditional coffin with which his landlords are trying to initiate him in the meaning of life ("Now, you're going to learn the only thing a man needs to know"), he cannot accept the teaching he is offered: "To die is to live."[52]

Liberation is not far away, however: in a passage reminiscent of these moments when the Sartrian hero becomes suddenly aware of his freedom, Philibert reaches the end of his quest:

> No more God, so I was all alone. When I was a kid they
> planted fears in me that grew as tall and thick as corn in
> the garden. . . . Without God I felt as if I'd been amputated,
> but I was a man, hostie! I could say God does not exist,
> but me I exist. . . . Ah! for Christ's sake, listen to me. . . .
> God does not exist, but me, I exist. . . .

Still, past teachings continue to assert their weight:

> Sometimes an angel, or one of the saints, or even God him-
> self used to come and nibble in the corner of my room like
> rats coming out of the sewer. Sometimes I could feel their
> little paws running across my chest in a panic when I
> couldn't get to sleep.[53]

Philibert's failure to answer his interlocutor's ironic comment,
"And you said there wasn't any God,"[54] except with a distorted
smile, hints at his enraged powerlessness to escape his conditioning and sheds some light on the novel's ambiguous denouement:
Philibert's apparent death in a fiery crash on "A phosphorescent
Cross of Christ [standing] in front of Philibert, like a tree, on the
road in front of his car."[55]

God and religion, it seems, are insurmountable obstacles, standing as it were on the path of his (and Quebec's, as well) free
development. His self-destruction and the concommitant removal
of the obstacles (cleansing by fire) seems to be the only way to
make it possible, for others at least, to achieve complete liberation—just as Carrier's diggings into Quebec's Dark Years and
unveiling of their true nature will make it possible for Quebec
to rid itself of its crippling psychological complexes.

Such an interpretation is consistent with the novel's ending
and with the general tone of Carrier's trilogy. The "Ninth Marvel
of the World" has chosen to make Philibert his heir, on the
material as well as on the psychological plane: "You're truly my
son. *Tu es mon fils.* Don't forget."[56] We might read in this
bilingual profession of faith a suggestion that the future for the

little man in Quebec—as well as for the little men in general—lies in acceptance of the dual and today multiplural nature of the Canadian experience. At the same time, the giant's insistence on the need to maintain links with the past—its true version rather than the imposed fable—is consistent with the very *raison d'être* of Carrier's literary endeavor: to recapture Quebec's true past so as to assume full responsibility for the making of her future.

Obviously, Carrier's account of Quebec's Dark Years is a far cry from the innocent world of *Maria Chapdelaine* where silent and zombie-like characters meekly accepted their assigned role in the divine order of things. He, like his contemporaries, gives voice to "the nocturnal protests of a people frustrated in its joys by a religion nurtured on the ideas of death."[57] Carrier's protagonists are flesh and blood individuals who have been crippled by years of religious teachings but whose appetite for life, as evidenced by the many lusty peasants who inhabit his novels, remains in force.

Carrier's trilogy corrects the distorted view of yesterday and, though it destroys the refuge in which some found solace, it dismantles, by the same token, its necessary counterpart, the prison in which Quebec was slowly suffocating: "Such was the situation. It is important therefore to unveil the forces which lead man to self-mutilation and make an inventory of the damages which ensued, so as to react in a better way later on."[58]

The events which have shaken Quebec during these last two decades attest to the depth of the mutilation and humiliation the Quebeckers have experienced in the course of their history. These events brought about a cultural mutation characterized by an unparalleled unleashing of the forces of freedom which, in turn, made a reassessment of the past possible. Indeed, if Quebec is to find the identity it is searching for, if Quebec is to be more than "one of the last countries where the Middle Ages are spiritually perpetuated,"[59] and yet, keep its cultural distance from the Anglo-Saxon world, it is imperative that it be provided with a true assessment of its past and that it participate fully in the making of its future:

> We will have to learn to live with our past, without attempting to enlarge it beyond measure, or erasing it so as to enlarge ourselves. We must become familiar with our ancestors, return them to their true size, and demystify the events which have been handed down to us.[60]

Carrier's novels provide us with such a reassessment. His speleological diggings into the Quebec night have brought to life a new world teeming with vitality and far more congruous with today's Quebec than that of most of his predecessors.

> Carrier symbolizes the new maturity of Quebec, the final transcending of the suppressed and self-conscious adolescent stage of social evolution. And this new maturity is permitting honest self-appraisal for the first time, cold, hard examination instead of blind rage or bemused nostalgia.[61]

NOTES

1. Guy Rocher, *le Québec en mutation* (Montreal: Hurtubise HMH, 1973), 27-28.
2. Louis Hemon, *Maria Chapdelaine* (Paris: Livre de poche, 1934), 241.
3. Hugh Bingham Myers, *The Quebec Revolution* (Montreal: Harvest House, 1964), xi.
4. Quoted in J. Huston, editor, *Répertoire national, Recueil de littérature canadienne* (Montreal: Valois, 1893), 396-397.
5. H. R. Casgrain, *le mouvement littéraire au Canada* (Montreal: Beauchemin et Valois, 1884), 368.
6. George-V. Fournier, "Roch Carrier: A Quest for the Authentic," *Ellipse*, 4 (Summer, 1970), 35.
7. Roch Carrier, "Comment je suis devenu écrivain?" quoted in *le roman contemporain d'expression française* (Sherbrooke: CELEF, 1971), 271.

8. *Ibid.*, 270.
9. *Ibid.*, 271.
10. Roch Carrier, *la guerre, yes sir!*, translated by Shelia Fischman Toronto: Anansi, 1970), 1.
11. *Ibid.*, 2.
12. *Ibid.*, 24.
13. *Ibid.*, 85.
14. *Ibid.*, 86-88.
15. Jean-Cleo Godin, "le théâtre—Rire à pleurer," *Etudes Françaises*, VII, 4 (1971), 429.
16. Carrier, *la guerre*, 97.
17. *Ibid.*, 46.
18. Ronald Bérubé, *"la guerre, yes sir!*, de Roch Carrier: humour noir et langage vert," *Voix et Images du pays*, III (Quebec: les Presses de l'Université du Quebec, 1970), 159.
19. Carrier, *la guerre*, 89-90.
20. *Ibid.*, 98.
21. Bérubé, *op. cit.*, 25.
22. Carrier, *la guerre*, 23.
23. *Ibid.*, 31-32.
24. *Ibid.*, 27.
25. Bérubé, *op. cit.*, 156.
26. Carrier, *la guerre*, 104-106.
27. *Ibid.*, 94.
28. *Ibid.*, 48.
29. *Ibid.*, 99.
30. *Ibid.*, 108-109.
31. Margaret Atwood, *Survival* (Toronto: Anansi, 1972), 218.
32. Roch Carrier, *Floralie, Where Are You?*, translated by Shelia Fischman (Toronto: Anansi, 1971), i.
33. Roch Carrier, *la guerre, yes sir!* (Montreal: Editions du jour, 1968), 104.
34. Pierre Chatillon, "Roch Carrier—*Floralie, où es-tu?*", *Etudes Françaises*, V, 4 (1969), 493.
35. Ronald Sutherland, *Second Image* (Toronto: New Press, 1971), 63.
36. Carrier, *Floralie*, 23.
37. Mark Levene, "Floralie, Where Are You? Roch Carrier," *Canadian Forum*, LVI (June 1971), 36.
38. Carrier, *Floralie*, 26.
39. Pierre Chatillon, *op. cit.*, 493.
40. Carrier, *Floralie*, 31.
41. *Ibid.*, 27-30.

42. Ronald Sutherland, "Crossing the Thin Line," *Canadian Literature*, 44 (Spring, 1970), 88.
43. Carrier, *Floralie*, 106.
44. *Ibid.*, 107.
45. *Ibid.*, 74.
46. Ronald Sutherland, *Second Image*, 92.
47. Roch Carrier, *Is It the Sun, Philibert?*, translated by Shelia Fischman (Toronto: Anansi, 1972), 17-19.
48. *Ibid.*, 28.
49. *Ibid.*, 87.
50. *Ibid.*, 2.
51. *Ibid.*, 51.
52. *Ibid.*, 57-58.
53. *Ibid.*, 81.
54. *Ibid.*, 81.
55. *Ibid.*, 94.
56. *Ibid.*, 90.
57. Anne Hebert, "les enfants du sabbat," *L'Express* (6-12 octobre, 1975), 60.
58. Bérubé, *op. cit.*, 150.
59. Hebert, *op. cit.*, 60.
60. Rocher, *op. cit.*, 63.
61. Ronald Sutherland, "Catching Up: Notes on Some Recent Cataclysms," *Saturday Night* (August 1972), 13.

Kin Hubbard And Journalistic Humor In The Midwest

WILLIAM McCANN

The Midwest has produced an extraordinary number of journalistic humorists, outstanding among whom are Eugene Field, George Ade, Ring Lardner, Peter Finley Dunne, James Thurber, George W. Peck (of Peck's Bad Boy), Charles B. Lewis (M. Quad), David Ross Locke (Petroleum V. Nasby), and Kin Hubbard (Abe Martin) whose career and achievements are reviewed below in some detail. The foregoing list is by no means exhaustive, but one must resist the temptation to add to it, recalling Constance Rourke's warning against the "excessive antiquarian pride" that causes one to label newly discovered old comic specimens "early Maine or late Arkansas."

Some of these writers of comic columns in a daily newspaper—*the* important medium of Midwestern literary humor—were called "Crackerbarrel Philosophers" or "Rustic Sages." They employed an ancient and honorable comic device that was not even new when Montesquieu invented a provincial character as commentator on men and institutions in his *Persian Letters.* "The first hundred years of American humor," Gilbert Seldes remarked with only mild exaggeration, "are the written records of the crackerbarrel philosophy: the reduction to print of the conversations around the stove at the cross-roads store."

A significant number of journalistic humorists assumed the name and characteristics of other persons, a transformation performed not so much to establish a fictional character who would acquire its own permanent being, (although this sometimes happened), but merely to mask irreverent or sardonic views. With rustic anecdotes, shrewd aphorisms, and genial but sometimes edged commentary—couched most often in rural dialect—these crackerbarrel philosophers dispensed horse sense, interpreted provincial eccentricities, and exposed the lesser corruptions of American political life. From Hosea Bigelow through Josh Billings, Petroleum V. Nasby, Bill Arp, Mr. Dooley, and Artemus Ward to Kin Hubbard's Abe Martin, there was a succession of unlettered, rustic wise-acres. They were social caricaturists of a sort, and for the most part keen observers of human affairs. Given to acid commentary on human frailty (leavened at times with wry geniality), they arraigned man's follies and pointed out the imperfections of his institutions.

Implicit in their work was a low-keyed glorification of the common sense of the common man directed against pretensions to superiority. This as much as anything else explains the wide appeal of crackerbarrel philosophy. "It is curious," Charles Henry Smith the creator of "Bill Arp" wrote, "how we are attracted by the wise, pithy sayings of an unlettered man. It is the contrast between his mind and his culture. We like contrasts and we like metaphor and striking comparisons. The more they are according to nature and everyday life, the better they please the masses. An old thought, dressed up fine for centuries, suddenly appears in everyday clothes." And Mark Sullivan noted that "The characters of song and story that Americans really loved were the ones who emulated sloth, obeyed no routine, and left diligence to the ant and bee. The village vagabond, if he had wit and personality, was better loved and longer remembered than the local nabob who built the town hall and tried to perpetuate his name by fastening it to an urban extension."

By the 1920s, American humor was rapidly becoming urbanized largely through the work of Robert Benchley, E. B. White, Thurber, S. J. Perelman, and others of the *New Yorker* group. However, evidently in response to the nostalgic yearnings of readers who came from small town and rural surroundings, "country oracles (were) still syndicated in papers throughout the country," Constance Rourke wrote in American Humor (1931), "even though the character presented is fast disappearing." And critic Jesse Bier was surprised to find that the "relatively mild and rural" Abe Martin should be so popular in a time of "highly antithetic or ascendant urban comedy"; and that Will Rogers should rise to such "bland heights of fame." (Hubbard once said of his friend Rogers' success that it was "the only time when having enough rope didn't end disastrously"). The popularity of both humorists may be attributed, as Bier suggests, to "nostalgia in a period of accelerated urban growth." Their work provided a respite from the acidity and tension of the urban humorists who were gradually superseding them. During the transition, as Bier says, "the public valued the fading types all the more as they became anachronized." In the 1930s, radio comedians adopted some of the formats and stances of earlier journalistic humorists. Fred Allen's Senator Claghorn was one case, and Archie Gardner used a variation of Dunne's Mr. Dooley format for "Duffy's Tavern." The only two widely known newspaper humorists today, Art Buchwald and Russell Baker, would doubtless acknowledge their indebtedness to Field, Dunne, and Kin Hubbard, among many, many others.

Josh Billings (Henry Wheeler Shaw, 1818-1895), one of the first crackerbarrel philosophers and also one of the best, recognized early in his career the difficulties of his craft. "It may look easy to those who have never tried to write a half column of material," he said, "and it *is* easy to those who never tried it. But to those who have tried it, and have even succeeded but a few

inches, it is a good deal like lifting things that are tied down. . . .
The power of a comic essay resides in its ideas, either original or
admirably stolen, not in its words strung lazily like a snake sun-
ning himself in the sand. . . . All real strength is short, things
are hoisted with a jerk; comic essay writers must ram pages into
paragraphs."

Kin Hubbard (1868-1930) was the last widely known humorist
to use the crackerbarrel-philosopher format, and many believe
he was the best of them all. Born in Bellefontaine, Ohio, Hubbard spent his life in the Midwest, though he became nationally
known through the syndication of his "Abe Martin" column.
Hubbard grew up in Bellefontaine, a county seat town, where
his father published a weekly newspaper. From his maternal
grandfather, who toured the Midwest for years with a theatrical
stock company, Kin (who was christened Frank McKinney Hubbard) got an enduring love of show business. He quit school
in the seventh grade and, though he showed an early talent for
drawing, aspired to be a showman. He hung around visiting tent
shows whenever possible and achieved local renown as a producer
of minstrel shows. His easy-going, affectionate parents let him
take off for trips with travelling shows, for which he worked
at menial jobs, but he usually came home after a few weeks to
resume work on his father's newspaper. "I was what's called a
'natural artist,' " Hubbard said, "one with no knowledge of drawing, no idea of perspective or color." After a brief hitch as a
cartoonist on a paper at Mansfield, Ohio, he was persuaded by a
friend to take a modest job on the *Indianapolis News*. During the
Roosevelt-Parker Presidential campaign of 1904, he did political
cartooning. "I was employed solely as a caricaturist," Hubbard
said, "attending conventions, local, state, and national, supplying
the *News* with single columns and splatters, and touring Indiana
with political celebrities."

After the election of 1904, Hubbard looked around for other
subjects and formats. He soon came up with the character, Abe
Martin, whom he conceived as an amiable but shrewd and
sardonic loafer, living in Brown County, a beautiful, hilly,

wooded region some forty miles south of Indianapolis. "I located Abe in Brown County," Hubbard said, "on account of the topography and the primitive condition of things. No telephone, railroad, or telegraphy, and few roads." Hubbard actually didn't visit the county until long after he had made it famous. Abe Martin was a lazy, village know-it-all, dressed in baggy pants, oversized boots, and a shabby black coat, the personification and embodiment of Mark Sullivan's single-gallused "village vagabond."

In December, 1905, Hubbard began to turn out for the back page of the *News* a daily box of two or three sharp, satiric, unrelated sentences attributed to Abe Martin, who often quoted and described other Brown County Characters—Wes Whipple, Burly Sapp, Martin Tingle, Miss Fawn Lippincutt, Tipton Bud, Tilford Moots, Uncle Niles Turner, an aged idler and prevaricator, and others. Hubbard's characters owed much to his sensitive observation of relatives and friends in Bellefontaine during his boyhood. It was a town, he once wrote, that could be "identified by the two sparrows on the south end of the water tank near the Big Four depot, . . . the town was so lonely that owls flew out of their way for many miles to spend a few days there."

One of Hubbard's daily columns might read: "Mrs. Tipton Bud's niece writes that they're gittin on fine in Kansas, an' that her husband will soon have enough money to get a divorce from. . . . The first thing to turn green in the spring is usually Christmas jewelry." The two sentences would be set beneath a picture of Abe Martin, and each day the picture showed the same character in a new pose and a different background. His drawings of Abe varied little, it seemed to most viewers, but Hubbard insisted on doing a new one each time.

In sharpness of insight and pungency of expression Hubbard is often compared with his distinguished predecessor, Josh Billings, a skilled maker of homely, laconic epigrams, "Keep a cow," said Josh, "and the milk won't have to be watered but once." Like Billings, Hubbard was a master of the one-sentence quip. He liked to take a well-known proverb, such as, "Those who seek to please everybody, please nobody," particularize the idea and come up with: "Burly Sapp was over to the poor farm the other day to see an old friend that used to publish a paper that pleased everybody." Someone's definition of an aphorism as a "proverb coined in a private mint" describes many of Hubbard's sentences. And Hubbard evidently agreed with Josh Billings that "wisdom can be smuggled into a man's mind by a good-natured proverb better and deeper than it can be mortised in with a wormwood mallet and chisel."

W. H. Auden, who thought aphorisms were essentially an aristocratic genre of writing, said that the aphorist who "adopts a folksy style with 'democratic' diction and grammar is a cowardly and insufferable hypocrite." But Auden nevertheless included a number of Hubbard's "Folksy" creations in his *Viking Book of Aphorisms*. Among them: "A loafer always has the correct time," "Nobody ever forgets where he buried the hatchet," and "The hardest thing is writing a recommendation for someone you know."

It was in aphorisms phrased in graphic, homely language that Hubbard excelled, rather than in his longer pieces. However, he wrote longer essays, usually for week-end publication, and called them "Short Furrows." Some were very funny, perhaps none more so than "A Letter From the Front," originally published in 1918:

A LETTER FROM TH' FRONT

Mrs. Min Nugent, cook o' th' New Palace hotel, has received th' follerin' interestin' letter from her son Stew, who is somewhere in France with th' American expeditionary forces:

DEAR MAW:

Well, here I am. I hope you are well. We had some trip comin' over. Cigarettes galore. A piece of shrapnel jest now broke th' last pane o' glass in my window as I write. I have enough terbacker t' last a week. Unless some has been sent since I left I'll probably be without some days before some comes. I'm billeted on th' parlor floor of an ole historic chateau with a mantle piece that goes back t' th' renaissance. My shoes are dryin' on th' mantle. Cigarettes should be mailed at intervals o' two days apart t' assure a steady, unbroken flow. Eatin' t'backer, too, only cigarettes is th' most important. . . . I'm writin' now with a pencil as a piece of flyin' shrapnel jest busted my fountain pen th' sheriff give me when I enlisted. Tell him I'm out o' fountain pens agin, but would rather have cigarettes. It's wonderful how indifferent you git t' danger over here. I'm not spendin' any o' my pay as I want t' loaf a couple o' years when I git home, so any cigarettes or t'backer you send me is jest that much saved. I wouldn' give much fer this historic chateau after th' shrapnel gits thro' with it. . . . I'm finishin' this letter this mornin' as a piece of shrapnel put my candle out last night an' no matches wuz t' be had. Th' French people wuz certainly glad t' see me but they have scarcely enough cigarettes fer 'emselves, an' are tired out an' poor after fightin' so long, so I hate t' ask 'em fer 'em when friends kin send 'em t' me so easily any time. It don't look right t' take 'em from 'em an' I know you would not want me t' do so. It's different with eggs, which are plentiful. I can't talk any French an' I can't tell what ther sayin, but I wouldn' ask 'em fer cigarettes, an' you wouldn' either if you could see what they've been up against. Are there any cigarette clubs at home? Some o' the boys say ther's clubs in ther towns that gather money with which t' buy them an' send them t' them. Girls send them th' same as socks, an' believe me, th' boys are glad t' git 'em. I hope you are well an' strong an' able t' work fer many years t' come. You should be glad you've got a good, easy cookin' job when you think o' th' poor ole women over here plowin'. Ther haint nothin' in loafin'. I'm goin' to work some when I git back. I'm goin' over t' th' mantle an' git my shoes as soon as th' shellin' lets up a little. Mark your packages care A. E. F. You cant carry a pipe over here very handy. Shrapnel knocks 'em out o' your mouth. You bet I've got my three cigarette cases distributed where they'll stop th' most schrapnel. It don't look like I'd ever git my shoes as ther's a constant hail o' schrapnel. Don't worry about me.

> Your lovin' son,
> STEW,

A.E.F. France.

(Put this on all cigarette packages sure.)

In 1910, George Ade wrote a laudatory article in a national magazine (*American Magazine,* May 1910) about Hubbard, comparing him with Billings and Artemus Ward. "His comments on men and affairs," Ade said, "prove him to be a grim iconoclast, an analytical philospher, and a good deal of a cut-up. . . . The funny man who comes to bat daily cannot hit a three-bagger every time, but Kin Hubbard has a high per centage." (Kin himself thought that "one really good paragraph in six days is a fine week's work.") Fred Kelly, Hubbard's biographer, thought that Ade's article caused the syndicates to become interested in Abe Martin. In any case, they now came to Hubbard, one of them signed him on, and his column became an immediate success. Before long, his daily box was appearing in more than three hundred newspapers. In the size of his readership he was the only humorist of the time who rivalled Will Rogers. Rogers himself declared that, "Kin Hubbard is writing the best humor in America."

Despite his success Hubbard resisted the blandishments of New York journalism and stayed on at the *Indianapolis News.* "I've had a couple of chances to go to New York," he said, "and make something of myself, but like a friend I used to have, whose uncle wanted him to go to Denver and take charge of a big drug store said, I'd rather stay right here where I can play in the band." Hubbard seems to have been wholly unimpressed with the trappings of worldly success.

Hubbard's satire was the work of a man inclined to take his own short-comings and those of his fellow creatures indulgently. Unlike Peter Finley Dunne, who was sometimes moody, cynical, and depressed, Hubbard was genial and friendly and an extrovert.

Though he experienced some serious personal setbacks, he did not follow, say, Lardner or Thurber, into deep, persistent pessimism. The prevailing side of his nature was a salty, good-humored sanity and a genial scepticism that never turned to bitterness and disillusionment. He was capable nevertheless of turning out sharply edged satire. Now and then in his humor, there was a show of teeth, a flash of the knife:

"Tell Binkley jumped into his new $3,000. tourin' car and hurried as fast as he could to the poor farm but arrived too late to see his mother before she died."

***

"Uncle Mort Hickman, nearly ninety-eight, after cuttin' and splittin' four cords of wood yisterday, wuz found frozen stiff in th' lane leadin' to th' house by his four sons, who had been away attendin' a billiard tournament."

***

It was sentences like these, no doubt, that prompted Franklin P. Adams to remark that, "There is more healthy hate in Kin Hubbard's paragraphs than in anything written these days." Hubbard was a realist as well as a humorist, of limited scope, it is true, but within honorable limitations, definitely of the first order. He avoided exaggeration, burlesque, and crude caricature, and could puncture the myths of Midwestern rural and small-town felicity as thoroughly as E. W. Howe, Hamlin Garland, or Edgar Lee Masters. His villains did not always come to bad ends and were not especially hateful. His heros and heroines were not very dignified, the victims not very sympathetic. "When Lem Moon was acquitted fer th' murder of his wife," said Abe Martin, "and old Judge Pusey asked him if he had anything to say, he replied: 'I never would have shot her if I'd knowed I had to go through so much red tape.'"

Henry C. Carlisle, in his anthology of satire, observed that, "Crackerbarrel commentary on national affairs became the mainstream of political satire for a century after Seba Smith." Though Hubbard commented less on politics than Mr. Dooley, he nevertheless managed to do so many times. He especially enjoyed watching Indiana politics, was an ardent Democrat, and a life-long admirer of William Jennings Bryan. But so good-natured was his political commentary that he seldom irritated Republican readers. William Howard Taft's jovial face always reminded him, he said, "of a man who has just found a dime in an old vest." Politicians and political hacks, however, came in for some of his ridicule and at times it had considerable bite:

"Now and then an innocent man is sent to the legislature."

***

"The election isn't far off when a candidate can recognize you across the street."

***

"There's some folks standin' behind the President that ought to get around where he can watch'em."

***

"Politics make strange postmasters."

***

"Some defeated candidates go back to work and others say the fight has just begun."

As Norris Yates has pointed out, Hubbard was sceptical about the optimistic myths of the "rational, informed citizen." Abe Martin said, "You kin lead a feller to the polls but you can't make him think." Hubbard was uneasy about the indifference and stupidity and malice he observed sometimes in the "common man." And he shrewdly depicted the contrast between the thinking man and unthinking dullards in a small town setting, where the life he cherished was threatened by the automobile and increasing social complexities. There were indeed some soft spots in crackerbarrel commentary. Robert Benchley satirized them in a clever parody: "I could go on lookin' at life like this forever, just a sittin' an' a lookin' an' a dreamin', with only an occasional attack of nausea." But Hubbard was less subject to sentimental vertigo than most of his brethren. He was steady, sardonic, and shrewd.

A definite promise of humor is nearly always irredeemable. But in the following sampling of Abe Martin's sayings the redemption rate is remarkably high:

"When a feller says, 'It ain't the money but the principle of the thing,' it's the money."

***

"It must be great to be rich and let th' other feller keep up appearances."

***

"It's no disgrace to be poor, but it might as well be."

***

"Gibson Peel, whose graduation essay, 'The Age of Opportunity,' caused no end of comment, has decided, after explorin' several fields of endeavor, t' take the agency fer th' Little Duchess Rug Beater."

***

"Miss Fawn Lippincutt has lowered her skirts fer Lent."

***

"There's always somebody at any dinner who eats all the celery."

***

"The hardest thing t' disguise is yer feelin's when you put a lot of relatives on the train fer home."

***

"We like little children because they tear out as soon as they git what they want."

***

"There isn't much to be seen in a little town, but what you hear makes up for it."

***

"Th' only time some fellers are ever seen with their wives is after they've been indicted."

***

"One good thing about livin' on the farm is that you can fight with your wife without being heard."

***

"Cause there's no place like home is the reason so many girls work in stores."

***

"Ike Moon, who will be operated on t'morrow, will leave a wife and three children."

***

"If capital an' labor ever do git together, it's good night fer th' rest of us."

***

"Th' feller that's mean around home is allus th' life and sunshine of some Lodge."

"Humor, in the proper hands, can be made as dull and respectable as philology or epistemology," Stephen Leacock said. Writing about humor and humorists is, to be sure, an awkward business. The underbrush of light literature too often crashes with the sounds of heavy-footed persons and their unwieldy bodies. "Being serious about humor is one of the great follies of the academician," said Professor C. Carroll Hollis in an excellent serious article about rural American humorists. One hopes that Kin Hubbard would be amused rather than appalled at an attempt to recall and celebrate his comic spirit.

An article on Hubbard should not end without quoting the only sentence he penned for publication that editors of his day declined to print. Kin never agreed with their contention that the sentence was in bad taste. Most humorists today would be delighted to come up with it. The sentence read, "Nothing annoys a vulture like biting into a glass eye."

How Hot Is The Scarlet Letter?

HUGO McPHERSON

"What we did had a consecration of its own. We felt
it so!"
> —Hester Prynne, Chapter XVII,
> *The Scarlet Letter.*

"I'm as pure as the driven slush."
> —Tallulah Bankhead.

"I liked Cary so much I had him twice."
> —Mae West.

Nathaniel Hawthorne was one of the first North American
writers who talked about female children who were real bastards.
His "Pearl" of *The Scarlet Letter* was regarded by the Puritan
community of Salem as a witch's child, yet Pearl grew up to leave
New England behind, and marry well in Europe.

It wasn't too much later that George Moore and Thomas
Hardy would write about other little bastards in *Esther Waters*
and *Tess of the D'Urbervilles.* After that, the female bastards
proliferated in English literature, and the male bastards, who

were eventually recognized as sons of nobility because they had a strawberry mark on their shoulder, went into decline. Boys can be noble bastards, but in America's developing mythology, apparently girls shouldn't. Instead, they should move from *A* to *B*, and become brassy bitches; or even to *D* for diamonds. The syndrome might be called Women's Revenge.

Women's Liberation and Women's International Year suggest that the *intellectual* tables have also been turned. Despite Hawthorne and Henry James, men have not been the first to support women's rights strongly (*cf.* George Eliot); women have increasingly recognized their rights and powers; and they don't need to have a strawberry mark on the shoulder to relate them to nobility.

Russel Nye's *The Unembarrassed Muse* and Northrop Frye's *The Secular Scripture* bring us again—in different ways—to the image of women in popular culture and art. Without debating either view, I went to go back to *The Scarlet Letter,* because I think that we have too long deceived ourselves about this book, and about the new images of women that have brought us Sophie Tucker, Mae West, Jean Harlow and a recent member of the Channing family who proclaims that "Diamonds are a girl's best friend." In all this, we must not forget the incomparable Brits: When Jean Harlow met Margot Asquith she said: "I'm pleased to meet you Margot." Ms. Asquith replied: "The 't' is silent as in Harlow." To-day's girls like to camp.

The case which I want to present is very simple. It deals with three questions:

1) Is woman (Eve), the Dark Lady, responsible for the fall of man?
2) Is man *equally* involved in what capital "P" Puritans described as the Fall?
3) Has a blonde woman—we remember the famous article of F. L. Pattee, "Puritans Preferred Blondes"—outstripped the Dark Lady?

More questions, somewhat frivolous: Did Congressman

Wilbur Mills' affair with a Latin stripper (1975) make him less competent in his professional role? Was his disgrace her fault or his? Or was it strange that the blonde goddess Marilyn Monroe became the wife of a playwright, a liaison which soon got back to Chaucer when the lady became known as A. Miller's tail? If these recent happenings still make headlines, then the Scarlet Letter is still very hot, but the sexy lady has passed from Eve to Miss Clairol; and the morality has changed from scarlet scripture to mass media.

D. H. Lawrence recognized in his *Studies in Classic American Literature* that Hawthorne was both devious and wise. Conventional criticism has insisted that Hester Prynne's story was an account of sin, expiation and forgiveness in the traditional Christian pattern. This implies even more: sin, isolation, suffering, repentance, and finally reconciliation or forgiveness. We all make our mistakes. But in Puritan terms there was *no* forgiveness for certain sins. The adulterer or adulterous person was forced to wear a scarlet *A*, or was branded with an *A* on the forehead; or simply executed. In seventeenth-century New England, the *A* was very hot.

Now, how did Hawthorne feel about all this in the conventional town of Salem, Massachusetts, in the 1840's? He was an artist, and presumably a sexy chap; and neither sex nor art (apart from sombre portraits and polite water-colours) were warmly welcomed in the houses of the complacent people who lived on Chestnut Street, though sex was probably well known around the harbour, and Transcendental blue-stockings—including Sophie Peabody Hawthorne—could find John Flaxman's drawings of the Greek myths enchanting.

After Hawthorne left Bowdoin College, Maine, he stayed at home for twelve years "as though under enchantment"—a kind of odyssey—learning how to write short stories. He liked his college nickname, "Oberon." Then one day, while visiting the intellectual Peabodys, he saw a daughter, Sophia, descending a staircase—dressed and swanlike, not at all like Duchamp's cubist nude, which has been described as "an explosion in a shingle factory." It was love at first sight. She usually stayed upstairs because she suffered from migraine headaches. But she soon became Nathaniel's "dove," and finally proved to be one of the toughest wives in American literary history. She didn't like her lovely man smoking cigars and drinking champagne with the young buck Herman Melville in the days when they lived seven miles apart in Lenox and Pittsfield, Massachusetts; the tobacco made her curtains smell. After Hawthorne died (she had indeed loved him dearly), she edited his letters. Some of the unacceptable passages she cut out with scissors; others she inked out, but these have been retrieved by Randall Stewart through infra-red photography—such innocuous phrases as "Una fell on her bum."

So now, back to Hester Prynne, her scarlet letter, and Hawthorne's rehabilitation of her. Hawthorne was torn between three views of human experience. He loved the multi-levelled symbolism of Shakespeare, the allegory of Spenser and John Bunyan, and the clarity of Swift. No problem there. But the cruel Puritan view of a totally fallen mankind was against his instincts. Neither could be accept Pope's paradox—"Reason the card, but passion is the gale" (there is no real woman in Pope's scenario); nor, though he felt himself a New England "isolato" in Melville's sense, he could not fully embrace Shelley's idea that "I am a man whom the world loves not," or indulge in the passive lover's role of "Indian Serenade"—"I faint, I die, I fail . . ." (See Cleanth Brooks on Shelley in *The Well-Wrought Urn*.)

Then what *could* he do about Hester-Esther-Eve? and what could he do about the questing artist Nathaniel? *The Scarlet Letter* was his major analysis of the problems of the American past, and the roles of sexy ladies and artistic men—problems which had an historic continuity from Hester and Arthur/Author in the seventeenth century to the "Custom House" world of the mid-nineteenth century, and on into the perverse era of twentieth-century America.

The basic narrative of Hester is this. She was a gorgeous English girl, exotically beautiful in a British but Near-Eastern sense, who naively married a tired old scholar called Roger Chillingworth. Un-jolly Roger sent her to the Massachusetts colony in advance of his own voyage. By the time he reached Boston, Hester had had an affair with the brightest young clergyman of the town, and produced an infant known as Pearl. Hester was on public trial in the civic square when Roger appeared incognito. The site was flanked by the church, the cemetery and the prison ("The dark flower of civilization"). Roger would not recognize Hester as his wife. The preacher, Dimmesdale, could not admit his guilt, though he exhorted sinning Hester to reveal publicly the paternity of her child. Hester refused because she loved Dimmesdale; so the community or tribunal condemned her to wear a scarlet *A* on her left breast for life, and to live on the outskirts of the town as a fallen woman.

Now, let's look a little more closely at this red-hot situation, and the people involved. In Puritan terms, there was a clear conflict between Head and Heart. Reason, the law of the church and the *Old Testament* were seen as divine law. The Heart was corrupt, and a very frail guide to probity; indeed, the Heart got out of hand at puberty. In this community, Hester and Arthur were heinously out of line.

Yet Hawthorne's character groupings in *The Scarlet Letter* deny both Alexander Pope and the Puritan-Christian view of human character. The real situation in Hawthorne's romance is this:

1) A luxurious, sexy dark lady—intelligent, gifted, and passionate.
2) A dusty old scholar, Chillingworth, who married her to "warm the cold chamber of his heart."
3) An imaginative young stud, Dimmesdale, who could only function in the New World as a man who praised God. He was a brilliant graduate of Cambridge, but he could not subdue dark passions when he met Hester.
4) Governor Bellingham, a bachelor, who represented the British aristocracy and the military. English roses did not

thrive in his garden; instead it produced pumpkins, etc.— "lumps of vegetable gold."

5) Mistress Hibbins, his sister, who remained in a darkened room all day, and went out on her broomstick at night to do the devil's work, since in that society she could not function as a real woman.

6) Pearl—the unacknowledged, rebellious little bastard who combined the qualities of both Hester and Dimmesdale; she was "the union of their two natures." But in Puritan New England, this Pearl was castigated as the Devil's child.

The centre of Hawthorne's vision, then, was something more than a simple Head-Heart conflict. Instead, we have the luxurious, gifted Hester Prynne at the apex of a triangle—officially married to the scholar Chillingworth, but in fact in bed, at least once, with the imaginative Dimmesdale. Both men deny their relation with Hester; and Pearl, except for her mother's love, is treated as a little crazy head.

Let's now look more closely at names. Hawthorne avoided such blatantly obvious names as Doll Tearsheet or Lady Sneerwell, but he was in that tradition. Hester is etymologically Esther —a mother figure and protector of the home and hearth. Chillingworth is a wise and worthy man, but not very hot, except in terms of hell-fire. Dimmesdale is spiritual, imaginative and creative, but in Puritan New England (outside of legal wedlock), he can express his passion only by ejaculating grand sermons. Pearl, who unites the gifts of her erring parents, has no place in the Puritan community; but her name—unless Hawthorne had forgotten the *Bible* and *Pilgrim's Progress*—suggests a "pearl of great price," the soul. (We should not forget that Hawthorne named his first daughter Una, after the sacred lady of Spenser's *Faerie Queene*; and Una is Truth.)

Thus in Puritan society neither the wise old man, Chillingworth, nor the imaginative, passionate young man, Dimmesdale, could cope with the problems presented by women such as Hester-Esther, or even admit their "marriage" to her, let alone acknowledge the bright, rebellious presence of Pearl.

A critic who shall be nameless once told me that he always taught *The Scarlet Letter* as a bad novel because the last chapter was so obviously contrived as a means of tying up loose ends. For me, the last chapter is essential for Hawthorne's statement. In the penultimate chapter, Dimmesdale decides to mount the public scaffold in daylight, and calls for Hester Prynne:

> "Hester Prynne," cried he, with a piercing earnestness, "in the name of Him, so terrible and so merciful, who gives me grace, at this last moment, to do what—for my own heavy sin and miserable agony—I withheld myself from doing seven years ago, come hither now, and twine thy strength about me. Thy strength, Hester; but let it be guided by the will which God hath granted me. This wretched and wronged old man [Chillingworth] is opposing it with all his might! with all his own might, and the fiend's! Come, Hester, come! Support me up yonder scaffold!"

In this scene, Pearl, who had earlier accused her father of moral weakness—"Thou wast not bold, thou wast not true!"—now kisses him on the lips:

> A spell was broken. The great scene of grief in which the wild infant bore a part, had developed all her sympathies; and as her tears fell upon her father's cheek, they were the pledge that she would grow up amid human joy and sorrow, nor forever do battle with the world, but *be a woman in it.* [my italics.]

Then the strange concluding chapter. Pearl and Hester go to Europe, and Pearl marries well. She has inherited the qualities of her father and mother, and she has also inherited all of Chillingworth's wealth, since he, "with no more devil's work to do," withered away and died. The great irony is that this witch-child, now "the richest heiress of her day, in the New World" might "at a marriageable period of life, . . . have mingled her wild blood with the lineage of the devoutest Puritan among them all." But in seventeenth-century New England there was no place for a complete woman, or an artist like Dimmesdale. And Hawthorne evidently felt that the lovely lady and the artist were equally rejected in the America of the mid-nineteenth century.

With Pearl happily married, Hester returned to Boston: "Here had been her sin; here, her sorrow; and here was yet to be her penitence." She became a friend to all the troubled people who visited her cottage:

> She assured them, too, of her firm belief, that, at some brighter period, when the world should have grown ripe for it, in Heaven's own time, a new truth would be revealed, in order to establish the whole relation between man and woman on a surer ground of mutual happiness.

So much for suffering, maternal, *A*ngel, *A*ble Hester. She is finally buried beside her lover, king Arthur/Author Dimmesdale beneath a tombstone which in heraldry would be described as "ON A FIELD, SABLE, THE LETTER *A* GULES."

But if Hawthorne was a champion of Hester, and the Dark Ladies of his later romances, he was also a bit frightened of their power, even though they were not the destructive Eve-Circe figures that Puritans feared. In *The House of the Seven Gables, The Blithedale Romance,* and *The Marble Faun,* a tender, intelligent, seductive, but essentially passive blonde appears, and wins the hero's heart. Melville, too, especially in *Pierre,* was torn between a sweet blonde and a fascinating dark lady. In English writing, as in Moore and Hardy, the theme of un-wed mothers as pure women was taken up; and female bastards are to-day celebrated for their lack of conventional parentage.

The curious turn in American popular culture is that the Dark Lady may still be seen as a vamp, but the tender blonde is no longer tender; instead she tends to run the show, and to manipulate the men who would manipulate her. The *A GULES* has apparently proceeded to *B* (brass) and even to *D* (diamonds). Men retain a certain kind of power as "sugar-daddies", but they have lost the power which they exercised in Puritan New England. The Scarlet *A* is no longer hot, except, perhaps in middle-America and Canada. Faulkner celebrated the *A,* earth-mother figure, in Eula Garner, but Eula's daughter was deafened by World War II bombs in Europe; and in *The Mansion* she succeeded only by assisting tacitly in the murder of Flem Snopes, the most despicable member of the new commercial order.

But Eula Garner's daughter was an exception. The blondes have a precarious hold on their power. Some of them commit suicide (Carol Landis, Marilyn Monroe, etc.); and some lament (to invert Sophie Tucker) that "A hard man nowadays is good to find." Tragically, the *A*, which for Hawthorne really meant *A*lpha, the self—the mixed-up human Heart—is cold, or at best luke-warm. Hester-Esther no doubt still lives as a genuine earth-mother; but the rhine-stoned broad is having a well-deserved revenge on imperial men.

NOTE

The critical literature on Hawthorne is now so extensive that there is no point in attempting to compound academic folly. For those who wish to look further, the principal sources for this article are, in alphabetical order:

Bell, Millicent; HAWTHORNE'S VIEW OF THE ARTIST (New York, 1962).

Cowley, Malcolm, ed.; THE PORTABLE HAWTHORNE (New York, 1948).

Crews, Frederick C.; THE SINS OF THE FATHERS (New York, 1966).

Fiedler, Leslie A.; LOVE AND DEATH IN THE AMERICAN NOVEL (New York, 1960).

Fogle, Richard Harter; HAWTHORNE'S FICTION: THE LIGHT AND THE DARK (Norman, Oklahoma, revised ed., 1964).

Hoffman, Daniel G.; FORM AND FABLE IN AMERICAN FICTION (New York, 1961).

Kaul, A. N.; THE AMERICAN VISION (New Haven, 1963).

Levin, Harry; THE POWER OF BLACKNESS: HAWTHORNE, POE, MELVILLE (New York, 1958).

Male, Roy R.; HAWTHORNE'S TRAGIC VISION (Austin, Texas, 1957).

McPherson, Hugo; HAWTHORNE AS MYTH-MAKER (Toronto, 1969).

Stein, William B. HAWTHORNE'S FAUST: A STUDY OF THE DEVIL ARCHETYPE (Gainesville, Florida, 1953).

Waggoner, Hyatt H.; HAWTHORNE: A CRITICAL STUDY (Cambridge, Mass., revised ed., 1963).

The ideas about the blondes' revenge are widespread in popular literature; I acknowledge subjective debts to Marshall McLuhan, Buckminster Fuller, and several sexy periodicals of popular culture.

Richer in Esteem:
A Reappraisal of
John Burgoyne

J.E. MORPURGO

History has a perverse way with the reputation of generals. Victory, even consistent triumph, may not frank a passport to enduring fame and defeat can sometimes elevate its victim to a niche in the gallery of folk-heroes that is denied to conquerors. Robert E. Lee is remembered with pride not only by his Southern countrymen but also by the heirs of those who forced him to Appomattox; Ulysses S. Grant has long-since shambled out of the affections of all but a few cold-hearted students of strategy. To this day Rommel holds his place in the admiring reminiscences of his former enemies high above those who led them when they chased him out of Africa.

A realist addressing young men in military academies anywhere in the world might well recommend to them that, if they wish to ensure that the bubble sought in the cannon's mouth does not burst too soon, the best that they can do for themselves is to die whilst in battle and in high command, and that it does not matter overmuch whether they find death in the hour of glorious victory or in the moment of disaster. Nelson is among the immortals not so much because his battle-honours were many as because his mortality was established when he was adding Trafalgar to their number (though it must be admitted that his conquest of Emma Hamilton contributes the endearing quality of human frailty to his almost godlike infallibility as a commander). Wolfe died young, in battle, and in superbly-contrived triumph, but nothing has subscribed quite so much to his lasting fame as the fact that the general he defeated became a folk-hero in three countries by dying on the same field—which must make Quebec in all history the text-book battle for aspirants to military glory. Sir John Moore, J. E. B. Stuart, Stonewall Jackson, George Custer: all died at the head of armies that were either defeated or doomed to eventual destruction; all have survived as paragons of valour in the annals of their countries and in the world's store of legend.

Measured thus, by the scale of continuing fame, victory would seem to be useful, defeat no disqualification, but death in victory and death in defeat are well-nigh ineluctable as sureties. By the same scale the one certain route by which a general can reach oblivion is that he be humiliated in his only major campaign—and live to argue the reasons with his own disbelieving countrymen.

Already long before Saratoga, John Burgoyne had gathered to himself such a host of enemies in Britain as, could they have been transported to New York, must have made the American forces seem but indifferently powerful opponents. When he disgraced himself in battle the delight of these home-grown adversaries was scarcely less delirious than the rejoicings in the United States, and the pleasure that they took from continuing to castigate him for his shame was almost enough to compensate them for the shame that he had brought upon the Army. As Bernard Shaw wrote in *The Devil's Disciple:* "Burgoyne's surrender at Saratoga made him that occasionally necessary part of our British system, a scapegoat." Once he had served this purpose, and suffered also for his arrogance towards them, it was his enemies' intention to expunge his name forever from British military history.

Almost they succeeded. The convenient forgetfulness of the British would have reduced Burgoyne to a minute entry in the more voluminous reference-books were it not for the inconvenient tenacity of American national mythology. Still, two centuries after the surrender at Saratoga, Burgoyne is for Americans an effigy for public burning, a representative caricature of bumbling, bullying, choleric and effete Britishness, the symbol of all that they escaped through the wondrous achievement of revolution:

> Is he to conquer—he subdue our land—
> This buckram hero, with his lady's hand?
> By Caesars to be vanquished is a curse,
> But by a scribbling fop—by Heaven—is worse.

Not for Burgoyne that unqualified respect for the defeated enemy which the British still hold for Rommel and the Americans (if less patently) even for Cornwallis. These two gained credit with their opponents for their cleverness and boldness, as generals who, having fought a good fight, were brought eventually to doom by commanders, their equals in military art, leading armies superior to their own in competence and military fervour, and supported by the unmatchable heavy artillery of a God who comes always (if occasionally only just in time) to the support of those whose cause is righteous. Saratoga spelled for the United States the first substantial and breath-taking discovery that the braggart oratory of council-chamber and street-corner could be translated into battlefield reality. Here, almost as much as in Independence Hall, the American nation finds its origins. On this battle-honour the United States Army built its pride.

For two centuries, the Americans have reiterated their disdain for Burgoyne and the British have persisted with their furtive reluctance to mention his name, so that now any attempt to restore his reputation must seem like asking the College of Cardinals to canonize Judas. Yet for all his faults—and his faults were many—John Burgoyne was no mean representative of his country, his age and of the three crafts which he practiced: as soldier, parliamentarian and playwright. Erase that one disaster at Saratoga and there is left a substantial record as military philosopher and reformer, a career as a shrewd and generally honest politician, and a corpus of dramatic literature which, even though it is by immutable standards undistinguished, is yet worthy of comparison with the work of any of his contemporaries except the two indisputable geniuses, Sheridan and Goldsmith. Above all there remains the impression of a man possessed of those two qualities, versatility and honour, which his century prized above all others.

Saratoga remains, seemingly the immovable and insurmountable obstacle to Burgoyne's entry even into the outer halls of a pantheon. But though Burgoyne bore, and still bears, the opprobrium, he was in truth the victim and not the author of the disaster. The concept of an invasion from Canada designed to split in two the forces of rebellion was politically sound and, in military terms, elegant. That concept was not Burgoyne's alone (though after it had failed his enemies credited him with its invention) but he approved of it and spoke up for it.

Almost it worked. Ticonderoga was taken and Ticonderoga was regarded by many as the key to victory in New York. Against heavy odds Burgoyne won the first battle of Saratoga, the battle of Freeman's Farm, and three weeks later, at Bemis Heights, with only 1500 troops he held off attacks by an enemy four times as strong. Eventually he was brought to defeat not so much by the skill of his opponent, Horatio Gates, who for all that he had served previously with Burgoyne in the British Army (or perhaps because of that) and for all that he had a close family connection with Burgoyne's arch-critic, Horace Walpole, had an exaggerated respect for Burgoyne and for the British soldiers under his command and was therefore reluctant to attack his beleaguered enemy. (Gates, like Burgoyne himself, had less admiration for Burgoyne's German troops, but neither he nor Burgoyne saw it as any cause for shame to British arms that the King of Great

Britain and Hanover should use his German subjects and his German allies. The *canard* that George the Third used German *mercenaries* was not put about by American generals but by American propagandists and continued by American historians. (A latter-day British observer must allow himself the parenthetical comment that the appearance of the Baron von Riedesdel at Saratoga is no more "shocking" than the appearance of the Comte de Rochambeau at Yorktown.) Tactically Burgoyne was defeated by the bold but virtually mutinous intervention of Benedict Arnold. Strategically the fate of his force was sealed when Howe moved against Philadelphia instead of advancing to link up with the army from Canada. Burgoyne's last chance of fulfilling his mission vanished when Clinton gave up his attempt to relieve the troops at Saratoga. But the principal architect of disaster was not Gates, Arnold, Howe or Clinton, nor yet Burgoyne himself, but Lord George Germain. Had Germain's instructions to British generals in North America been specific, the derelictions of Howe and Clinton would not have occurred. Indeed, had the British Government recognised the impossibility of conducting North American campaigns from London, had they sent to New York a Supreme Commander with entire authority, and a headquarters' staff competent to transmit his orders to all generals in the field, the confusions, delays and arguments which bedevilled the British during the Revolutionary War could have been reduced to insignificant proportions.

The decision was never made and Burgoyne was just one of several British generals who suffered on the battlefield for the negligence of Westminster. Yet the humiliation at Saratoga was not entire and the compensations plucked from disaster can be marked to Burgoyne's credit and to his alone. His army had lost the tactical struggle and consequently the strategic objectives of his campaign were never achieved; but at the conference-table he routed his conquerors. Poor Gates, an honest, dogged and slow-witted British Army officer who had turned to the American cause without either sacrificing his integrity or sharpening his wits, was bamboozled by Burgoyne into accepting that the

British forces had not capitulated; though deprived of all capacity for using military muscle, even so the British commander would concede no more than a "Convention" with Gates whereby his men were allowed free passage back to England in return for the promise that they would never again fight in North America.

Congress was more cunning than Gates. Realising that Burgoyne's troops could be used by the British to relieve an equivalent number for service in America it repudiated the Convention and held Burgoyne's men prisoner for the duration. The decision was expedient but hardly honourable. Gates was shamed and Burgoyne alone could claim that he had come out of the affair with his reputation for probity unimpaired.

Claim it he did, vehemently and vociferously when he arrived back in London—having been granted by the Americans the privilege of repatriation that was denied to his subordinates.

His enemies in Britain were less kindly than his American opponents and he was never given the opportunity that he demanded for self-justification before a court-martial. Calumnies were spread about him. It was argued (perhaps with justice) that he should have returned to America to join his troops in captivity. It was said of him that he had failed in America with intent, because his political instincts led him to favour the American cause, an accusation that might have been levelled with some force against the Howes or even against Clinton but not against Burgoyne who, despite his friendship with many of the Whig leaders and despite his ancient and continuing animosity towards Germain, had always regarded himself as a King's man.

Burgoyne was never again given a field-command and he was denied (or perhaps out of pique he denied himself) any of those public honours which Britain uses as rewards for conquering heroes, as balm for the pride of generals who have failed and as prizes for all who have a plethora of influential friends.

In North America Burgoyne lost an army. A year earlier he had lost his wife. His romantic elopement with Lady Charlotte Stanley in 1751 had cost him years of seniority in the Service but, by the standards of his class and time, the marriage had been a success, not merely because it had won for him eventually the patronage of Lady Charlotte's powerful family but also because there was between husband and wife genuine affection and mutual understanding which had helped them to hold their marriage firm for twenty-five years even though Lady Charlotte could not share her husband's enthusiasm for soldiering and even though he demonstrated, frequently and publicly, his unwillingness to share her belief in monogamy. When the news of his wife's death on 5 June, 1776 reached Burgoyne in Canada he had written to Clinton that all that he was now was "an unconnected cypher in the world, the partner lost which made prosperity an object of solicitude. Interest, ambition, the animation of life is over." All that was left for him was the honour of being "finished in a professional grave."

With so much else even that had been denied him by Fate and Gates, by Congress and by the King, back in England, unjustified, a failure and a widower, he should have been a broken man. But no one, not even the King, could deprive him of his seat in Parliament, and he struck back boldly against his opponents by shifting his political affiliation to the Whigs and going far towards vindicating his military reputation by his frequent, sensible—if somewhat prolix—interventions in parliamentary debates on Army affairs. And nothing, not even disgrace or personal sorrow, could take from Burgoyne his zest for being entertained and for entertaining others. He was seldom out of debt; gambling, women and half-pay saw to that; but he was never idle.

Soon the "scribbling fop" was back at his scribbling. His first dramatic piece, *The Maid of the Oaks* had been staged at Drury Lane in November 1774, a few weeks before its author left to join Gage in Boston. Horace Walpole dismissed it in scathing terms such as he devoted to all Burgoyne's activities, military, political, personal or theatrical:

> There is a new puppet-show . . . as fine as scenes can make
> it . . . and as dull as the author could not help making it.

But David Garrick, better-qualified than Walpole to judge an entertainment, though just as prejudiced in Burgoyne's favour as Walpole was perfervid in animosity, pronounced the show "a great success," and *The Maid of the Oaks* survived in the repertory for several months and in book-form enjoyed for many years a considerable vogue.

The Maid of the Oaks is, in truth, a heavy-handed and stylized piece, remarkable only for its sentimentality and for its portentous morality so utterly out of keeping with Burgoyne's own inclinations and activities. For two dreary acts Burgoyne preaches on the blessings of pastoral life and on marriage as the highest estate, the perfect union of true hearts. And, at the end, the pastoral idyll envelops even the hypocritical and sinful visitors from the city, and marriage, as all other virtuous institutions, triumphs over sinfulness, dissimulation and greed. The twentieth century reader may smile that advocacy of this kind should come from Burgoyne, Londoner-born, energetic participant in all the amoral delights that his London had to offer, and the beneficiary of patronage that came from marrying into an influential family. That smile is the only pleasure that he can wring from *The Maid of the Oaks*.

The later plays, the post-Saratoga plays, were so much better than *The Maid of the Oaks* that it is tempting to argue that the disappointments, frustrations and tragedies which he had experienced in his career and in his personal life had heightened Burgoyne's sensibility and equipped him with understanding which he had lacked when ambition and potential were equally matched.

Burgoyne's second essay into the theatre, *The Blockade of Boston,* like John André's famous Philadelphia *Mischianza,* had been no more than an entertainment designed to sustain the morale of officers bored by not-very-active service, but his third, *The Lord of the Manor,* for all that its targets for satire were most of them ephemeral, had the virtues that come from a writer who knows his characters. Burgoyne had been bemused by the pastoral idyll which he had created in *The Maid of the Oaks.*

Had he met his Maria she would not have remained a maid for ten minutes. But Sergeant Sash, Corporal Dill and Corporal Snip are caricatures only in the sense that they are exaggerations of reality and the reality that is the British soldier Burgoyne understood and respected more than any other playwright of his time. An eighteenth century audience was never averse to a resounding platitude, and Burgoyne gave them many to applaud, but as they listened to his hero, Trumore, his contemporaries must have heard the voice of the author, the man who had gone to America a happily-married man ambitious for honour and returned disgraced to an empty home and an unforgiving nation.

> A passion for my country is the only one that ought to have
> competition with virtuous love; when they unite in the heart
> the actions are inspiration.

Armed with knowledge of the author's circumstances which later generations have let slip the more charitable members of his audience transposed bathos into pathos.

The Lord of the Manor was staged just six years before *The Marriage of Figaro.* To compare the two operas is tantamount to comparing the angels at play with an entertainment contrived by a small-town operatic society which draws some of its strength and inspiration from a nearby military base. Yet, like all operas, both demand of the audience the abandonment of all sense of reality. Sergeants do not indulge in musical soliloquy but the possibility that they might do so is no more unthinkable than the sudden interruption of normal dialogue by a duet between a personal maid and a valet. Mozart's marvellous genius and da Ponte's rare competence as a librettist overcame the essential illogicality of opera. Burgoyne's composer, William Jackson of Exeter, was a not insignificant representative of a generation of English musicians all capable of writing a charming or—when need be—a rumbustious tune, but he was no Mozart, and Burgoyne was most certainly no rival to da Ponte, but the dramatic faults in *The Lord of the Manor,* like the faults in *The*

Marriage of Figaro, are those which are endemic to the *genre.*

The fall of the Whigs led to Burgoyne quitting politics and thus gave him more time for gambling, for the arms of Susan Caulfield, who in the fulfilment of matrimonial duties as in all else but title had taken the place of his dead wife, and for the theatre. In 1785 he published an adaptation of a serious French libretto, *Richard Coeur de Lion.* The opera was not performed in public until after Sheridan had staged at Drury Lane Burgoyne's outstanding success, *The Heiress.* Then it failed, and it is in no way memorable except as proof that Burgoyne was a considerable linguist.

The Heiress is a different matter. The plot is thin and moves forward in a flurry of coincidences. No less than in *The Maid of the Oaks* the characterization is simplistic and appears to be formed more by the names of the participants (Lord Gayville, whose title represents the cheerfulness of his country residence; Mr. Rightly, the honest lawyer and Mr. Alscrip, his devious colleague; Chignon, the prissy French hairdresser; the social climbers, Mr. and Mrs. Blandish). But the play has pace, the wit is sharp and the social comment incisive:

> Our young men are flimsy essays; old ones political pamphlets; coquettes, fugitive pieces; and fashionable beauties, a compilation of advertised perfumery, essence of pearl, milk of roses and Olympian dew.

Or again, in the last act:

> . . . and really Miss Alscrip. I see no reason for your being dispirited; there may be many ready-made titles at market, within reach of your purse.

And, both pointed and revealing of the author's bitterness:

> The public eye, in this country, is never long deceived. Believe me and cherish obscurity. Title may bring forward merits, but it also places our defects in horrid relief.

With *The Heiress* Burgoyne made little more than £200 but he won at last the respect of Horace Walpole:

> Burgoyne's battles and speeches will be forgotten, but his delightful comedy of The Heiress will continue the delight of the stage and one of the most pleasing domestic compositions.

And so said all the critics, not only in England but also in France and Germany. One newspaper hinted that if Burgoyne's writing continued to improve—"if he proceeds as much as he has done, advancing as much beyond his *Lord of the Manor* as that was beyond *The Maid of the Oaks*"—he might yet write the comic masterpiece for his age. Another supported this view in rhyme, suggesting even that Burgoyne could out-write his friend Sheridan:

> Burgoyne, perhaps, unchill'd by creeping age,
> May yet arise and vindicate the stage;
> The reign of nature and of sense restore,
> And be whatever Terence was before.

Sheridan! Terence! These were insignificant names to a man who, with *The Heiress*, had at long last won the public glory that had been denied to him in his prime profession. Now he would prove his quality by improving upon the quality of Shakespeare. He planned to re-write *As You Like It* in eighteenth century verse and to have it staged as an opera. Gout and other inhibitions brought on by "creeping age" slowed the great endeavour and, on 4 August 1792, all Burgoyne's work was ended. The *Gentleman's Magazine* reported

> Died . . . at his house in Hertford Street, Mayfair, the Right Honourable John Burgoyne, a Privy Councillor, Lieutenant-General in the army, Colonel of the 4th Regiment of Foot, M.P. for Preston, and author of the much celebrated comedy entitled *The Heiress* . . . He has died richer in esteem

than in money; in the saving or securing of that he had no talent. Of all the gay, the witty, and the fashionable, who eagerly sought his acquaintance, and whose minds were impressed by the elegance of his conversation and the variety of his talents, very few were present to drop the tear over departed genius. . . .

The obituary-writer made no secret of the fact that Burgoyne died—as so often he had lived—insolvent; but the sly hint that the acquaintances who had fawned upon him in life refused him the gesture of attending his funeral was no more justified than the accusation, expressed in the notice only by flagrant omission, that the Army which he had served for so long at the last rejected his right to military honours. There were close friends and admirers who wished to salute Burgoyne, and their number included many whose names stand still high above his in the record of British achievement. Sir Joshua Reynolds had preceded Burgoyne to the grave by a few months, but there was Sheridan, Fox, Robert Adam, and, for all that they had come to parliamentary disagreement, the Younger Pitt. The senior officers who had served under him even in defeat were loyal to the end (one was the executor of his will) and—perhaps the greatest of all tributes to his life—he was mourned by non-commissioned officers and private soldiers as no other predecessor in high command since Wolfe and as few of his successors other than Nelson and Moore. The artists, dramatists, politicians and general officers who loved and admired him did not attend his funeral because he had specifically requested that they stay away. The streets were not lined with troops and old soldiers because, in one of those strangely contradictory gestures which were part of his make-up, the man who had been so eager for public acclaim had insisted also that there should be no previous announcement of the details of the funeral.

He was buried alongside his wife in the North Cloister of Westminster Abbey and thus came to rest at last, and as it were through the distinguished patronage of her family, just outside the hallowed space where Britain memorializes her greatest sons. The inscription on his coffin made no reference to *The Heiress* and none to his parliamentary constituencies, but only to his military rank and his membership of the Privy Council.

Saratoga was ignored and this same shrugging-off of an inconvenient memory was evident in most of the obituary-notices. But, because of Saratoga, the author of the inscription, the writers of the obituaries—and most subsequent historians—have shrugged-off also Burgoyne's greatest claim to enduring fame: as a military reformer. And, because of Saratoga, Burgoyne's reforms were still-born. His tactical philosophy and, above all, his theories of man-management could be proved valid only by military success. That was denied him. Consequently the British Army had to wait for Sir John Moore and Wellington before Burgoyne's tactical notions could be put into practice and not until after the Crimean War was the Army prepared to move towards Burgoyne's view that the British soldier should be treated as a thinking and essentially human human-being. Because of Saratoga and because so much time had passed since Burgoyne had first prompted reform no credit for progress has ever been ascribed to him.

His military thinking was developed long before the Revolutionary War and was largely founded on close observation of French and German armies exercised during the period when he was out of the Service and living on the Continent with his new bride. The Prussians, he insisted, were the best-disciplined troops in Europe and the French the worst but the machine-like response to orders instilled into Prussian soldiers ("trained, like spaniels, with the stick") was useful in the crises of battle, and so too was the devotion to the regiment and the flag which the French acquired as "the point of honour." "A just medium between the two extremes," wrote Burgoyne, "is the surest means to using English soldiers to perfection."

His ideas he codified in 1759 and 1760 when he was commissioned to raise the 16th Light Dragoons. More than any other field-officer of his generation he appreciated that modes of discipline and methods of training are the grammar upon which is founded the doctrinal language of battle-field tactics. Light cavalry, he argued, must be adaptable, and capable of rapid movement either *en masse* or in small, independent units. To this end every officer, non-commissioned officer and private soldier must be immediate in his response to orders but no less ready to act for himself when the circumstances required initiative. Soldiers cowed by harsh discipline would never respond as Burgoyne wished—"An Englishman will not bear beating as well as the foreigners." Even, he forbade swearing at his dragoons!

A troop, a regiment or an army, he insisted in terms that might have come from a Second World War general, is only as good as its junior officers; and to a generation which regarded a commission in the Army as an excuse for gentlemanly indolence, he preached a series of sermons full of heresies against the prevailing professional code. On-duty officers must abide strictly by the rules of military hierarchy but off the parade-ground all officers were equals and something of this relaxation could be applied even between commissioned and other ranks: his officers were to obtain "an insight into the characters of each particular man" and on occasion, "such as during stable or fatigue duty . . . may slacken the reins so far as to talk with their soldiers, nay, even a joke may be used, not only without harm but to good purpose."

Again in terms that were not to become common in training-manuals until the twentieth century, Burgoyne demanded of his officers that they make themselves competent in any task which their men were called upon to perform:

> I hope I shall not appear finical, if I recommend to officers sometimes to accoutre and bridle a horse themselves until they are thoroughly acquainted with the use of each strap and buckle. . . .

Farriery, grooming, the feeding of horses, some knowledge of veterinary science; all this and more that most armies of the time regarded as troopers' technology but far beneath the dignity of gentlemen, Burgoyne willed upon his junior officers. It was not his intention, he claimed, to offer them instructions "as the orders of a commanding officer, but as the sentiments of a friend"; nevertheless, the bark of seniority was audible: he was not slow to tell his officers that they were "as much particularized by their youth and inexperience as by their rank and fortune."

Burgoyne's programme for the training of a young officer included much more than practical subjects and transcended by far those barrack-square exercises which, two centuries later the British Army poet, Henry Reed, was to epitomize by the refrain "to-day we have naming of parts." A good officer must prepare himself for his profession— "A short time given to reading each day . . . will furnish a great deal of instruction"—and not only books in English but also in French, then the language of the best military thinkers. He must study mathematics and must learn to sketch, "to practise taking views from an eminence, and to measure distance with his eye." Above all—advice which Burgoyne did not often follow himself—"an officer ought to write English with swiftness and accuracy."

When Burgoyne drafted these instructions to the officers of the 16th Light Dragoons not one European country had established a military academy that could be recognised as a predecessor to Sandhurst or West Point, and the British Army still regarded exercise in the hunting-field, the gaming-table and the ball-room as the best preparation for a military career.

Not for another one hundred and fifty years did any major military power establish a Staff College, yet on this, too, Burgoyne had his ideas as early as 1765. No less than junior officers, he urged, their seniors must apply themselves to continuous professional study. In an age when artillery was despised as an arm not quite worthy of manipulation by gentlemen, Burgoyne considered the possibility of supporting light cavalry with highly mobile horse artillery. When he came to command in North America he advocated the use of saturation-bombardment as a counter to the ungentlemanly aptitude in the use of cover shown by American infantrymen. So enthusiastic was he for the advancement of the artilleryman's craft that he subverted the implacable convention of the period and gave the command of one of the wings of his invading force to a Gunner, Major-General William Phillips, and so convinced was he that artillery wins battles that the number of guns his force dragged into New York State from Canada was out of all proportion to the custom of the time. Sadly for Burgoyne his tactical philosophy had outstripped technical and logistic possibilities. The comparative immobility of his clumsy artillery-pieces and the problems experienced in keeping them supplied with ammunition over a long and difficult line of communication with bases in Canada were contributory causes for the disaster at Saratoga.

Indeed, in action Burgoyne failed to live up to the promise of his own military intellect. The fault was, for the most part, not his and it was not he alone who suffered the consequences. Saratoga spelt the beginning of the end for Britain's American empire, but for the British Army it spelt also a delay of forty years before the first of the reforms which Burgoyne had projected was implemented; and not until after the Crimean War—a century later—did Burgoyne's theories of officer-training and man-management become commonplace.

Because he failed in battle his military virtues were forgotten and his missionary zeal ignored.

Burgoyne was bombastic, vain, a gambler, a wencher and a spendthrift. His political career was insignificant and within ten years of his death his fame as a playwright was already vanishing. Yet a memorial was raised to John Burgoyne even before he was dead. It is there in the words of that extraordinarily literate sergeant, Roger Lamb (written in the moment of Burgoyne's disgrace), the undimmed affection of the ordinary British soldier:

> He possessed the confidence and affection of his army in an extraordinary degree, that no loss or misfortune could shake the one, or distress or affliction the other . . . not a voice was heard throughout the army, to upbraid, to censure or blame their general.

And the memorial stands yet, prouder than paeans and more enduring than granite obelisks. Speak the name of Burgoyne even amongst those who would not claim for themselves historical sophistication and back comes, not Preston or Brooks's, not *The Lord of the Manor* or *The Heiress*, not Portugal or the 16th Light Dragoons, not even Saratoga. Back comes, as immediate today as it was when first it was heard, the nickname he was given by the private soldiers under his command: Gentleman Johnny.

Lord Kames and American Revolutionary Culture

GILMAN M. OSTRANDER

After a long neglect, the Scottish jurist, Henry Home, Lord Kames, is regaining much of the reputation he enjoyed during his own lifetime as a major figure in the Scottish Enlightenment.[1] Less distinguished as an original thinker than his most brilliant colleagues and sometime proteges, David Hume and Adam Smith, Kames is perhaps more interesting today as the crusty doyen of the Edinburgh intellectual establishment than as philosopher. Nevertheless, his writings in the fields of moral philosophy and aesthetics, as well as those in law, education, and agricultural science, won him acclaim and influence abroad as well as at home. At the time of his death in 1782, his reputation was at its height. In America, new editions of his most influential writings continued to appear for a century thereafter, but it was upon the Revolutionary generation of Americans that Kames exerted the greatest influence.

Among Kames's writings, two works were notably influential in America as elsewhere: *Essays on the Principles of Morality and Natural Religion* (1751) and, especially, *Elements of Criticism* (1762). *Essays* was Kames's own statement of the Scottish philosophy that Francis Hutcheson had founded a generation earlier, essentially by systematizing Lord Shaftesbury's modifications of John Locke's psychology and philosophy. From Shaftesbury, the Scottish philosophers derived the belief that man possessed senses, or faculties, other than the five that Locke would allow him. They believed that man universally possessed an innate common sense and that he additionally possessed an innate moral sense and that through the instinctive exercize of these faculties, man was capable of intuiting truth from error and right from wrong, as well as intuiting accurate aesthetic judgments regarding beauty, and the reverse of it, in all of its forms.[2]

Kames's *Essays on Morality and Religion* advanced no very original theses, but it provided a comprehensive reconsideration of moral philosophy that took into account the current literature on the subject, including the skepticisms of Berkeley and Hume, which it sought to refute. Kames's *Essays* would be followed during the next generation by numerous interpretations of the Scottish philosophy, including those by Adam Smith, Adam Ferguson, Thomas Reid, and Dugald Stewart, and these works would supercede Kames's *Essays* in influence. However, it was not until the 1760's that the works of these writers began to appear, except for Smith's *Theory of Moral Sentiments*, published in 1759. Until then, two contemporary works held the field, so far as the Scottish philosophy was concerned: Kames's *Essays on Morality and Religion* and Hume's *Enquiry Concerning the Principles of Morals* (1751).[3]

Elements of Criticism was more original in conception and more enduring in influence than *Essays*. Kames accepted from Shaftesbury and Hutcheson the conception of virtue and beauty as related qualities to which the moral sense of mankind naturally responded. Both aspects of the moral sense received extensive attention in *Essays*; in *Elements of Criticism*, Kames limited his subject to the aesthetic sense of man and to the rules according to which literature and the arts conformed to this aesthetic sense. *Elements* won immediate international recognition and, so far as the English-speaking world was concerned, it remained a basic text on criticism for a half century and more. At least thirty-one American editions of it were printed, the first of them appearing in 1796. Together with *Lectures on Rhetoric and Belles Lettres* (1783) by the Reverend Hugh Blair, whom Kames had assisted in his career as he earlier had assisted Hume and Smith, *Elements of Criticism* remained the authoritative handbook in America throughout the period of the early Republic and, to a lesser extent, thereafter.[4]

Jonathan Edwards was very likely the first American intellectual to read Kames's *Essays on the Principles of Morality and Natural Religion* (as well as the first to read Hume's *Enquiry Concerning the Principles of Morals*).[5] He appears to have read both works at the time he was preparing his own essay on *Freedom of Will*, which appeared in 1754, and he was later incensed to learn that his own essay was being cited in Scotland in support of the arguments of Kames against the possibility of man possessing any real liberty to act on his own volition. The unqualified determinism advanced by Kames was at the time embroiling him with the Scottish Church, and Edwards had no wish to be falsely implicated in the charge. To a friend in Scotland, Edwards wrote an extensive letter comparing in detail the differences between him and Kames on this subject, a letter which came to be added as an appendix to subsequent editions of *Freedom of Will*.[6]

That is not to say that Edwards was not influenced by Kames's essay, however, or, for that matter, by Hume's. Edwards wrote of Hume's work that he was "glad of an opportunity to read such corrupt books, especially when written by men of considerable genius," since it gave him "an idea of the notions that prevail in our nation."[7] As contemporaries writing at the same level of abstraction as Edwards, Hume and Kames provided the kind of intellectual stimulation that was not so readily available to him in his native America. As such they were bound to influence his thinking, if only in reaction to their arguments.

If Edwards was the first American to become familiar with the works of Hume and Kames, Benjamin Franklin probably was the first to become well-acquainted with the two philosophers personally. Scotsmen had been notably prominent among Franklin's more intellectual associates in Philadelphia and later in London,[8] and when he heard that he had been awarded an honorary doctorate by St. Andrews University, Franklin was moved to pay his first visit to Scotland in 1759.[9] While in Scotland, he became the house guest of David Hume and of Lord Kames, among others, and he wrote Kames following his visit that the occasion had been ". . . Six Weeks of the *densest* Happiness I have met with in any Part of my life; and the agreeable and instructive Society we found there in such Plenty has left so pleasing an Impression on my Memory that, did not strong Connections draw me elsewhere, I believe Scotland would be the Country I should chuse to spend the remainder of my Days in."[10]

Franklin remained a friend and correspondent of both Hume and Kames thereafter, but it does not appear that he ever studied their writings with the care that Edwards did. In any case, Franklin had arrived at a world view of his own before he ever made the acquaintance of these Scottish philosophers, and so had Edwards. It was upon the younger Revolutionary generation of American intellectuals that Kames (and, to a greater extent than is generally recognized, Hume) exerted a formative influence through their writings.

Douglass Adair has convincingly demonstrated the importance of Hume, writing as political scientist rather than philosopher, to the constitutional theory argued by James Madison in the Tenth Federalist Paper.[11] Gilbert Chinard and Adrienne Koch have more concretely established the importance of Kames, the moral philosopher, to the social theory that Thomas Jefferson summarized in the Declaration of Independence.[12] Jefferson's natural rights argument is commonly labeled "Lockian," which, in a general way, it certainly is. But if Jefferson believed that "Locke's little book on government is perfect as far as it goes,"[13] this famous quotation itself implies that the treatise did not go far enough to suit Jefferson. Jefferson, himself, had been trained in the post-Lockian Scottish school that endowed mankind with a moral sense which Locke had not discovered in man's psychological makeup, and the Declaration reflects this Scottish influence.

Jefferson received his Scottish education at William and Mary College, where the faculty was entirely composed of Anglican ministers, except for one Scottish layman, a recent graduate of Marischal College at Aberdeen University.[14] In a well-known passage from his "Autobiography," Jefferson wrote: "It was my great good fortune, and what probably fixed the destinies of my life, that Dr. William Small of Scotland was then Professor of Mathematics . . . from his conversation I got my first views of the expansion of science, and of the system of things in which we are placed. Fortunately, the philosophical chair became vacant soon after my arrival at college, and he was appointed to fill it *per interim*; and he was the first who ever gave in that college, regular lectures in Ethics, Rhetoric and Belles Lettres."[15] Jefferson, who held the Anglican faculty of the college in contempt on moral as well as intellectual grounds, was Small's student as well as his "daily companion" from 1760 to 1762. It was during this period of his life that Jefferson chiefly formulated his own moral philosophy under the generously acknowledged guidance of his Scottish mentor.

The text, or one of the texts, from which Jefferson originally learned his moral philosophy was Lord Kames's *Essays on Morality and Natural Religion*. Jefferson copied passages from this work extensively in his *Commonplace Book of Philosophers and Poets*, and the conception of human nature and natural rights that resulted from his studies was Kamesian rather than Lockian.[16] Jefferson accepted the un-Lockian and distinctly Scottish conception of the "moral sense" as an innate human feeling that all human nature shared. Furthermore, Jefferson also accepted Kames's own interpretation of the moral sense as being capable of progressive development both in the individual and in the society. In the margin of his own copy of Kames's *Essays on Morality and Religion*, Jefferson commented extensively on his own agreement with Kames's statement that the law of nature concerning moral feelings of men and of society, in Jefferson's words, "cannot be stationary. It must vary with the nature of man, and consequently refine gradually as human nature refines." Jefferson went on in his marginal comments to enlarge Kames's argument into an assertion of a natural basis for human progress in history.[17] This Scottish emendation of Lockian psychology— this "moral sense" or "moral sentiment" or "moral faculty" that functions in the heart and not in the head—together with Kames's developmental interpretation of it, remained basic to Jeffersonian social thought throughout his life.[18]

Where Locke's Creator would have endowed all men with the natural right to life, liberty, and property, the Declaration specified life, liberty, and the pursuit of happiness. This idea that the pursuit of happiness was the natural right of all mankind was not simply an idiosyncratic belief of Jefferson's. It was a belief which was characteristic of mid-eighteenth-century thought generally, whether in France, England, Scotland or America, but there were regional variations in enlightened interpretations of it. The English interpretation that appears in Pope's *Essay on Man* (1733) and in William Paley's *Principles of Moral and Political Philosophy* (1785) was that God had evidently distributed happiness more or less equally among all classes of society, and that that was that. The Scottish conception of happiness as a natural right, being the realization of the natural human sentiment of benevolence, was substantially Jefferson's version of it. According to the Scottish, as well as the Jeffersonian, theory of it, the moral sense impelled men and women to act in harmony with the interests of society as a whole and at the same time to gain pleasure from doing so.

At the heart of Jeffersonian democratic thought there is this Scottish conception of a moral sense, as well as of a common sense, inherent in all mankind. Thus Jefferson advised young Peter Carr in 1789 that it would be "lost time to attend lectures" in moral philosophy, since "The moral sense, or conscience, is as much a part of man as his leg or arm" and as likely to be comprehended by the ploughman as by the professor. "This sense is submitted indeed in some degree to the guidance of reason," he added, "but it is a small stock which is required for this; even less than what we call common sense."[19] For Carr's fuller understanding of morality and religion, Jefferson recommended that he read the relevant essays by Kames and Hume.

In his copy of Kames's *Principles of Morality and Religion*, Jefferson underscored Kames's comments on the moral sense of savages.[20] In 1814 he wrote that "Men living in different countries, under different circumstances, different habits and regimens, may have different utilities," but regardless of these circumstantial differences, he sincerely believed "in the general existence of a moral sense."[21] This central Jeffersonian belief probably derived from Professor Small's instruction; it certainly derived from his study of Kames's *Essays*.

Although Jefferson acquired a substantial collection of the writings of Kames, he does not appear to have been much influenced by Kames's most widely influential work, *Elements of Criticism*. Jefferson advised others to read the great writings in English literature from Shakespeare to Pope, in order to improve their writing styles, rather than to read Kames or Blair or any such manual. Elsewhere, however, for would-be writers who were not as confident of their own literary styles as Jefferson evidently was of his, Kames's *Elements of Criticism* was grasped as the key to literary achievement.[23] This was strikingly the case with the group of Yale undergraduates who became known as the Conneticut Wits, led by Timothy Dwight, Jonathan Trumbull, David Humphreys, and Joel Barlow. Nothing they gained from the curriculum at Yale appears to have inspired in these young men the hope that they might be able to create a worthy American literature. Rather it was their discovery, outside of class, of Lord Kames's *Elements of Criticism* that persuaded them of the possibility of creating a literature that would compare favorably with European literature, according to those universally applicable standards of taste that they were led through their reading of Kames to believe they could master.[24]

Kames taught them that, as was the case with ethics and the universally operative moral sense in human nature, so ". . . upon a sense common to the species, is erected a standard of taste . . . for ascertaining in all the fine arts, what is beautiful or ugly, high or low, proper or improper, proportioned or disproportioned. And here, as in morals, we justly condemn every taste that swerves from what is thus ascertained by the common standard."[25] Later on, as an instructor at Yale, Dwight introduced Kames's *Elements of Criticism*, with its argument concerning an aesthetic "internal sense" that literary aspirants in provincial New Haven and Hartford shared equally with the literati of London.[26] The zealous republicanism of the Connecticut Wits, even while most of them retained their old convictions concerning the propriety of degrees and stations in society, is to be appreciated in terms of their patriotic literary ambitions for their new nation, as well as for themselves, to present themselves on an equal footing with men of letters everywhere.

Beyond considering its subject philosophically, *Elements of Criticism* is a how-to-do-it book. There is a chapter on wit, replete with illustrative examples, explaining what wit is, the various ways in which it is created, and the various errors that the would-be wit should avoid. There is a chapter on dramatic and epic verse, similarly defining the subject and prescribing the appropriate literary methods. There are other chapters dealing with other aspects of the use of language in various literary forms, all of them illustrated by appropriate examples. Presumably anybody, anywhere, in any literary time, could write epic verse and produce wit by following these instructions. *Elements of Criticism* appeared to show the Connecticut Wits the way "to soar as high as European bards," as John Quincy Adams wrote of them admiringly during a visit to Hartford in 1785.[27] Both the rather remarkable literary achievements of the Connecticut Wits and the obvious limitations of these achievements are to be understood in the context of Kames's arbitrary book of rules, which the Connecticut Wits studied and followed.

The American influence of *Elements of Criticism* long outlasted the influence of *Essays on Morality and Natural Religion*, which, even for Jefferson came to be superceded by later Scottish and French moral philosophers. At least twenty-two American editions of *Elements of Criticism* appeared after 1835, and an editor of the 1855 edition declared in the preface that "There seems to be no other work even at this date, that is fitted to supply its place, nor, without great disadvantage to the cause of educaion, can it be laid aside."[28]

By 1855, the Presbyterian minister, Eliphalet Nott, was entering his fifty-first year as president of Union College and as professor of the senior course in Moral Philosophy, which appeared in the college catalog under the title of "Kames." The text for the course was Kames's *Elements of Criticism*, as had been the case since before Nott had taken the course over in 1804.[29] During the passage of a half century, Nott had found much to criticize about the text, and *Elements* had been reduced in his classroom to the role of butt of Nott's awesome ridicule. Nott attacked Kames's mechanistic resolutions of all aesthetic and moral problems, as well as Kames's attribution to humans alone of capabilities, such as the power to reason, which Nott could discover in dogs and other animals. But Nott was apparently less removed from Kames in his thinking than he allowed his students, and perhaps himself, to believe. When he came to write his own manual, *Help to Young Writers* (1836), Nott drew heavily upon the text written by Hugh Blair, Kames's junior colleague in the Scottish intellectual establishment of the eighteenth century, whose views on morals and taste differed little from those of Kames.[30]

Upon attacking Kames's assertion of reason as a faculty that separated man from animal, Nott arrived emphatically at the conclusion that the only sense which man alone possessed was the moral sense.[31] Nott thought of himself as an inconoclast, and evidently his students shared this view of him, but by the end of the century, academic psychology and philosophy had substantially obliterated the Scottish "moral sense" along with the rest of the optimistic, egocentric, and fatally unevolutionary Scottish synthesis. This Scottish synthesis succumbed to naturalism in science and to pragmatic relativism in social thought.

Later on, however, in the course of America's experience with fascism and communism abroad and McCarthyism at home, American intellectuals faced what Edward A. Purcell, Jr., has called the crisis of democratic theory, arising chiefly from the fact that relativism in political theory admitted of no absolute values by which antidemocratic ideologies could be condemned.[32]

The scientifically questionable way out of this dilemma for many pragmatic liberals was to accept relativistic and pluralistic American democracy as a positive, perhaps even an absolute, value in itself. Still, these relativist-pluralist defenders of American democracy have not been content to assume the amoral position of defending American democracy merely for its utility as a self-serving mutual benefit society for the various groups within its membership. There is evidently thought to be a moral content to democratic life deriving from a moral principle —however imperfectly realized in practice—that somehow resides in the national community as a whole. The Declaration of Independence remains the basic document of American democracy, and the Kamesian "moral sense" version of the Lockian natural rights argument evidently continues to be accepted as an article of faith a century after it fell into disrepute as a scientific truth.

NOTES

1. The two major recent works on Kames are: Ian S. Ross, *Lord Kames and the Scotland of His Day* (Oxford, 1972) and William C. Lehmann, *Henry Home, Lord Kames and the Scottish Enlightenment* (The Hague, 1971). A study in the Twayne series, Arthur E. McGuinness, *Henry Home, Lord Kames* (New York, 1970), examines Kames's *Essays on Morality and Religion, Elements of Criticism,* and *Sketches of the History of Man.*

2. James McCosh, *The Scottish Philosophy* (Hildesheim, 1875) is a comprehensive biographical account; Gladys Bryson, *Man and Society; The Scottish Inquiry of the Eighteenth Century* (New York, 1945), describes the pattern of thought that emerges in com-

mon from the writings of David Hume, Lord Kames, Adam Smith, Adam Ferguson, Thomas Reid, and Dugald Stewart.

3. *Ibid.*

4. William Charvat, *The Origins of American Critical Thought, 1810-1835* (New York, 1936), 30-32.

5. Andrew Hook, *Scotland and America; A Study of Cultural Relations* (Glasgow, 1975), 28.

6. Edwards, . . . *Enquiry into* . . . *Notions of* . . . *Freedom of Will* . . . (New York, 1924), 290-300.

7. Quoted in Peter Gay, *A Loss of Mastery; Puritan Historians in Colonial America* (Berkeley, 1966), 91-92.

8. Carl Van Doren, *Benjamin Franklin* (New York, 1938), 271-72; Verner Crane, *Benjamin Franklin and a Rising People* (Boston, 1954), 91.

9. J. Bennett Nolan, *Benjamin Franklin in Scotland and Ireland, 1759 and 1771* (Philadelphia, 1938).

10. Franklin to Kames, Jan. 3, 1760, Leonard W. Labaree and Whitfield J. Bell, Jr., eds., *The Papers of Benjamin Franklin*, 9 (New Haven, 1966), 9-10.

11. Adair, "That Politics May be Reduced to a Science: David Hume, James Madison, and the Tenth Federalist," *Huntington Library Quarterly* 22 (1957), 343-60.

12. Chinard, *Thomas Jefferson, Apostle of Americanism* (Ann Arbor, 1929), 29-30; Koch, *The Philosophy of Thomas Jefferson* (New York, 1943), 17-18; 29; 45; 52.

13. Jefferson to Thomas Mann Randolph, Jr., May 30, 1790, Julian P. Boyd, ed., *The Papers of Thomas Jefferson*, 16 (Princeton, 1961), 449.

14. Dumas Malone, *Jefferson, the Virginian* (Boston, 1948), 51-55.

15. Dumas Malone, ed., *Autobiography of Thomas Jefferson* (New York, 1959), 20.

16. Chinard, *Jefferson* and Koch, *Philosophy of Jefferson, op. cit.*; Wilson Smith, *Theories of Education in Early America, 1655-1819* (Indianapolis, 1973), 127-29.

17. Koch, *Philosophy of Jefferson*, 17-18.

18. Jefferson to Thomas Law, June 13, 1814, Adrienne Koch and William Peden, eds., *The Life and Selected Writings of Thomas Jefferson* (New York, 1944), 640.

19. Jefferson to Peter Carr, Aug. 10, 1787, Boyd, ed., *Jefferson Papers*, 12 (1955), 14-19.

20. Roy H. Pearce, *Savagism and Civilization* (Baltimore, 1953), 95.

21. Jefferson to Thomas Law, June 13, 1814, Koch and Peden, *Writings of Jefferson*, 640.

22. Jefferson to Peter Carr, Aug. 19, 1785, Boyd, *Jefferson Papers*, 8 (1953), 407.

23. Charvat, *Origins of American Critical Thought*, 31-32.

24. Leon Howard, *The Connecticut Wits* (Chicago, 1943), 26-28; 47-49.

25. Kames, *Elements of Criticism* (1762), III, 365.

26. Howard, *Connecticut Wits*, 47.

27. Quoted in Robert A. East, *John Quincy Adams, The Critical Years* (New York, 1962), 26.

28. Charvat, *American Critical Thought*, 30.

29. Codman Hislop, *Eliphalet Nott* (Middletown, Conn., 1971), 237.

30. Hislop, *Nott*, 253.

31. *Ibid.*, 241.

32. Purcell, *The Crisis of Democratic Theory; Scientific Naturalism & the Problem of Value* (Lexington, Ky., 1973), 233-72.

Nonsense Poetry and Romanticism

A.J.M. SMITH

Let us begin by looking at a text:

> He said that you had been to her,
>   And seen me here before:
> But, in another character
>   She was the same of yore. . . .
>
> They told me you had been to her,
>   And mentioned me to him:
> She gave me a good character,
>   But said I could not swim. . . .
>
> I gave her one, they gave him two,
>   You gave us three or more;
> They all returned from him to you,
>   Though they were mine before. . . .
>
> My notion was that you had been
>   (Before she had this fit)
> An obstacle that came between
>   Him and ourselves and it.

This is part of the evidence read by the White Rabbit at the trial of the Knave of Hearts. Strictly speaking, this is not exactly nonsense—certainly not complete nonsense. An obstacle *is* what comes between people and things, and gets in the way and impedes progress. A good character *is*—especially in the Victorian times of Lewis Carroll—a very desirable, indeed an essential possession. And the poem's progression is logical. Actually, as a matter of fact, these verses are a realistic and quite recognizable 'imitation of nature'. It is an overheard and slightly secretive, possibly scandalous, bit of conversation: the *him* and *you* and *her* and *I* are perfectly clear and well-defined to the speaker and (presumably) to the person or persons addressed. It is only we, the readers, who are overhearing something not addressed to us, who find it meaningless or obscure. In self defence we call it nonsense.

Now here is another poem—by a writer quite as much admired as Lewis Carroll, and in some respects quite as difficult. As in the case of the first piece I shall begin *in medias res*:

> So they loved, as love in twain
>   Had the essence but in one;
> Two distincts, division none;
>   Number there in love was slain.
>
> Hearts remote, yet not asunder;
>   Distance, and no space was seen
>   'Twixt the turtle and his queen:
> But in them it were a wonder. . . .
>
> Property was there appalled,
>   That the self was not the same;
>   Single nature's double name
> Neither two nor one was called.
>
> Reason, in itself confounded,
>   Saw division grow together;
>   To themselves yet either neither;
> Simple were so well compounded. . . .

Superficially there is a good deal of resemblance between these two pieces of verse: the puzzling playing with numbers, for example,—*one, two,* and *three* in the White Rabbit's poem; *one* and *two* here. And the turtle and his queen—are they not, we wonder, related to the Walrus and the Carpenter, who wept to see such quantities of sand and so many oysters.

But no, of course not. The turtle here is that turtle whose voice in the springtime is heard in the land—the amorous cooing dove. And this poem is not nonsense, but paradox. It is deadly serious, though not solemn, or dull. It is, of course, by William Shakespeare, who is here making good use of the then fashionable metaphysical conceit to express his awareness of the way in which lovers may through the union of the flesh become mystically united, one unique and fiery Phoenix that is at once *both* and *neither*.

This poem *sounds* like nonsense not because it has no meaning, or too little meaning, but too much—too much to be apprehended all at once in the intuitive flash that sometimes enlightens the good reader as well as the good poet.

But we must not be contemptuous of nonsense. "None but a man of extraordinary talent can write first-rate nonsense," said De Quincy. "None but a man of extraordinary taste can appreciate first-rate nonsense," added Carolyn Wells. "Don't tell me of a man's being able to talk sense," said William Pitt, "everyone can talk sense. Can he talk nonsense?"

Absence of sense, of course, is not nonsense. Mere babbling idiotic drivel is very far from nonsense. Nonsense may be either (1) words without sense which yet convey a tone, a mood, an atmosphere that has appropriateness or a significance that is independent of, and perhaps contrary to, logic; or (2) words conveying ridiculous or absurd ideas. The best examples of (1) are some refrains of folk songs and old ballads and the Dadaist poetry that originated in Zurich in 1916 and was intended to function as an anarchist's bomb. Carolyn Wells cites *Jabberwocky*, but Carroll's portmanteau words are not surrealist. They are really intellectual constructs, very self-conscious, and very logical.

Much of the comic element in Lewis Carroll, indeed, is not due to nonsense or the absence of logic but, conversely, to too much logic, or the application of logic to situations that do not usually get it, or that do not need it, or that cannot bear it. And this is to get to nonsense the wrong way round, back to front, left to right, Through The Looking Glass.

Nonsense poetry is not poetry without law (such a thing would be a contradiction in terms), nor does it present a world without law—that is left for the Dadaists. Instead, it creates a world where other, mysterious or even unknown, but always consistent laws exist, and are enforced. We are on the other side of the looking glass, or the dark side of the moon. The area of nonsense poetry is something like the world of non-Euclidian geometry and variable quanta, where space is curved, and the square-root of minus-one has, if not meaning, at least *being*.

In childhood we enter this world in all innocence. It is the land of heart's desire, where dreams come true and wishes are horses; and it can be entered by a simple act of the will—aided by the imagination. It is the happy world where cows jump over the moon and dishes run away with spoons—situated somewhere between Banbury Cross and The Great Rock Candy Mountain. This is the world of Mother Goose, the first great nonsense poet, and the folk songs and singing games of primitive people.

I would like to make clear however, that though the topsy-turvy laws of the nonsense world prevail, the characters, the properties, and the décor of this childlike or primitive poetry are simple, natural, and real—spoons, dishes, horses, bramble bushes, pails of water, bean-stalks (even though gigantic ones); and the living persons who move through these strange dramas are real, homely, living, and convincing—Jack and Jill, a butcher, a baker, a candle-stick maker, a queen, a knave, farmers, millers, princesses, step-mothers. It is only a step for them to move out of the faery world of nonsense into Chaucer.

This world, then, is real, and the people are ordinary. It is only what happens to them, or what they do (and the queer inverted logic that motivates them or governs their reactions to experience) that is nonsensical, out of this world, *super.*

Professor Elizabeth Sewell, the English philosopher and critic, in an interesting article on "Lewis Carroll and T. S. Eliot as Nonsense Poets," has observed that "The genre or game of Nonsense has strict rules." The aim, she points out, is to "construct with words a logical univere of discourse meticulously selected and controlled." The process involved is directed towards analysing, breaking-up, separating the material into a series of "discrete counters." "Whatever is unitive is the great enemy of Nonsense, to be excluded at all costs."

Nonsense, then, is the imposition of an arbitrary and non- or extra-logical unity upon disparate elements of experience. This is done out of pure innocence in the wildest of the nursery rhymes or in such magical poems as the Tudor lyric "The bailey beareth the bell away"—which may seem nonsense to us only because the key to its meaning has been lost.

There is another unconscious but less innocent kind of nonsense to be found in the inspirational ejaculations of religious enthusiasts, the "numerous host," in Dryden's words, "of dreaming Saints." Here almost the only record of their visionary (or nonsensical) language that has passed into poetry is in the parodies or satires of men who laugh at their nonsense from a rational point of view. Samuel Butler makes fun of Ralph, the squire of the sectarian knight Sir Hudibras, in these terms:

> What e'er men speak by this *New Light,*
> Still they are sure to be i' th' right.
> 'Tis a *Dark-Lanthorn* of the Spirit,
> Which none see by but those that bear it.
> A Light that falls down from on high
> For Spiritual Trades to couzen by.

and Dryden demolishes such people in a single line:

> The Spirit caught him up, the Lord knows where.

I myself, in a poem called "Resurrection of Arp," could not

resist taking a crack at this kind of not-innocent but ignorant and reprehensible Nonsense:

> He spoke another language
> majestic beautiful wild
> holy superlative believable
> and undefiled
>
> by any comprehensible
> syllable
> to provoke dissent
> or found a schism . . .

These are attacks on a false sort of nonsense produced by ignorance and cupidity. They are to be sharply distinguished from the rich and intuitive Nonsense of children and primitives.

True nonsense poetry, however, can be reached through knowledge and sophistication, as well as through naivete and innocence. Freud has pointed out that the world of primitive imagination, the world of nonsense in one of its aspects, is also the world of the neurotic; and Surrealism in art and poetry tends to confirm him. But modern Surrealism came rather late; it was very self-conscious; and it had many predecessors. Among them are two Victorian gentlemen, who taking up verse as a sideline (one was a clergyman and the other a painter) soon demonstrated a mastery of nonsense poetry that has made them immortal— Lewis Carroll (that is, the Reverend Charles Dodgson) and Edward Lear. Both of them were men of learning and experience, men with great literary and critical sophistication. Carroll was a skilful logician and an accomplished mathematician; Lear was a landscape painter of charm and originality; but the sophisticated and varied talents of each found their most fruitful expression in humour and imagination. Each created a comic world.

Let me begin with Lear. I suppose everybody knows one or two of his poems: *The Owl and the Pussy Cat* or *The Jumblies* or *The Dong with the Luminous Nose.* When we read these poems we are in the very heart of romance. It is like reading *Ulalume* without being bothered by the mawkish melancholy or *Kubla Khan* without suspecting that there may be a hidden meaning we ought to look for. We are at once transported to a magical land beyond the blue horizon where everything is rich and strange—the landscape, the foliage, the geographical names, and the creatures that dwell there. The sounds and sweet airs, as Caliban phrased it, that give delight and hurt not, which twangle in our ears and (if we have any sense of wonder and any sense of humour) dissolve us into ecstasies. Indeed, when I read the best of Lear it is of the enchanted island of *The Tempest*, of snatches of music from the songs in *Comus*, of bits of Poe and Coleridge, and echoes of the song of Mariana in the Moated Grange that I am irresistably reminded. . . .

Listen:

> And all night long they sailed away;
>   And when the sun went down,
> They whistled and warbled a moony song
> To the echoing sound of the coppery gong,
>   In the shade of the mountains brown . . .

Or again—another nocturnal picture, but this time sterner, darker, more full of an intenser horror:

> When awful darkness and silence reign
> Over the great Gromboolian plain,
>   Through the long, long wintry nights;—
> When the angry breakers roar
> As they beat on the rocky shore;—
>   When storm-clouds brood on the towering heights
> Of the hills of the Chankly Bore . . .

Here we have a typical romantic landscape—wild, grotesque, rugged, and calculated (like romantic art in general) to make an assault on the nerves by the addition of strangeness to beauty—as in another poem:

> Paint me a cavernous waste shore
> Cast in the unstilled Cyclades . . .

That is not Lear, or Shakespeare, but T. S. Eliot. Yet that is exactly the kind of painting Lear gives us and the romantic world into which he transports us. Then Why, I can hear you asking, is Lear funny, while Shakespeare, Eliot, and the others are not? The answer lies in incongruity, hyperbole, and a transformation of the sublime into the ridiculous and the ridiculous into the sublime. But illustration is better than explanation, quicker, easier, and more immediately convincing. Let me continue the quotation from Lear:

> Then through the vast and gloomy dark
> There moves what seems a fiery spark,
>   A lonely spark with silvery rays
>   Piercing the coal-black night,—
>   A meteor strange and bright:—
>   Hither and thither the vision strays,
>   A single lurid light.
>
> Slowly it wanders,—pauses,—creeps,—
> Anon it sparkles,—flashes and leaps;
> And ever as onward it gleaming goes
> A light on the Bong-tree stems it throws.
> And those who watch at that midnight hour
> From Hall or Terrace, or lofty Tower,
> Cry, as the wild light passes along,—
>   'The Dong!—the Dong!
>   The wandering Dong through the forest goes!
>   The Dong!—the Dong!—
>   The Dong with the luminous nose!'

First of all, notice here the succession of romantic words: *vast, gloomy, lonely, strange, vision, lurid, wild, wandering,* and *luminous.* Could any better or more complete series be found to define and characterise the spirit of Romanticism as it mani-

fested itself at the end of the eighteenth century and the beginning of the nineteenth in the Gothic novel and the poetry
of Poe and Coleridge and the early Tennyson? A poet like Carroll or Lear, cutting across—or rather, inverting—all logical
associations, deliberately produces a mirror world where meaning cuts fantastic capers to an absurdly endearing accompaniment
of music.

In the case of Lear, who is closest in this respect to Poe, we
almost attain an absolutely pure poetry, a self-sufficient melody,
which depends on alliteration, assonance, and a heavily accented
beat, and (here like Milton also) on romantic or exotic proper
names. But unlike Poe, or such imitators of Poe as Thomas Holley
Chivers—Lear never quite attains it. He gives us nonsense not
lack-of-sense—"The Dong with the Luminous Nose," not "Ulalume" or a stanza like this one by Chivers:

> Many mellow Cydonian suckets,
>   Sweet apples, anthosmial, divine,
> From the ruby-rimmed berylline buckets,
>   Star-gemmed, lily-shaped, hyaline:
> Like the sweet golden goblet found growing
>   On the wild emerald cucumber tree,
> Rich, brilliant, like chrysoprase glowing,
>   Was my beautiful Rosalie Lee.

These anthosmial apples and the wild emerald cucumber tree
might well have been native to the Great Gromboolian Plain,
but Lear did not go so far as to mention them. So that the
question of what is Nonsense Poetry and what Romantic Poetry
perhaps comes down to no more than a question of Intention, a
subject I must leave to scholars and academic critics.

But to return to our text from Lear: I do not think the Dong
poem is satire. Lear is not making fun of romantic excesses. He
doesn't disapprove of romanticism; but he *does* parody it; he *does*
criticize it—for all parody is a form of criticism, though it may
be (as here) *appreciative* criticism.

And yet even this implies some sort of denigration.

What does Lear object to in the Romantics? Their half-heartedness, I think. They don't go far enough along the road to excess, along the causeway to Nonsense. They are timid; they draw back. They pretend that their fantasies are not fantasies at all, but something real, something sensible, and perhaps, if it can be worked, something profoundly significant. Blake, of course, is the romantic poet who has succeeded best in putting this over on posterity. Poe made a valiant effort and for a long time got away with it. He took in foreigners like Baudelaire and Valéry, and enthusiasts like Swinburne, but as a poet he is pretty well relegated to the place where he really belongs—the realm of nonsense.

Lear was wiser from the start—more honest, and more courageous. Without a moment's hesitation he took romantic poetry to its logical and final end, and with a greater awareness of the nature of reality than that possessed by the later Surrealists he created a new world of nonsense and provided a pure poetry with which to celebrate it. His poetry is at once an extension of romanticism and a parody of it, but the parody is oblique and allusive. Lear loves the Romantic masters, and he only gently presumes to correct them—by showing them how their job ought to have been done.

Here and there, of course, the masters have excelled him at his own game. Lear gives us his wild and strange incantations filled with resonant and romantic-sounding proper names: the Hills of the Chankly Bore, the Great Gromboolian Plain, the lakes and the Terrible Zone, and the rocks of the Zemmery Fidd. Fine as this is—and indubitably nonsense—it hardly equals Milton's invocation to the fierce gods of the Oriental world who seduced the Chosen people wandering in the wilderness of their own Terrible Zone:

> From Aroer to Nebo, and the wild
> Of southmost Abarim, in Hesebon
> And Horonaim, Ston's realm, beyond
> The flowery dale of Sibma, clad with vines,
> And Elealé to th' Asphaltic Pool . . .

This is magnificent, and it may not be nonsense, but it sounds like nonsense, inspired magniloquent nonsense, nonsense raised to its highest power;—and it prepares the way for Coleridge's dream:

> In Xanadu did Kubla Khan
> A stately pleasure dome decree
> Where Alph the sacred river ran
> Down to a sunless sea . . .

But you all know the immortal incantation. This is a step forward in the direction of 'pure poetry', which is not very far indeed from pure nonsense. Alph, the sacred river, does not have to run very far before it flows into the Great Gromboolian plain overshadowed by the Hills of the Chankly Bore.

We do not need to read very deeply in Lear's *Nonsense Songs* and the earlier *Book of Nonsense* (1846) to realize that this landscape painter turned comic poet was soaked in the literary tradition of early nineteenth century Romanticism, though he looks back to the ballads and ballad refrains of an older time, to nursery rhymes, and (as we have seen) to Milton. But the poet he most resembles, and whom he most admired, was Tennyson.

If we take our stand with those entranced watchers "From Hall or Terrace or lofty Tower" whose fascinated gaze follows the wild gleam moving along through the blackness of the night we may perhaps think of another early Victorian poet, Lord Macaulay, and his poem describing how the news of the defeat of the Spanish Armada flashed along from beacon to beacon and from promontory to promontory from Beachy Head to Skiddaw. But when in the next stanza of *The Dong with the Luminous Nose* we read that

> when the sun was low in the west
> The Dong arose and said,—

we expect him to say—for remember the Dong is lamenting a

lost love, a Jumblie girl, with her sky-blue hands and her sea-green hair, who had sailed away with her people back home across the sea in a sieve—we expect him to say (shifting the gender of the pronouns, of course)—

> My life is dreary,
> She cometh not, he said.
> He said I am aweary, aweary,
> I would that I were dead—

with Tennyson's Mariana in the Moated Grange. But Lear knew better. What the Dong actually said is something more prosaic, and truer, and less like nonsense—

> What little sense I once possessed
> Has quite gone out of my head.

To go from Lear to his great contemporary Lewis Carroll is like turning from Shakespeare to Ben Jonson or from Milton to Dryden; that is, from wild imagination to wild unreason. Carroll takes us down the rabbit hole or through the looking-glass into a topsy-turvy world of left-hand right-hand reversal. "In a mirror," writes Martin Gardiner, in his invaluable piece of parody-pedantry, *The Annotated Alice*, "asymmetrical objects are not superposable on their mirror images." The rule in *Through the Looking Glass* is "Go the other way." To approach the Red Queen Alice walks backward. Tweedledum and Tweedledee are mirror-image twins. . . . The White Knight sings of squeezing a right foot into a left shoe. . . . The King has two messengers, one to come and one to go. . . .

In a sense, nonsense itself is a sanity-insanity inversion. The ordinary world is turned inside out, upside down, sideways, and backward. The inversion theme occurs in the first Alice book too. Alice wonders if cats eat bats or bats eat cats, and she is told that to say what she means is not the same as to mean what she says. In *Sylvie and Bruno* we learn about 'imponderable,' an anti-gravity wool that can be stuffed into parcel-post packages to make them weigh less than nothing, a watch that goes backward, black light, and a purse with outside inside and inside outside. Here nonsense is trespassing in the world of relativity and science fiction.

As might have been expected twentieth-century poetry has not altogether ignored this theme. Robert Graves comes to mind at once. Though classical in form (as Carroll as a poet also is) Graves is one of the most romantic of modern poets. He is also one of the most distinguished nonsense poets, and the theme of the inversion of mirror-images and the reversal of logic that is the essence of serious nonsense is found in several of his poems—in none more truly Carrollian than the brilliant metaphysical lyric called "The Terraced Valley":

> In a deep thought of you and concentration
> I came by hazard to a new region:
> The unnecessary sun was not there,
> The necessary earth lay without care—
> For more than sunshine warmed the skin
> Of the round world that was turned outside-in. . . .
>
> Neat outside-inside, neat below-above,
> Hermaphrodizing love.
> Neat this-way-that-way and without mistake:
> On the right hand could slide the left glove.
> Neat over-under: the young snake
> Through an unyielding shell his path could break.
> Singing of kettles, like a singing brook,
> Made out-of-doors a fireside nook.
>
> But you, my love, where had you then your station?
> Seeing that on this counter-earth together
> We go not distant from each other;
> I knew you near me in that strange region,
> So searched for you, in hope to see you stand
> On some near olive-terrace, in the heat,
> The empty snake's-egg perfect at your feet.

But found you nowhere in the wide land,
And cried disconsolately, until you spoke
Immediate at my elbow, and your voice broke
This trick of time, changing the world about
To once more inside-in and outside-out.[1]

We learn from this poem—what we learn also from *Sylvie and Bruno*, and more surprisingly in its Victorian context—that E-V-I-L is simply L-I-V-E backward. And we find asserted too that Love cannot live in the world of Nonsense poetry. Nonsense poetry, it seems to be implied is an Anti-love poetry, and to whatever extent this is true nonsense poetry in this one respect cannot be considered as romantic.

No sooner have I written this than I come to doubt it. How naturally and unconsciously we have come to identify love with romance and to think that any criticism of it must be anti-romantic. The most romantic, as well as the greatest of Lewis Carroll's poems is, I am sure no one will deny, "Jabberwocky"; and that is certainly much closer to a hate poem than a love poem.

"Jabberwocky" is a linguistic *tour de force*, a semantic *jeu d'esprit*, an exercise in the fine art of logical unreason, and a triumphant demonstration of Carroll's great invention, the portmanteau made of words, words capable of holding several meanings at once, an invention that has had an immense literary influence. It has made Joyce's *Finnegan's Wake* and Empson's *Seven Types of Ambiguity* possible—if not unnecessary or redundant. And the *explication de texte* that the author furnished in *Through the Looking Glass* prepared the way for the New Critics of the day before yesterday.

Yet while "Jabberwocky" is one of the most original poems ever written, it is also, like so many of Carroll's pieces, a parody not of any particular poem but of a genre, a type, an attitude, and an age. Carroll, even more than Lear, is a critic of romantic excess, a thoroughgoing rationalist, and in this poem it is the medievalist side of the romantic movement, with its idealisation of the Age of Chivalry and its love of the heroic, exemplified in the epic conflicts between Knights and Dragons which is held up in the dry light of wit for our scrutiny and rejection. If the poem throws a somewhat withering beam forward to the Mookes and the Gripes it also casts a somewhat baleful glare backward at *The Faerie Queene.*

NOTE

1. "The Terraced Valley" from COLLECTED POEMS 1955 by Robert Graves. Copyright © 1955 by Robert Graves. Used by permission of Doubleday & Company, Inc.

Nathaniel Hawthorne: "Conservative after Heaven's own fashion"

MILTON R. STERN

Essays in *festschriften* often have no relation to the person honored other than the fact that they appear in a book dedicated to his name. But in presenting this condensation of one section of a book in progress, a study of the political dimensions of American literature, I honor Russel B. Nye as a master and teacher who led me toward an understanding of literature as not only a matter of traditions, conventions, techniques, and aesthetics, but finally as a matter of public culture, as the most compelling penetration of history. In presenting this chapter, I ask only that Russel Nye not be judged in any way by whatever might be bad about my essay, over which he had no control, after all, but by the lasting influence exercised by a great teacher and scholar who defines directions for literary study, whether his students march into them triumphantly or stumble waveringly in their attempts to follow the example of the pathfinder.

My teacher made me sensitive to overtones to which otherwise

I would have been deaf. So, I felt Nye-esque vibrations when I read William Charvat's letter to Fredson Bowers, explaining that until he had read Bowers' "ur-text" of *The Marble Faun*, Charvat had never realized what a parenthetical style Hawthorne employed—the correspondence is in the front matter in the Centenary edition of *The Marble Faun*. Charvat's remark rang a bell for me, for I had long felt that beneath the veilings of Hawthorne's self and characters, there was also an essential veiling of his style, an evasiveness, that somehow placed his social and political sense of self, his literary marketplace, and his literary themes in a fragile and uneasy, though highly significant, relationship. By the time I had satisfied myself about the nature of the problem, I had come to see that in Hawthorne's richest, most deeply flawed book, one important perspective on and explanation of the style—the very *syntax*—was historical and political. I cannot offer that demonstration here, for it requires more space than I have. In fact, that demonstration led me to a very long chapter on Hawthorne, which led me to return to the development of Melville's political vision, which led me to the book on which I am still at work. But here, I wish to take the commonplace that Hawthorne was conservative, and to examine it briefly within the political ambience of his literary marketplace in order to suggest the deeply political dimensions of the literary act.

Grant me, reader, that had we but pages enough and time, I would amplify and demonstrate my definitions; grant me, too, the necessity for almost impossible condensation here, and grant me, therefore, T. E. Hulme's useful distinction between romanticism and classicism as a set of rubrics (despite all the many and pointed modifications and exceptions we would both wish to make) under which we may sanely and usefully set the poles of radicalism and conservatism. I use Hulme as a beginning point from which to add my own observations.

In his famous essay, "Romanticism and Classicism," the avowedly anti-romantic, conservative Hulme defines the romantic as one who has a conception of human identity as inexhaustible in resources and possibility. Man is essentially divine. To release the naked inner being is to release goodness, innocence, and love. The romantic imagination sees the past as restrictive, as a pool of examples of the misuses of human energies and the repression of aspiration. Through his study of history, the romantic therefore repudiates the past. His analysis of the past leads him to embrace the future as a process of destruction of old limitations and a realization of cosmic identity expressive of the limitless potential of human identity. For Hulme, therefore, the romantic imagination tends to be cosmic and general, for the history of the future is not specific, existing rather in categories of largeness, light, and nobility. The romantic emphasizes feeling, and his rhetoric tends toward large categories and cosmic imagery. The past is seen as great waves of movement in a struggle toward liberation, toward full realization of the potential of the human soul; and the present is seen as a vast revolutionary and intense moment surging toward the millennial state of being in that future that lies on the other side of the ultimate triumphant revolution. History is seen as progressive, the human being is seen as perfectible, and nature is seen as an interconnected series of symbolic examples of the process toward the future. Institutions, especially religious institutions, and the discipline of institutional dogma and ritual become impertinences, blasphemies, and impediments.

The classicist, or conservative, conceives of human identity as limited. Man is essentially brutal, selfish, mean, and ignorant. To release the naked inner being is to release savagery. Because of the fallen nature of man, the future will be a continuation of past experience and is not to be hailed as millennium but is to be seen as a cyclic repetition of the past. Consequently, the past is not to be repudiated but is to be honored as a pool of precedents. The present becomes the moment in which the future is to be controlled by adjustment to the past. Control and decorum rather than liberation become the meaningful terms in a discussion of a regulation of human behavior. The conservative imagination tends to be sober rather than jubilant, legalistic rather than subjective, for the future can be only the same area for the necessary control of human beings that the past has been. The classicist emphasizes rule and precedent and his rhetoric tends towards dryness and specificity.

In his view of man and history—and of God as the process of man and nature— the romantic tends toward radicalism, toward revolution. His stance is future-facing; he tends to celebrate the modern; he announces the self and freedom and universal equality and transcendence; he is a member of what Emerson called "the party of hope." In his view of man and history—and of God as an unknowable and supreme master—the classicist tends toward conservatism, toward counter-revolution. His stance is past-facing; he tends to repudiate the modern; he announces subordination and discipline and hierarchy and limitation; he is a member of what Emerson called "the party of memory." In poetics and politics, the romantic tends toward change and experiment; the classicist tends toward a defense and polishing of established principles. The radical rebels against the establishment; the conservative represents the establishment. Between these two huge poles swings the pendulum of basic political beliefs. It is relatively easy to mark the romantic radicalism of Whitman and Thoreau and Emerson, but apparently confusing to mark that of Hawthorne. It is relatively easy to mark the classicist conservatism of Andrews Norton and the later Orestes Brownson, but apparently confusing to mark that of Hawthorne. Hawthorne's romantic radicalism and classicist conservatism must be understood in a context of the complexities and intricacies visited upon my condensed categories by the inescapable facts of history. One of the major facts is that of a basic paradox in which the political success of romantic radical principles creates—like any political success—a political establishment. By the time of Hawthorne's milieu and the conflicts of vision between the Nortons and the Emersons, the revolutionary, radical principles of Enlightenment Deism, which had opened the door in so many ways (not the least of which was its attraction to its own vision of primitivism) to romanticism, had been rhetorically co-opted into the new establishment. That is, the surface ideologies and terminologies of progress, equality, human divinity, approaching millennium defined in the new American Eden, had become the rhetoric of patriotism, of acquiescence to the status quo, had become, in short, the rhetoric of the conservative.

Neither all conservatives nor all radicals philosophically examine the roots of their attitudes. One is philosophically a radical or a conservative when he understands the relationship of his own identity to the romantic or classicist visions of man, history, nature, and God. But insofar as one identifies with and champions the status quo or opposes it, insofar as one has attitudes without deep or examined philosophical understanding of them, we must distinguish between the philosophical foundations of radicalism and conservatism on the one hand and their modal manifestations on the other. In an America in which good business and millennial identity tended to be equated, acquiescence in the status quo, or modal conservatism, was an expression of loyalty to the hardened surfaces of what paradoxically had once been radical philosophy. To put it another way, philosophical conservatism in Hawthorne's America was at odds with modal conservatism, for to suggest that man and history might not be progressive and that America might not be (or not about to be) millennial, was to be at odds with the established values of one's society and was to feel oneself the lone outcast. It was enough to give a philosophical conservative an uneasy and untrue community with romantic radicals, who also objected to the ruthlessly undeviating custom-house orientation of their society. The serious difference, of course, was that Hawthorne, as philosophical conservative, objected to his bourgeois culture because it proclaimed so freely, in its materialistic triumphs, its rhetorical beliefs in the shibboleths of romantic radicalism; however, Hawthorne's romantic radical colleagues in the arts, also outcast loners, objected to their bourgeois culture because its proclamation of those shibboleths was merely rhetorical and were in opposition to the continuing revolution of the spirit that our Thoreaus called for in the New England milieu they shared with Hawthorne. The ironic transference, in which the beliefs and rhetoric of romantic radicalism became the modal conservatism of a conventional, commercial society, alienated both radicals and philosophical conservatives.

The irony created a strange community among artists of opposing visions. For insofar as they indicate outcast opposition to or ingroup defense of what is, the modes of radicalism and conservatism suggest personality types as well as ideological poles. Because conservatism leads toward a defense of established values and institutions, the modal conservative tends toward acquiescent membership in his society. Conversely, because of the romantic foundation, the modal radical tends toward opposition to his society and therefore toward an inevitable degree of isolation. Because the logic of conservatism tends toward social membership, it tends toward conformity to the status quo and identity with the church, the custom house, the court, and the marketplace. Because the logic of radicalism tends toward social isolation, opposition, and dissent, it tends toward introversion, toward membership in anti-establishment and in experimental groups, or toward solitude. The romantic loner, through the perceptions of his unorthodoxy, observes the established society with which he has little acquiescent intercourse. The conservative tends to represent established institutions; the radical tends to be their outcast critic. And in Hawthorne's literary milieu, it was easy for all seclusive and reclusive personalities to feel at least one bond, if no others: that of estrangement from a society that proclaimed its cheerful, noonday custom house materialism as the millennial New Eden.

Within his own temperament and desires, Nathaniel Hawthorne was both social representative and social outcast. Along with his philosophical conservatism, his personality kept him from ever finding a comfortable home in modal conservatism, with all its implications of public gregariousness and millennialistic rhetoric. Yet despite his vocation, which I will suggest was one of modal radicalism, his deep beliefs kept him from ever finding even a momentary resting place in philosophical radicalism. With rare exceptions, such as "The Artist of the Beautiful," which, despite its interesting moment of complex ambivalence, is almost totally in sympathy with romantic idealism, Hawthorne's fiction indicates an essential conservatism implicit everywhere and explicit in tales like "Earth's Holocaust."

In the complications of real life, even though Hawthorne's philosophical conservatism, together with his temperament, impeded his full immersion in the modal conservatism of gregarious acquiescence in the status quo, nevertheless it also prompted him toward that very acquiescence. Hawthorne's literary marketplace left him no doubt that the real man, the real American, was the citizen of the custom house, and in his "Custom House" introduction to the *Scarlet Letter* he announced how much part of him had always hungered to be a solid burgher among solid burghers. (One need not embellish Hawthorne's famous and constant desire to open an intercourse with the world and to take an amiable and accepted place in established society.) Hawthorne's world in the first few decades of the nineteenth century was one in which the *general* experience (blacks and many Irish immigrants excepted) was that of the cottager, farmer, and artisan—the respectable worker—rather than that of the debased peasant or lumpenproletariat. On a personal level, Hawthorne's experiences, unlike Melville's, were never those of men engaged in the underdog life of bestial labor. His view of the ongoing community, together with his philosophical conservatism, made him certain that there was a rich and shared wisdom in the high priority that common folk assign to the daily meal and yearly income and lowly cottage joys rather than to the theories of change that were to revolutionize and liberate them. Not all the visionary theories under the sun could stand finally against the mundane understanding, richly bred from experience, pain, and necessity, that it was best to rest content with the bird in the hand. Part of Hawthorne was like Flaubert observing the bourgeois Sunday promenaders and saying, *"Ils sont dans le vrai."*

This aspect of Hawthorne's conservatism was the nexus between his otherwise opposed philosophical conservatism and modal conservatism. It was the socially oriented expression of his insistence that limited human beings inevitably must settle for what is because of their common and absolute brotherhood in an imperfect and incomplete world of inescapable sin. The insistence that one should not abandon his accepted and established place in the social community is clear in pieces like "Wakefield." Sin's ubiquity is a constant in tales like "Young Goodman Brown," as its mysterious obtrusiveness is in tales like "The Minister's Black Veil," as its inescapability is in tales like "The Birthmark." From a conservative understanding of the inevitable initiation of all men, however shallow, into sin, pain, and limitation ("Rappaccini's Daughter," "My Kinsman, Major Molineux") arose Hawthorne's compassionate sense of fraternity, sympathy, and kindness and his sad but wistful conservative willingness to accept defective human society *in status quo.* To recognize the truth of one's limited human nature was to recognize one's mutual identity with all humankind. Thus, "Be true! Be true!", the call for an honest assessment of one's inner self at the end of *The Scarlet Letter,* arises in Hawthorne from the same conservative source as the desire to open an intercourse with the world.

I suggest that there is politics as well as psychology in the fact that Hawthorne hung shyly back in isolation from what he so deeply desired, in the complexities of the conflict between his philosophical conservatism and his modal conservatism. For to "Be true! Be true!" to his philosophical conservatism, made Hawthorne feel the strain of his modal conservatism in saying to his new Young America that it was in final, human fact no different from all the human enterprises that had ever had their glorious beginnings. To deny that the commercialistic young Republic was the new Eden was to repudiate the nationalistic fervor that dictated the conditions of acceptance or rejection in the literary marketplace, conditions that Poe, too, felt very deeply. The public was much more ready and willing to support the implications of "The Grey Champion" than those of "The

May-Pole of Merrymount." This conflict was deep in the center of Hawthorne's literary choices, not only in his themes and failures of theme, but in the very form and structure of his fiction. It was the conflict that had him saying two things at once to his marketplace. One was, "I am a real man, I am an American, I belong." The other was, "You are self-deceived, you are without wisdom or self-knowledge, I repudiate you." In his prefaces he applauds the cheerful, sunlit common sense of his own dear, happy, native land and yet, as in "The Custom House," opts to be a citizen of somewhere else. He applauds the bustling mediocrity of his noonday society, yet insists on ruins, mosses, lichens, and shadows for "true" fiction. He devotes an entire fiction, *The Scarlet Letter,* to dramatizing the "true" message that the shadowy, shady, fallen dark lady of sorrow and painful experience is the one who reveals the path to redemption, and then, at the end, he intrudes a statement which calls for the stereotype of the traditional Christian American Puritan Un-stained White Maiden as the lady who will lead us all to redemption. In *The Marble Faun* Hawthorne comes to pieces in the most interesting and significant ways when he does the same thing he did in *The Scarlet Letter,* and allows that moral fungus, Hilda, to inherit the stage and the moral role, for after all, she is the "daughter of the Puritans," an "American girl," the as-sumed self-image of his marketplace audience. The problem of endings extends from the novels (the conclusion of *The House of the Seven Gables* offers fascinating intricacies and contradic-tions) to the tales as well. "Young Goodman Brown" ends just at the point that Hawthorne really has begun another novel, for the discovery of what is "true" isolates the protagonist from his society, which is Hawthorne's problem precisely. (This ending offers more complexity than I hint at here, and one would wish to look carefully at the political implications of the endings of "Rappaccini's Daughter," "Ethan Brand," and several others of Hawthorne's most famous tales.) The parenthetical asides in *The Marble Faun* often—astonishingly often—are signs of the author's dissociation of himself from the politically uncomfor-

table implications of the "truth" of his philosophical conservatism. In subtle ways, in syntax and action and statement,
Hawthorne's fiction is a c onstant sign of his confronting and
breaking up on the problem of being "true," of being a romancer,
of being a philosophically conservative artist on the one hand, and
being an accepted member of the "real" society of American men
engaged on the other hand in the values and business of the
established world. In short, the political relationships of Hawthorne's themes to his marketplace, together with whatever
qualities of his psyche defined the limits of his courage, define the
failure of nerve that creates many of the ambiguities and rich
failures in his fiction. His writing was to become one deeply
political act of autobiography in his attempt to discover, through
his fiction and its characters, how his own identities as a man, a
citizen, and an artist could be reconciled and unified.

The literary marketplace, through the editors and reviewers,
left no doubt that popular acceptance and success were allied to
modal conservatism. Not only that, but the public identification
of one's person had, as always, political overtones. The stereotypes that arise from the conservative perspective, for instance,
express a division between "good, solid citizens," "decent, sober,
sensible folk," with "their feet on the ground," and "long haired
poets," "muddle-headed visionary dreamers," "free lovers,"
"atheists," "reformers," and "radicals." Conversely, the stereotypes that arise from the radical perspective express a conflict
between "liberated," "free," "progressive" and "heroic" leaders of
"heroic struggle" against the "materialistic" conformities and
"reactionary forces" of the "repressive establishment." Hawthorne's marketplace defined one's maleness as well as one's
Americanness. Whatever "visionary" and "poetic" literature was
accepted was largely the business of the "ladies magazines," to
which "real men" could look with condescending and conventional amusement and reverence as the "finer stuff" of which the
"fairer sex" was made. The men's magazines featured heroes
who were men of the military, of business, or the state, men of the
"real" world—and those magazines by and large left *fiction* to

the ladies.[1] Yet even the "uplifting" and "aspiring" tremulousness of the ladies magazines was largely mere sentimentality which reinforced rather than challenged the conventional values of the status quo, and which, therefore, drew the contempt of the isolated artists, as it did in Melville's parodic opening sections of *Pierre* and as it did in Hawthorne's famous complaint to W. D. Ticknor that "America is now wholly given over to a damned mob of scribbling women, and I should have no chance of success while the public is occupied with their trash—and should be ashamed of myself if I did succeed."

But Hawthorne is a bit less than totally honest here. Though there was much to merit his scorn in popular publications with titles like *Pearls of the West, The Bower of Taste,* and *Friendship's Offering* and in the bustlebound writings and editings of successes like Catherine Sedgwick, Sarah Josepha Hale, and Lydia Sigourney, the plain fact remains that it was within that very market, in gift-book annuals like *The Token,* as among the few outlets for fiction open to a native writer, that Hawthorne first published his work and took his initial steps toward literary success. We are so accustomed to the picture of Hawthorne as "the obscurest man of letters in America" at the beginning of his career, a picture of a man who would not write for the trashy marketplace but who would reserve his best only for the choice, discerning, elite audience that recognized quality and greatness, that we tend to forget the facts. Sophia, Julian, and Nathaniel Hawthorne himself created and perpetuated this picture of uncompromising and quietly, contentedly waiting genius, and, only partly true, it is a picture that tends to remain as a whole truth.

But another truth is that Hawthorne always longed for *popular* success. When, retrospectively, he looked back on himself as being so obscure at first, he conveniently forgets the fact that almost at once he was welcomed, identified, and hailed as a writer of great quality by that very discerning few he supposedly cherished and who were supposedly all he cared about. When he was only seventeen he wrote his mother in ways that made it clear that beneath the quiet surface was a burning desire to win great literary fame. If one reads at one sitting all of Hawthorne's prefaces chronologically arranged (a most useful and illuminating experience which I commend to all), several significant and repeated motifs emerge. Not the least of these is a recurrent soft chiding, a quiet moaning and sighing, a sweet, continuing recrimination: "American readers, I don't care that you never made me a success in the *popular* marketplace." The quietly amused and self deprecating poise with which Hawthorne breathes this disclaimer becomes suspicious when considered in its unremitting continuation, and especially when considered in the light of the fact that he continued to voice it long, long, long after he had been hailed as America's greatest living writer, long, long, long after he had monopolized that discerning audience he claimed was the only "gentle reader" at whom he aimed his writings. He protests too much.

Another truth is that for somoene who "should be ashamed of myself if I did succeed" in that popular market, Hawthorne tried damned hard to make himself ashamed. Even at the very beginning, in contrast to the general quality of the market, Hawthorne's work was so noticeable that he became an instant success with the editors, who clamored to have his work not only for the annuals but also for newspapers and magazine publication. S. G. Goodrich, who published the highly successful *Token* in Boston, constantly put Hawthorne into print. The 1837 volume, for instance, was practically a Hawthorne issue, containing eight of his pieces. In the eighteen thirties, when, as "the obscurest man of letters in America" he was learning and breaking into his trade—in that same popular market he deplored—Hawthorne averaged newspaper, magazine, or gift book publication approximately at the rate of one piece every seven weeks. Of course, as Poe recognized, it was true that Hawthorne became the prime American example of the man who attained great literary distinction without great popular success, but one must always remember the modifications: Hawthorne had greater popular success than he led us to believe; Hawthorne wanted popular success in the very market he insistently despised;

Hawthorne was a man of much greater ambition for literary fame than he ever admitted; Hawthorne entered, was trained in, and competed in the popular literary marketplace. It was inevitable that Hawthorne, in his wistful hunger for the social *modes* of his philosophical conservatism, should define himself in deep ways within the context of that established marketplace, which voiced the sentimentalized values of the status quo.

As for being a man and being an American, what did the marketplace say about "visionaries" and "poets?" One of that "damned mob of scribbling women," Sarah Josepha Hale, showed what the role was even from the sentimental distaff side, which, as I have said, reinforced rather than opposed the conventional and stereotypical view: even when recommending *Fanshawe* to her readers, Hale made perfectly apparent the priorities created by the needs and activities of the thriving young nation. If, as she asserts, "the time has arrived when our American authors should have something besides empty praise from their countrymen," she makes the assertion in a significantly left-handed way: "Our institutions and character demand activity in business; the useful should be preferred above the ornamental; practical industry before speculative philosophy; reality before romance. But still the emanations of genius may be appreciated, and a refined taste cultivated among us."[2]

The male response was what one might expect. Charles Fenne Hoffman, in an 1838 review of the *Twice-Told Tales,* offers a singularly ambiguous compliment to Hawthorne. Specifying the "types of the soul of Nathaniel Hawthorne" as "a rose bathed and baptized in dew—a star in its first gentle emergence above the horizon," he then goes on to put matters in their proper perspective: "Minds, like Hawthorne's, seem to be the only ones suited to an American [literary] climate. Quiet and gentle intellect gives itself, in our country, oftener to literature, than intellect of a hardier and more robust kind. Men endowed with vigorous and sturdy faculties are, sooner or later, enticed to try their strength in the boisterous current of politics or the Pactolian stream of merchandize. . . . Thus far American authors, who have been most triumphant in winning a name, have been of the gentler order. We can point to many Apollos, but Jove has not as yet assumed his thunder, nor hung his blazing shield in the sky. . . . Yet men like Hawthorne are not without their use; nay, they are the writers to smooth and prepare the path for nobler (but not better) variants, by softening and ameliorating the public spirit." Significantly, Hoffman reserved his highest praise for Hawthorne's realistic evocation of native actualities: "His pathos we would call New England pathos . . . it is the pathos of an American, a New Englander. It is redolent of the images, objects, thoughts, and feelings that spring up in that soil, and nowhere else. The author of *Twice-Told Tales* is an honor to New England and to the country."[3]

As Mrs. Hale put it, "reality before romance." The nationalistic overtones of the two reviews are typical; also typical is the shared assumption that national identity, vocational identity, and sexual identity are interrelated: the "real" male is the man who creates the millennial emergence of America in business, martial glory, politics, industry. That is, the identification of the "real" Ameircan *man* is one of modal conservatism. The man who chooses to transcend that identification in "visions" or "dreams" or "poetry" is the romantic who does not quite belong. In sum, Hawthorne, the *philosophical conservative* who could not quite happily be a *modal conservative,* much as he longed to be, was also a *vocational radical,* and these three categories mark the internal tensions and contradictions and ambivalences that are the political intricacies of the relationship between Hawthorne's life and fiction—which lead me to suggest that his fiction is in many ways a groping, political autobiographical exploration of his identity within his culture. Almost always, Hawthorne's pleas for the romance, his pleas to be liberated from the delineation of actualities, are protests against nationalistic and modally conservative identifications of the functions of the American writer, as "The Custom House" makes explicit and as does the introduction to *The Marble Faun,* where he makes plain his need to escape those "actualities" which "in America" are "so terribly insisted upon."

What I suggest is that the genres of Hawthorne's marketplace —the sketch and the novel, the tale and the romance—themselves have heavily political overtones. Whatever is associated with "reality" appeals to the modal conservatism of that marketplace; whatever repudiates it is called strongly, often angrily, into question. By temperament as well as by his philosophical conservatism, Hawthorne was driven to the romance, for not only the nature of his own imagination but also the nature of his marketplace led him toward disguised, highly fictive, allegorical representations of a philosophically conservative theme that his modally conservative marketplace would neither relish nor accept. Another way to say it is that the conflict between the modal conservatism of the marketplace and the philosophical conservatism of his vision led Hawthorne paradoxically toward the vocational radicalism of the romancer. And in every way Hawthorne became conscious of the implications of the genres of the marketplace. The implications have particular importance for a man of Hawthorne's hungry ambitions and divided inclinations. To be an American is to deal in "acutalities" in the "Eden" around one. To be an American writer is to evoke those actualities. To be a "manly" American writer, a "Jove" rather than an "Apollo," is to embrace conservative genres dedicated to originally radical assumptions hardened into celebrational shibboleths of the status quo—is to write sketches and novels, not tales and romances. The evocation of actualities, in short, is the techniques of verisimilitude ("reality:" this is what it's "really like") wedded to the materials of shop, office, home, village square, church, Custom House—the "manly" qualities—by means of an elevating sentimentality and "poeticizing"—the "finer" or "feminine" qualities—so that what emerges is a highly retouched photograph purporting to show that in "actuality" the "common" experience of "everyday" American life is the experience of the happy, the redeemed, the Edenic, the "new" in history. In terms of "actualities," the sketch and novel had patriotic uses implicitly and un-consciously built into them by the social context, as the tale and romance could too easily become suspiciously "un-American."

Woe betide the writer who took the wrong kind of imaginative liberties with "actuality!" One clerical reviewer took Hawthorne to task because *The Scarlet Letter* "involves the gross and slanderous imputation that the colleague pastor of the First Church in Boston, who preached the Election Sermon the year after the death of Governor Winthrop, was a mean and hypocriti-cal adulterer. . . . How would this outrageous fiction, which is utterly without foundation, deceive a reader who had no exact knowledge of our history!" The reviewer's outrage is motivated, of course, by the need to vindicate one's own, but there is more to it than that. The grounds upon which the critic bases his attack is a didactically utilitarian view of literature as history, of literature as "actualities:" "Seeing that many readers obtain all their knowledge of historical facts from the incidental implica-tions of history which are involved in a well-drawn romance, we maintain that a novelist has no right to tamper with actual verities. His obligation to adhere strictly to historic truth is . . . to be exacted [and] . . . we venture to question his right to misrepresent the facts and characters of assured history." Not-ing the insistently public and contemporary nature of the setting of *The Blithedale Romance*, the reviewer remarks that if Haw-thorne "shaded and clouded his incidents somewhat more ob-scurely, if he removed them farther back or farther off from the region of our actual sight and knowledge, he would be safer in using the *privileges* of the romancer. But he gives us such distinct and sharp boundary lines, and deals so boldly with matters and persons, the truth of whose *prose life* repels the *poetry of his fiction*, that we are induced to *confide* in him as a *chronicler*, rather than *indulge* him as a *romancer*."[4]

Is it any wonder that in his prefaces Hawthorne repeatedly pleaded for the reader's indulgence to allow the romancer to "shade and cloud his incidents somewhat more obscurely," to "re-move them farther back or farther off from the region of our actual sight and knowledge"—and that at the same time Hawthorne complained that the "twilight" and "foreign" and "ancient" aspects of his writing left it without a sense of immediate, throbbing "actuality" or "life" peopled with "real" men and women? Despite the fact that generally the reviews of *The Scarlet Letter* and *The Blithedale Romance* were statements of high praise, the *assumptions* of the reviewer just quoted are entirely representative of the marketplace: good prose chronicling serves an educational and national function; romancing is permissible, but its poetry is a privilege to be indulged. The genres that the marketplace points Hawthorne toward are the sketch and the novel for acceptance and "confidence," the tale and the romance for "indulgence." Hawthorne's is not only the experience of the Surveyor of the Salem Custom House, who is aware of the extent to which American civilization is practical and secular and its values impatiently pragmatic and commercial, honoring good dinners above almost all else, but it is also the experience of a practitioner of romance in a literary marketplace which demonstrated in every nook and corner how art as a majority-sanctioned "official" enterprise is responsive to the values of the larger social establishment within which it is created.

When one scans the reviews of the nineteenth century, what becomes apparent is that although the terms "sketch," "novel," "tale," and "romance" were freighted with meaning, there was no consistent or systematic understanding of those meanings. For the sake of clarity, I invest some artificial precision in those terms, but it should be understood that what is artificial here is hardly something manufactured out of whole cloth. The meanings I intend have by now a generally received usage, and, more important, are indicative of the major tendencies of meaning in Hawthorne's day even though the terms often were used with confusing and irregular interchangability (see, for instance, the review quoted immediately above). I impute to Hawthorne's marketplace a consistency of terminology which did not in fact exist in every usage, though often it is observable, and which is, nonetheless, a true and useful indication of the kinds of categories that revealed the politico-literary matrix and context of Hawthorne's marketplace.

The romance and the tale were ostensibly a matter for "feminine" sensibility: they were ethereal, imaginary, and perhaps luxurious—a "poetry" to be "indulged" as a "privilege" of those who have time for "a refined taste cultivated among us." Although the very nature of the fictitious was often suspected (America suffered a long tradition of this) as a seductively pleasant, useless, and perhaps even misleading entertainment for idle hours, still there was fiction and there was fiction. The novel and the sketch ostensibly were more suited to the manly taste: their fictitiousness was only a didactically useful way of reporting actualities, and they had the useful function of sweetening the reader's morals and broadening his knowledge of the planet's affairs. The novel and the sketch were statisticable insofar as their characters and actions supposedly could be validated as actualities of a time and place, and their psychology could be explained by reference to actualities. Wrapped within the delight of fiction was the instruction of new ways to see "how things are." The sketch differed from the novel (aside from its much briefer length) only in that it might be reportage as well as fiction, but in either case it served the same didactic purpose as the novel. Of course, a tale might be a muscular, hard, and profound piece (Hawthorne's tales often were), and a sketch might be the lightest froth of merely fashionable and idle reportage and shallow sentiment (N. P. Willis's sketches often were); but the general supposition was that the romantic is moonlight and roses and dreams whereas the novelistic is beef and ale and "realities." And the tale is to the romance as the sketch is to the novel. It is interesting that Hawthorne never wrote about the conflict between imagination and legality, imagination and practicality, artistry and marketplace, without creating the familiar opposing clusters of imagery that persist in his work: moonlight versus noonlight, secluded nook versus public square, clouds and butterflies versus machinery, flowers versus laws, brooding versus action, ghosts versus matter, isolation versus sociability, past versus present, cloudland versus current events, dreams versus actuality, "somewhere else" versus "Salem," romance versus novel, tale versus sketch.

For the most part, for reviewers the tale and romance were good when, like the sketch and novel, they were homiletic, moral, and acceptably instructive. At worst, they were "morbid" (a favorite word) and "diseased:" the moonlight turned to hellfire, the roses to nightshade, the imagination to perversion, and the dreams to nightmare. They were morbid and diseased, also, if they did not offer acceptably respectable or patriotic materials and conclusions. For the most part, for reviewers the sketch and the novel were at their best when provocative of "high thoughts" and "deep truths" that befit a Christian gentleman; at worst they were merely dull. The sketch and novel were descended in the tradition of the Renaissance babies book and gentleman's book—they were of, for, and by the cultivated classes, inculcating, illuminating, dramatizing, explaining, and sugaring the values of the status quo. Although with the rise of the realism that grew out of "local color" regionalism on either side of the civil war, the sketch and the novel were to become instruments of radical dissent, generally they, like the *acceptable* tale and romance, were instruments of modal conservatism in Hawthorne's marketplace.

The bitter paradox at the heart of the distinction between genres is that although the reviews "terribly insisted" upon "actualities" as the literary commodity of most service to the nation, the romance—as several scholars since Matthiessen and Chase have pointed out—was the real vehicle of American literary genius, just as the novel was that of the English. A pragmatic nation of "realism" and progress, America supposedly was also a nation beyond all the historical realities she transcended. The very millennialism of the American self image, so very much part of modal conservatism, paradoxically bred an impulse toward transcendent actions and characters in philosophy and fiction— toward the romance. When Trollope, the Englishman, mused on a Hawthorne letter, that quintessential practitioner of the novelistic was well aware of national as well as temperamental differences between his art and Hawthorne's. He quoted the remark (which has become very familiar in Hawthorne criticism) Hawthorne made in a letter to his publisher James T. Fields: "It is odd enough," wrote Hawthorne, "that my own individual taste is for quite another class of novels than those which I myself am able to write. If I were to meet with such books as mine by another writer, I don't believe I should be able to get through them. Have you ever read the novels of Anthony Trollope? They precisely suit my taste; solid and substantial, written on strength of beef and through the inspiration of ale, and just as real as if some giant had hewn a great lump out of the earth, and put it under a glass case, with all its inhabitants going about their daily business, and not suspecting that they were made a show of." After quoting this revelation of Hawthorne's conservative tug, Trollope went on to say, "The creations of American literature generally are no doubt more given to the speculative,—less given to the realistic,—than are those of English literature. On our side of the water we deal more with beef and ale, and less with dreams. . . . But in no American writer is to be found the same predominance of weird imagination as in Hawthorne."5

The "feminine" and ethereal romance as well as the "masculine" and realistic novel had their nationalistic duties to perform. As an examination of "what is," the American realistic mode of "beef and ale" was called upon to be a celebration, not a criticism, of "actualities" in the redeemed new world. The "actualities" of the status quo were to be seen as the "actualities" of a new Eden. But in its insistence on being untied from the "actualities," the romance tended toward the uses of dissent.

In Trollope's conservative England, an old, consolidated nation hardening to empire, there was an established society to examine and criticize. Writers, like Dickens, used "actualities" to document their social criticism and to make the novel an instrument of the nay-saying that Melville cherished in Hawthorne's tales. Although England did not welcome dissent either, it was more secure as a civilization well established and long defined. In America, where the national self was adolescently insecure and

bumptious, there was not enough cultural identity to give away—
in the very essay in which Melville celebrated the dark nay-saying
of Hawthorne's *Mosses,* he also voiced an outrageously patriotic
cant for his "Young America" audience. And Poe felt his most
bitter, paranoid isolation from the literary establishment when he
challenged the supremacy of American literature as *a national
product.* Producing both patriotic sketches and romances and
tales of alienation, Hawthorne butted his head against the insistence that in America the actualities *are* the dream realized.
The "dream," he saw, had become nothing other than America's
own materialistic, imperial triumph of strength which proclaimed
its own beef and ale as a utilitarianism, pragmatism, and practicality that evidenced the extent to which Providence had smiled
on America. His plight, in which the marketplace insisted that
there was more than a hint of correlation between the romantic,
the unmanly, and the unAmerican, was shrewdly caught by a
British reader of *The Marble Faun.* With the distance of the
outsider, this reader saw clearly what Hawthorne's prefaces were
all about:

"There is a peculiar type of the American mind which is
strongly in revolt against American utilities, and which is pre-
disposed by the very monotony of its surroundings to hues of
contrast and attitudes of antagonism. We have seen the mani-
festation of this revolt in American literature in Edgar Poe and
even in Longfellow and Washington Irving. It is emphatically
the desire of idealists like these and of Mr. Hawthorne to escape
from the 'iron rule' of their country and the 'social despotism' of
their generation. They disdain to be parts of a complicated
scheme of progress, which can only result in their arrival at a
colder and drearier region than that they were born in, and they
refuse to add 'an accumulated pile of usefulness, of which the
only use will be, to burden their posterity with even heavier
thoughts and more inordinate labor than their own.' This impulse induces them to become vagrants in imagination and reality,
tourists in the old world of Europe, dreamers and artificers in
the older world of poetry and romance. . . ."[6] In going on to

note that the American response to the experience of Europe is characteristically more romantic, less matter of fact, less novelistic than the Englishman's, the reviewer touches on the intricate ironies in which monarchical old England and libertarian new America swap roles and literary genres within the context of freedom of literary dissent. The distinction between the novel and the romance, the sketch and the tale, was not merely a matter of literary definitions in America; but for a man who defined himself as a romancer it reflected most deeply in its implications the nature of the relationship between his membership in his American society and his identity as a man and as an artist.

In the last analysis, the sketch was no more "real" than the tale, or in its "manliness" any less subject than the tale to the sentimental and homiletic uses of the ladies' literary marketplace. While a gentleman might display tolerant and condescending amusement toward the lurid and luxurious qualities of fiction for ladies, nevertheless all genres and genders of literature were subjected by reviewers to conformity with standards of polite and relatively orthodox Christianity, respectability, and patriotism. Literature should be "profound" and make one "think," but always within the limits of acceptability. Acceptable literature, as Melville and Whitman were to discover, avoided the ruggedly original, the radically dissenting query, the deeply frightening and ugly dark areas of experience, or the highly eccentric. To be made to "think" by literature was to be brought to a pleasantly melancholy state of mind in a brooding consideration of experience that neither stretched nor basically challenged established values. To be merely entertained was pleasant enough, of course, but it was not "profound." On the other hand, excess of "profundity"—anything truly or acutely uncomfortable—was, as I have pointed out, "morbidity," and anything fanciful enough to be separated from the "actualities" was "subjective." A writer who was consistently "subjective" or "morbid" was accused of being "monotonous." The terms most commonly assigned to the entertaining or pleasant aspects of either sketch or tale, as well as to those features that created felicitous pictures of the native scene, were "light" and "sunshine." The term most commonly assigned to the "thoughtful" or "profound" aspects of literature was "shadow." Although a writer ran the risk of "monotony" if his works were all "sunshine" (he would be less substantial than the native genius demanded) just as he did if his works were all "shadow" (he would be "morbid" and, because gloom is not characteristic of the "actualities," the "real" in American life, he would also be "subjective"), clearly the market supported more happily those who were monotonously light than those who were monotonously umbrageous. As professor Crowley pointed out in his excellent book, "Goodrich [the publisher of the *Token*] put his finger on the public's preference for the simple and happy when he compared Hawthorne with Nathaniel P. Willis [who had achieved the popular success for which Hawthorne had always longed]. . . . 'Willis was all sunshine and summer, the other chill, dark, and wintry; the one was full of love and hope, the other of doubt and distrust . . . it is, perhaps, neither a subject of surprise or regret, that the larger portion of the world is so happily constituted as to have been more ready to flirt with the gay muse of the one, than to descend into the spiritual charnel house, and assist at the psychological dissection of the other.' "[7]

The best writers mingled light and shadow and created a highly touted "chiaroscuro."[8] The reviewers made it plain that Hawthorne could expect charges of monotony, subjectivity, and morbidity when he offered strong and uncompromising presentations of his philosophical conservatism in works of fancy, and that even in works of fancy he could expect a chorus of "chiaroscuro!" for his touches of humor, his pathos, his orthodoxy, his respectability, his nationalistic service of rendering cheerfully the "actualities" of his American region and history. Consistently, the works that were singled out as sketches were unexceptionably praised; the works that were singled out as tales received mixed responses—praise was lavish, disapproval was strong—depending upon whether they leaned toward sunshine or shadow. " 'The Birth-mark,' 'Rappaccini's Daughter,' and 'Roger Malvin's

Burial,' are the nettles and mushrooms of Mr. Hawthorne's mind," wrote one reviewer, "and certainly should not be tied up with a bouquet of flowers for the public. Perhaps we hate these tales the more, that they are bound in the same covers with 'The Celestial Railroad,' and 'Drowne's Wooden Image,' the happiest efforts of the author in sketch writing."[9]

The response was instructive when Hawthorne published the first edition of *Twice-Told Tales*. Except for Longfellow, who liked everything in the book, light and dark, and for Poe, who admired the dark tales and detested the sketches, by far the great majority of readers and editors agreed in pointing at pieces like "A Rill from the Town Pump" and "Little Annie's Rambles" as examples of the chiaroscuro they admired. Therein they found the proper sentiments whereby everyday American life was "profoundly" presented and thoughtfully examined with both humor and pathos. Hawthorne was not to forget the fact fourteen years later in his 1851 preface, nor was he to be unaware that only Poe and Melville were the consistent champions of the "darkness" in his work as the true and lasting greatness of his fiction. It is revealing that when Melville began his essay on Hawthorne's *Mosses,* he felt it necessary to repudiate the prevailing opinion that Hawthorne was a writer of "sunshine." Conversely, when Longfellow, who was very much part of the literary establishment as Poe was not, recommended Hawthorne to the *ladies,* he chiaroscuroed the blackness into a dappled shade of moral instruction and delicacy of taste: "Every woman owes [Hawthorne] a debt of gratitude for those lovely visions of womanly faith, tenderness, and truth, which glide so gracefully through his pages. . . . His tragedy is tempered with a certain smoothness; it solemnizes and impresses us, but it does not freeze the blood, still less offend the most fastidious taste. . . . Indeed, over all he has written, there hangs, like an atmosphere, a certain soft and calm melancholy, which has nothing diseased or mawkish in it, but is of that kind which seems to flow naturally from delicacy of organization and meditative spirit."[10]

Hawthorne's own letters reveal repeatedly that, like the

reviewers, the one thing he most feared in his fiction was "monotony," and even Poe cautioned Hawthorne against a too "prevalent tone."[11] And Henry F. Chorley, a friendly English reviewer, reflected the message of many American reviews when he said, "We have already so often expressed our pleasure in [Hawthorne's] gem-like tales . . . that none, we apprehend, will mistake for covert censure the recommendation we must now give him on the appearance of this second volume [the 1845 edition of *Twice-Told Tales*]—to beware of monotony. We do not say this because he chiefly loves the bygone times of New England. . . ."[12]

No, the love of New England and its bygone times would not earn charges of "monotony" or any other censure; it was part of what the American reviewers nationalistically cherished and praised in Hawthorne, for the "worthy characteristics of a truly National Literature . . . certainly are those of a polished and elegant cultivation. . . . All we think, write, and say, must be tempered and modified by the *Real*—both moral and physical— around us. . . . Ours must be an honestly American—if it be not too much to say—an Aboriginal Literature! as distinct from all others as the plucked crown and scalplock of the red Indian—as vast, as rude, as wildly magnificent as our Mississippi, our mountains, or our Niagara—as still as our star-mirroring lakes at the North. . . ." and "Hawthorne is National—national in subject, in treatment and in manner. We could hardly say anything higher of him. . . ." The moral reality to be found in the national actualities is that ". . . all that is wanted for the "perfectibility' of the Race is the requisite . . . conditions which will furnish . . . the capabilities for enjoying this Paradisiacal state a benevolent Providence has offered. . . . As an artist, in this respect, Hawthorne possesses the most consummate skill."[13]

Like Emily Dickinson, Hawthorne saw "New Englandly," and this native flavor in his romances, tales, and sketches was savored in the marketplace. But when his fictions departed into his philosophical conservatism, all but one or two of the scores and scores of commentators became uneasy in exactly the same way.

Indeed, as one of Hawthorne's "Custom House" practical fore-fathers of the establishment might have exclaimed on learning that from his progeny sprang "a writer of story books," "the degenerate fellow might as well have been a fiddler!" Even when *The Scarlet Letter* was praised as the high point of Hawthorne's production and perhaps even the summit of American literature, still even the friendly critics were disquieted by the subject matter of the book, by the gloom, and by the relationship between good Christian orthodoxy and the uses of a *national* literature. If there was one point upon which the reviewers agreed in hauling Hawthorne before the bar, it was the "immorality" and unAmerican quality of his "morbidity" and "subjectivity." For explicitly acceptable morality was American, just as well-selected American "actualities" were moral. In all the reviews, the categories of "actualities," nationalistic Americanism, morality, sweetness, uplift, "sunshine," "chiaroscuro," variety, and manliness were so intermeshed as to leave no doubt about the proper vocational function of a writer who wished to take his place within established society and to win success within the prevailing popular market. The same Whig periodical, for instance, that delighted in Hawthorne's apparent modal conservatism, could also despair of his immoral inability to deal with solid actualities and could mourn his morbid insistence upon philosophically conservative metaphysical romancing. "He has no genius for realities. . . . Between his characters and the readers falls a gauze-like veil of imagination, on which their shadows flit and move, and play strange dramas replete with second-hand life. An air of unreality enshrouds all his creation." The events of *The Scarlet Letter* have "little more than a reminiscent interest; when characters and customs were so different to all circumstance that jostles us in the rude, quick life of today," and are merely "pale shadowy ancestry . . . with whom we have no common sympathies." Although "Mr. Hawthorne deals artistically with shadows . . . we question much . . . whether the path he has chosen is a healthy one. . . . When an author sits down to make a book, he should not alone consult the inclinations of his own genius regarding its purpose or its construction. If he should happen to be imbued with strange, saturnine doctrines, or be haunted by a morbid suspicion of human nature, in God's name let him not write one word. Better that all the beautiful, wild thoughts with which his brain is teeming should moulder forever in neglect and darkness, than that one soul was overshadowed by stern, uncongenial dogmas. . . . It is not alone necessary to produce a work of art. The soul of beauty is Truth, and Truth is ever progressive. The true artist therefore endeavors to make the world better. He does not look behind him, and dig out of the graves of past centuries skeletons to serve as models for his pictures; but looks onward for more perfect shapes, and though sometimes obliged to design from the defective forms around him, he infuses, as it were, some of the divine spirit of the future into them, and lo! we love them with all their faults. . . . [But Hawthorne's] books have no sunny side to them."[14]

This review represents not only the response of the market-place but also the ways in which the shibboleths of romantic radicalism had hardened into the attitudes of whiggish conservatism. For when the same coin was turned over from censure to praise, and Hawthorne was seen as a man who evoked the regional "actualities" of redeemed American experience, the same Whig journal threw accolades in unmistakable and significant terms: "It happens that we have not only found Conservatism, but a good many other things we have asked for, in our national literature, expressed through the pages of Nathaniel Hawthorne." That Conservatism discovers that things as they are are quite good enough. "It is a favorite expression with regard to Hawthorne, that he '*Idealizes*' everything. Now what does this Idealization mean? Is it that he *improves* upon Nature? Pshaw! this is a Literary cant. . . . Talk to me of *Idealizing* the violet, and you talk nonsense . . . Hawthorne does not endeavor to improve upon the Actual, but with a wise emulation attempts—first to reach it, and then to modify it suitably . . . he is led by his fine taste to . . . make you see it in precisely that light in which . . . its highest beauty is revealed. . . . We can't get away from the physical, and just as our material vision informs the inner life will that inner life know Wisdom. When some of our crude Theorists have learnt to realize this truth . . . they will have come to the knowledge that one Fact of the external life is worth a thousand Dreams, and that they need not waste their lives in seeing sights that have no substance, and dreaming Dreams that have no reality; for if they will only wake up, and look at the real World as it absolutely is, they will find that they have a Paradise made to their hand." So when one looks into Hawthorne's attitudes, "there is a still more interesting and even wiser exhibition of the Ethical Conservatism of his mind, given in that fine allegory, 'Earth's Holocaust.' Here he represents a saturnalia of the reformers," men like Emerson and that whole "brawling tribe of Innovators—each of whom imagines he has certainly found the Archimedean lever, and is heaving at it in the effort to turn the world topsy-turvy."[15]

The summation of acceptability was voiced in a British review which summed up the American response to Phoebe as the "sunshine" in the "chiaroscuro" of *The House of the Seven Gables*: "surely this pretty creation [Phoebe] of Mr. Hawthorne's must stand for the Middle Classes of Society, to whom has been committed by Providence the mission of social reconciliation; which, once completed, the disunited are joined, the unblest, blessed, and the 'wild reformer' becomes a Conservative after Heaven's own fashion."[16]

When one considers the conflict between many of Hawthorne's romances and tales and their endings, the wonder is not that Hawthorne's fiction has as many failures of nerve as it does, that it reveals so many attempts to open a modally conservative intercourse with the world, but that it succeeds and is brave as often as it is. The identification of the signs of the tensions and failures in Hawthorne's writings is a demonstration of great intricacy, but well worth the candle because the significance of the details are of enormous importance. Only suggested most briefly here, they offer a direction for readings of Hawthorne's works, one in which what we know about the psychological dimensions of Hawthorne's life merges with the political dimensions of Hawthorne's world.

The problem was that for Hawthorne the philosophical conservatism in his mind was more of a reality than the new world of progress that his contemporaries announced lay all about them, either in American actualities if they were modal conservatives or in the possibilities of the spirit if they were romantic radicals. The fictive representations of Hawthorne's inner world were the messengers of truth, or reality, as he saw it, which he sent out to the deluded, chimerical outer world. As such, they were "subjective" representations of romance-writing as a vocation and of Hawthorne as a self. They were, in short, elements of autobiography. But the autobiography toward which Hawthorne was groping was one of discovery rather than memory; his necessity was not to define himself according to all the accumulated details of actuality, but according to a definition of himself as a prophet entitled to popular honor in his own land. What he had to do was to create himself in his vocation, within his time and place, according to the laws of a world perceived through his philosophical conservatism rather than according to the values of that time and place within which he wished to be identified. And given the obdurate power of organically felt cultural nationalism and the terrible insistence upon actualities, his only autobiographical and self-creating recourse was to substitute the inner for the outer world at the very same time that more than anything else he wished to open an intercourse with that world through the fictions so prompted. In short, the nature of his vision in combination with the nature of his external world turned him into a ghost whose instrument of communication doomed him to what he felt to be relative invisibility among the ordinary, daylight population of his time and place. It is not unfair to say that the larger, national values implicit in the editorial strictures and structures of the literary marketplace denied Hawthorne a fully embodied life—a denial about which he himself bitterly complained. His dilemma was that his hunger for popularity and esteem was one level of his need to discover and announce himself as both man and writer. His need to discover and announce himself forced him to the creation of the messengers from his mind. The message of those messengers announced the laws of Hawthorne's philosophically conservative vision. The primacy of those laws forced him to a recognition of the distance between his internal and external worlds. Recognition of that gap only exacerbated his need to close it and to belong, which exacerbated his need to discover and announce himself. The vicious circle of self-creation and opening an intercourse with the world was self-generating. The politics of adjusting his opposing worlds and selves to each other became the core of his fictions, an endless round of a fictive autobiography of discovery with which Hawthorne finally became despairingly bored and sickened unto death. The significance of his feeling himself turned into a ghost is, I suggest, in profound and complex ways, within the context of his national culture, the same as the significance of his continual plaint about his lack of literary popularity. The politics of his vocation lay at the center of the aching in his soul just as the aching in his soul lay at the center of the politics of his vocation.

NOTES

1. A useful study of the development, subject matters, editorial principles, and variety of Hawthorne's contemporary magazine market is by Theodore P. Greene, *America's Heroes: The Changing Models of Success in American Magazines* (New York, 1970).
2. *Ladies Magazine*, I (November, 1828), 526-27. J. Donald Crowley quotes the review on p. 42 of his book, *Hawthorne: The Critical Heritage* (London, 1970). Professor Crowley's book is an extremely useful work of high editorial intelligence. The edition relieves scholars of the task of digging through the reviews to discover an overview of the opinions of Hawthorne's contemporaries. I have checked through most of the original reviews, and in all but one or two cases I have found no need to flesh out Crowley's elisions from

the originals. In admiration for his work and as a testimonial to my own great debt to it, in the few references I make in this essay to contemporary reviews, I offer also in each case a reference to Professor Crowley's invaluable volume, which puts a reference library on each critic's desk.

3. *American Monthly Magazine,* V, n.s. (March, 1838). 281-283; cited in Crowley, pp. 60-61, 63.
4. All italics mine. Anonymous, *Christian Examiner,* LV (September, 1852), 292-294; quoted in Crowley, p. 251.
5. "The Genius of Nathaniel Hawthorne," *North American Review,* CCLXXIV (September, 1879), 203-22; quoted in Crowley, p. 515.
6. Anonymous, *The Times* (London, April 7, 1860), p. 5; quoted in Crowley, pp. 329-330.
7. Crowley, p. 6.
8. For a discussion of contemporary critical terms, see Crowley's instructive introduction to his book. Although he does not utilize the critical terminology for the same purposes I do, his introduction offers a seminal beginning point for critics interested in the suggestions I make in this essay.
9. Amory Dwight Mayo, "The Works of Nathaniel Hawthorne," *Universalist Quarterly,* VIII (July, 1851), 272-93; quoted in Crowley, p. 222.
10. *North American Review,* LVI (April, 1842), 496-499; quoted in Crowley, p. 82.
11. *Graham's Magazine,* XX (May, 1842), 298-300; quoted in Crowley, p. 93.
12. *Athenaeum* (August 23, 1845), 830-831; quoted in Crowley, pp. 95-96.
13. Charles Wilkins Webber, "Hawthorne," *American Whig Review,* IV (September, 1846), 296-316; quoted in Crowley, pp. 128, 131.
14. Anonymous, *American Whig Review,* XVI (1852), 417-424; quoted in Crowley, pp. 267-68, 269.
15. Webber, quoted in Crowley, pp. 126, 128-131.
16. Anonymous, "American Literature: Poe, Hawthorne," *Tait's Edinburgh Magazine,* XXII (January, 1855), 33-41; quoted in Crowley, p. 309.

John Dos Passos:
Reaching Past Poetry

LINDA WELSHIMER WAGNER

In 1920, Dos Passos' first novel, *One Man's Initiation—1917*, was published in England. In 1921, *Three Soldiers* appeared, and in 1922, his first and only poem collection, *A Pushcart at the Curb*. Of the three books, the second novel received the most acclaim (as a "realistic" war novel[1]); the other books went relatively unnoticed. For all its submersion among Dos Passos' forty published books, however, *A Pushcart at the Curb* may be one of his most interesting because it illustrates many qualities—both strong and weak—of the young writer's developing aesthetic. In poetry Dos Passos found and then polished some elements of the style that was to shape his later fiction.

Born in 1896, John Dos Passos was a restless Harvard undergraduate during 1913 to 1916, the same years that found E. E. Cummings and Robert Hillyer studying there. With them, Dos Passos helped edit the avant garde *Harvard Monthly* (where his essays, stories, and poems showed his knowledge of contemporary art).[2] As a member of the Poetry Club, he heard such innovators as Amy Lowell, Robert Frost, Vachel Lindsay, John Gould Fletcher, Conrad Aiken, and others[3]—and could disdainfully comment that too many Harvard students "chose to live in the 1890's."[4] For Dos Passos and his friends, as he reminisced, "Currents of energy seemed breaking out everywhere. . . . [American were] groggy with new things in theatre and painting and music."[5] More specifically, Dos Passos described this "creative tidal wave" in the 1931 introduction to his translation of Blaise Cendrars' poem, *Panama*:

> Under various tags: futurism, cubism, vorticism, modernism, most of the best work in the arts in our time has been the direct product of this explosion, that had an influence in its sphere comparable with that of the October revolution in social organization and politics and the Einstein formula in physics. Cendrars and Apollinaire, poets, were on the first cubist barricades with the group that influenced Picasso, Modigliani, Marinetti, Chagall; that profoundly influenced Maiakovsky, Meyerhold, Eisenstein; whose ideas carom through Joyce, Gertrude Stein, T. S. Eliot (first published in Wyndam's [sic] Lewis's "Blast").[6]

A key idea in this aesthetic revolution was that of the image, and Dos Passos frequently refers to the Imagist poets, particularly Ezra Pound and Richard Aldington; just as he often cites ideas that were first stated by Pound and F. S. Flint as early as 1913. The concentration on the concrete, the use of free or organic form, and of rhythms determined by the spoken phrase rather than that of the metronome—these so-called principles of Imagism were to lay the foundation for most modern poetry, and prose as well.[7] The new aesthetic might be destructive of traditional forms and attitudes, but as Dos Passos explained in 1923: "Explosions of fresh vitality in any art necessarily destroy the old forms."[8]

The poems finally collected in the 1922 *A Pushcart at the Curb* (and the manuscript in the Dos Passos collection at the University of Virginia suggests that the book was once nearly twice as long as the published version)[9] do seem influenced in some respects by the Imagist doctrines. Short poems like XV from

"Winter in Castile" are image-centered, highly descriptive, and succinct:

> The weazened old woman without teeth
> who shivers on the windy street corner
> displays her roasted chestnuts invitingly
> like marriageable daughters.[10]

Most of the longer poems also emphasize the image, although it may be only one part of a structure determined partly by the musicality of the total poem. Dos Passos' interest in the image is clear from his letters to Rumsey Marvin, the friend who was younger than he by several years. In 1915, he stressed that

> an idea or emotion has usually to be tied up in a picture, a figure of speech or something like that, before it is really available for poetry—in the highest sense . . . .[11]

In 1916, he wrote that "The game is to get musical-picture words and pack them with the desired emotion."[12] Later he referred to "concrete images," claiming to be interested in "originality" in their use before all else.[13]

Other of Dos Passos' comments to Marvin in his letters from 1915 to 1918 also suggest Imagist principles. A "modern" writer, according to both Dos Passos and the Imagists, was to use natural-sounding language rather than poetic diction. In 1918, Dos Passos took Marvin to task for using archaisms:

> In what language, except that of certain dead gentlemen, appears the word "smooth'st"? For heaven's sake man—write live language not dead Keats and Shelley. . . .[14]

Several years earlier, he had criticized Marvin's language as being "a little high falutin', even for poetry" and advised him "Try to run down the simple (not the hackneyed) and colorful words."[15] Dos Passos' own self-mocking poem, IX from "Nights at Bassano," illustrates the controversy surrounding both "poetic" language and "poetic" subject matter:

> O I would take my pen and write
> In might of words
> A pounding dytheramb [sic]
> Alight with teasing fires of hate,
> Or drone to numbness in the spell
> Of old loves long lived away
> A drowsy vilanelle. [sic]
> O I would build an Ark of words,
> A safe ciborium where to lay
> The secret soul of loveliness. . .
>
> But my pen does otherwise.
>
> All I can write is the orange tinct with crimson
> of the beaks of the goose
> and of the wet webbed feet of the geese. . . (99-100 *PAC*).

By shifting from the post-Victorian concept of suitable subjects for poetry to the geese of this poem, Dos Passos also supports his 1915 contention to Marvin that "Prize-fights are every bit as good a subject for poetry as fine ladies and illicit love affairs. . . . every subject under the sun which has any thing to do with human beings—man, woman or child—is susceptible of poetic treatment. . . . And, moreover, one of the prime reasons why American literature isn't is that we as a nation have not that feeling of the infinite beauty and infinite poetry underlying things—love, war, sunsets, tin pans, lawnmowers, etc etc—."[16] Contrasting Dos Passos' poems with those of Imagist poets like William Carlos Williams or H. D., however, shows some clear differences. Dos Passos seems to have been closer to the thinking of William Faulkner and Conrad Aiken in his feeling that, whatever its other properties, the modern poem should be "intensely musical."[17] The spare colloquial idiom of the modern

American street walker or butcher theoretically may be the stuff of art, but Dos Passos had great admiration for the poems of Stevenson, Tennyson, and Swinburne, as well as for the work of Richard Aldington and Ezra Pound. As he wrote to Marvin,

> Do write more—and read Keats' Eve of St. Agnes, Shelley's Adonais—there you will learn something about words. . . . The main thing is to write what you see as simply as possible No, not exactly, the main thing is to keep the proper average between the music of the thing, the meter and the words—and don't be afraid of any word if it seems to fit—sincerely.[18]

Frequently, Dos Passos' own poems are marked by heavy assonance, one means of creating a kind of musicality ("nights of clouds/terror of their flight across the moon./Over the long still plains/blows a wind out of the north;/a laden wind out of the north/rattles the leaves of the liveoaks/menacingly and loud." XIV, p. 41, *PAC*)

From this device, it is only a short step to one of Dos Passos' most pervasive techniques, the repetition of phrase or line, the use of refrain, whether or not conventionally placed. At its simplest, Dos Passos' repetition occurs to create a mood, often through imagery of color as in V from "Winter in Castile" which opens

> Rain slants on an empty square

and closes with the mournful "in the grey rain,/in the grey city." In more ambitious poems, Dos Passos uses repetition to vary mood rather than to maintain it, as in I of "Nights at Bassano" (a poem titled in draft "Rondel to our Lady of Abyssinia") and XIII, reminiscent of Vachel Lindsay, from "Winter in Castile":

> There's a sound of drums and trumpets
> above the rumble of the street.
> (Run run run to see the soldiers.)

> All alike all abreast keeping time
> to the regimented swirl
> of the glittering brass band.

Dos Passos also believed in the use of regular poetic forms so long as they achieved desired effects. Here, although the "run run run" line recurs as refrain, its context differs each time; and the author seems intent on achieving at least some effects which are unpredictable. The ending of this poem, for example, echoes key words from the opening stanza, but places them in a very differently toned image:

> old men in cloaks
> try to regiment their feet
> to the glittering brass beat.
> Run run run to see the soldiers (pp. 38-39, *PAC*).

This same density of verbal play—in both assonance and repetition—characterizes the Camera Eye and, to a lesser extent, the Biography sections of the *U.S.A.* novels.

Another part of Dos Passos' concept of musicality stemmed from his notion that free verse was never literally free, but "*meant* to have rhythm—it's not the same rhythm as so-called metrical verse; but it's a perfectly definite and sometimes quite *regular* cadence."[19] Line division and line placement in the poems usually help create rhythm or pace; in many places, the division that exists is expected, and borders on the uninventive. At other times, however, as in XI below, line arrangement works to create effective montage, a device Dos Passos admired throughout his career:

> Beyond ruffled velvet hills
> the sky burns yellow like a candle-flame.
>
> Sudden a village
> roofs against the sky
> leaping buttresses

> a church
> and a tower utter dark like the heart
> of a candleflame . . . (p. 34, *PAC*).

Even the recurring similes (a favorite figure of speech in these
early poems) cannot deaden the pace of this juxtaposition, the
technique that gives Dos Passos' poetry and fiction (particularly
the Newsreel sections of *U.S.A.)* its brisk tempo.

Important as these principles of musicality, the image, and
verbal structure were to Dos Passos' developing aesthetic, one of
the essential points of his credo was the concept of presentation,
of objectivity. The writer was to aim for the aura of distance.
His was the role of objective conveyor, and, although he might
use subjective elements in his presentation—and, indeed, his
choices of subjects and details were themselves subjective—he
was to avoid the explicit or the didactic. Method more than attitude was to be objective. Dos Passos' poems follow this directive
perhaps too well: nearly all the poems are montages of external
details—chandeliers, bells, soldiers, donkeys, children. The people
in the poems are also vividly externalized: he uses colors and
other graphic details but he seldom tells his reasons for being
drawn to the subjects of the poems. The *I* persona—to pervade
later American poetry—is almost never used, unless it occurs in
pastorals as narrative convention. The cumulative effect of the
poems in *A Pushcart at the Curb* is, then, relatively impersonal:
a reader knows more about Tivoli and camel travel than about
John Dos Passos. In fact, Dos Passos describes the poet in V from
"Quai de la Tournelle" as "a gardener in a pond// culling out
of the pool . . ./ gestures and faces" (p. 147, *PAC*).

The few exceptions to these characteristic objective presentations are all the more striking for their rarity. Several poems
picture the young poet as a classic Prufrock figure—unfulfilled,
searching, held back from various kinds of satisfaction because of
fear, thinking his life futile. At times the focus for his anguish
is a woman (usually slender and dark, shadowy in appearance

and detail); again, as in "Ode to Ennui," his malaise is undefined. More frequently, in the somewhat later poems, loneliness itself is the cause of his despair:

> O such a night for scaling garden walls;
> yet I lie alone in my narrow bed
> and stare at the blank walls, forever afraid,
> of a watchdog's barking (VIII, "Vagones De Tercera").

In "A L'ombre Des Jeunes Filles En Fleurs" he speaks of futility tumbling "like great flabby snowflakes about me" (*PAC*, p. 159) and in "Embarquement Pour Cythére" he concludes that the beautiful lady was only a dream, "a bitter dream."[20] If it were not that this theme recurs in Dos Passos' early fiction as well as his poetry, much of this self-image might be considered a traditional romantic pose. But the image cannot here be easily dismissed: it is too pervasive, fits too clearly with other autobiographical reflections (in his various memoirs, the Camera Eye sections of *U.S.A.* and the later novels). What some of the strongest of his poems in *A Pushcart at the Curb* seem to suggest is that Dos Passos did carry feelings of frustration into maturity. An isolato for many reasons, he continually tried to overcome his hesitancy about personal relationships. One of the clearest presentations of this view of the poet's persona is found in one of his later poems, VIII of "Phases of the Moon." An excellent poem in that repetition exists for meaning, not just rhythm, it opens with a powerful metaphor which is also "intensely musical":

> In me somewhere is a grey room
> my fathers worked through many lives to build;
> through the barred distorting windowpanes
> I see the new moon in the sky.

The image of the room—somber, closed off, even lost—with all its connotation of hollowness and separation from the moon establishes the poet as, once again, isolated (by the "distorting"

and "barred" glass) and also, more importantly here, the re-
cipient of his "fathers'" heritage. The multicareers of the successful John Randolph Dos Passos would be challenging to any
son, but especially so to the timid boy who, until he was sixteen,
could not so much as carry the family name.[21]

The next two stanzas give early and later events in the boy's
life, with the metaphor at the close of the third charging the
girl's role with greater importance than that of art.

> When I was small I sat and drew
> endless pictures in all colors on the walls;
> tomorrow the pictures should take life
> I would stalk down their long heroic colonnades.

> When I was fifteen a red-haired girl
> went by the window; a red sunset
> threw her shadow on the stiff grey wall
> to burn the colors of my pictures dead.

Rather than use the simile he so often resorted to, in this
poem Dos Passos turns to striking metaphors, occurring in both
single figures and in the dominant pattern of room, windowpane;
moon, shadow. The result is an exacting tautness, an accuracy
of emotion that none of his other poems—either published or
unpublished—matches. As the concluding stanzas continue the
earlier imagery, it assumes even greater personal and immediate
significance:

> Through all these years the walls have writhed
> with shadow overlaid upon shadow.
> I have bruised my fingers on the windowbars
> so many lives cemented and made strong.

> While the bars stand strong, outside
> the great processions of men's lives go past.
> Their shadows squirm distorted on my wall.

> Tonight the new moon is in the sky (pp. 200-201, *PAC*).

Interested as Dos Passos was in the process of poetry—and he saw it as reflecting his fascination for Flaubert's *le mot juste* as well as being important in its own right—his concern for subject matter soon began to overwhelm his absorption with technique. Increasingly his notebooks and letters include comments about characters and themes, and as his own experience broadened—through his foreign travel as well as his involvement in social and political issues in America—his views about literature grew more expansive.

In fact, his tone during the twenties as he discussed purely literary matters is often somewhat impatient. "I wasn't much interested in the labels on these various literary packages but I was excited by what I found inside," he recalls about these formative years; "at times I would find it hard to tell you whether the stuff is prose or verse."[22] This imagery of "package" surfaces again as he discusses his turn from poetry to the various kinds of writing in the mature novels. His impulses to write poetry later found outlet in what he calls the "poetic passages" of the novels: "I got to a point where there was no particular reason for making separate little packages."[23] And in the 1969 *Paris Review* interview, he admits, "I did quite a lot of that [poetry] but it took a different form . . . it got into certain rhythmic passages in *USA*."[24]

Considering the fact that there are very few long-line poems in the 1922 *A Pushcart at the Curb*, Dos Passos' later move into the prose-poem Biography and Camera Eye segments of the *U.S.A.* trilogy, and the various prose-poem sections of later novels as well, is linked most immediately with the writings of Walt Whitman. Early Whitman and not early Dos Passos would seem to be the chief ancestry for these sections. Although Dos Passos had long admired Whitman as both poet and seer, he appears to have re-discovered his writing with a new intensity once he was himself concerned with America as theme.

> Perhaps it was from living so much abroad as a child that I imbibed a stubborn love of my country that no amount of disillusion has been able to weaken. . . .[25]

It seems reasonable that Dos Passos, like Whitman, came to see himself as the chronicler of his country—and to feel the need for some new form of expression as vehicle for that chronicle.

What is, finally, most surprising (and, perhaps, most limiting) about Dos Passos' poems is that they are so thoroughly unAmerican. Foreign countries, scenes, characters, images—most of these early poems, like his journals, captured some impression from his travels, and Dos Passos' line of vision did not return to Manhattan/New York/America until 1923. The impetus for the greatest art, however, according to Dos Passos' aesthetic, was the ability to capture one's place; and his admiration for the writing of both Whitman and Cendrars attests to that recognition.

Dos Passos' prose-poem style, one element of the novels that he termed *chronicles*, was first anticipated, not in his formal poetry but rather in his 1926 contribution to "A Passaic Symposium," for *New Masses*. His strategy here was to mesmerize readers with an incantatory, heavily imaged prose scenario gauged to elicit sympathy for the striking workers in New Jersey. He focused first on "the people who had come from New York . . . talking of outrages and the Bill of Rights," the theoretical liberals who rode in "shiny sedans of various makes, nicely upholstered"; and then contrasted them with the deprived strikers. He used very few facts, relying almost totally on rhythm and poignant imagery. The piece ends, effectively, in a single-sentence paragraph that repeats the contrast between the liberals and the workers:

> The procession of taxis, shiny sedans of various makes, went back the way it had come, down empty streets protected by deputies with shiny new riot guns, past endless facades of deserted mills, past brick tenements with ill-painted stoops, past groups of squat square women with yellow grey faces, groups of men and boys standing still, saying nothing, looking nowhere, square hands hanging at their sides, people square and still, chunks of yellowgrey stone at the edge of a quarry, idle, waiting, on strike.[26]

He uses the same methods in his prose sketch of Sacco and Vanzetti, "The Pit and the Pendulum," in the August, 1926, *New Masses*; and then, in contrast, in the October, 1927, issue of the same magazine, includes a poem about their execution, " 'They Are Dead Now—' " which opens

> This isn't a poem
>
> This is two men in grey prison clothes.
> One man sits looking at the sick flesh of his hands—
> hands that haven't worked for seven years.
> Do you know how long a year is?
> Do you know how many hours there are in a day
>   when a day is twenty-three hours on a cot in a cell,
>   in a cell in a row of cells in a tier of rows of cells
>   all empty with the choked emptiness of dreams? . . . .[27]

Details, rhetorical emphasis through repetition and contrast, rhythmic incrementation—Dos Passos' techniques in his "poem" to Sacco and Vanzetti are much like those in his "prose" account of their imprisonment—and, most important, much different from his usual verbal arrangements when he writes "formal" poems. The fusion of necessity, outcry, demanding subject and his own concept of effective form seems to have led Dos Passos into a rhythmic shape that he, rightly, could not distinguish as either prose or poetry; but one which he used, frequently, throughout the rest of his writing career.

Most of the "Biography" sections from the *U.S.A.* trilogy are marked by the long-line movement, detail building on detail (often ironic), the passage at first marked by periods, but later moving cumulatively to the rising climax. Each has at least one repeated image, occurring at studied intervals. In the case of Gene Debs' portrait, titled "Lover of Mankind," the continuing imagery is that of the plain-spoken Midwesterner, and the brotherhood of like men. The biography opens with the unembellished recitation of facts:

> Debs was a railroadman, born in a weatherboarded shack
> at Terre Haute.
> He was one of ten children.
> His father had come to America in a sailingship in '49,
>   an Alsatian from Colmar; not much of a moneymaker,
> fond of music and reading,
>   he gave his children a chance to finish public school and
> that was about all he could do. . . .

and moves to longer units of description as Debs becomes the
important labor leader, rising to the inclusion of his own words,
with which Dos Passos so thoroughly agrees; then ending with
what Dos Passos sees as his betrayal—catalogues, colloquially
phrased and charged descriptions, the imagery of faith become
the imagery of betrayal:

> But where were Gene Deb's brothers in nineteen eight-
> een when Woodrow Wilson had him locked up in Atlanta
> for speaking against war,
>   where were the big men fond of whiskey and fond of each
> other, gentle rambling tellers of stories over bars in small
> towns in the Middle West,
>   quiet men who wanted a house with a porch to putter
> around and a fat wife to cook for them, a few drinks and
> cigars, a garden to dig in, cronies to chew the rag with. . . .

> And they brought him back to die in Terre Haute
> to sit on his porch in a rocker with a cigar in his mouth,
> beside him American Beauty roses his wife fixed in a bowl;
> and the people of Terre Haute and the people in Indiana
> and the people of the Middle West were fond of him and
> afraid of him and thought of him as an old kindly uncle who
> loved them, and wanted to be with him and to have him
> give them candy,
>   but they were afraid of him as if he had contracted a social
> disease, syphilis or leprosy, and thought it was too bad,
>   but on account of the flag

and prosperity
and making the world safe for democracy,
they were afraid to be with him,
or to think much about him for fear they might believe
him;
for he said:
While there is a lower class I am of it, while there is a
criminal class I am of it, while there is a soul in prison I am
not free.[28]

The idiomatic rhythms of this section (probably the most striking
single quality of these Biographies collectively), almost too stylized
in places, had fascinated Dos Passos for much of his writing
career—witness many of the characterizations in his fiction and
such poems as the unpublished "Two Engines over the Mountains" which has as epigram: "Pullman Porter: 'Yessir, we always
have two engines over the mountains.' "[29] The questions of
whether or not idiomatic language is poetic language rises
wherever modern writing is discussed; for Dos Passos, at this
stage in his artistic development, one assumes that it was.

Judging from the drafts and early manuscript versions of the
U.S.A. novels, Dos Passos' chief problem in writing these biographies was to include accurate information within the heavily
accented lines—the rush and tumble of impassioned or ironic
speech that he was attempting to approximate also had to be
factual. Included among his work sheets are notes and listings
of the concrete—places, dates, and events for respective subjects
of these profiles. Once he had absorbed these facts, one assumes,
he could fit them into the rhythms appropriate to the entry.

At times, changes from early versions to published suggest that
the final tone or form of a biography was a surprise to Dos
Passos himself. The biography of Andrew Carnegie, for example,
seems to have been much less satiric in its early version—or at
least less effectively satiric. As published in the novel, the piece is
titled "Prince of Peace" and its central irony works because

Carnegie is shown investing in philanthropic enterprises only in peace time. The heavy irony of the ending is, however, absent in the early draft which closes simply

> whenever he had a billion dollars he invested it.

As published, it reads

> whenever he made a billion dollars he endowed an insti-
> tution to promote universal peace
> always
> except in time of war (*FSP*, p. 278).

The manuscript draft in the University of Virginia collection also includes a heavy-handed couplet which Dos Passos, happily, deleted:

> Andrew Carnegie lies a-mouldering in the grave
> But his billions go marching on.

Apparently different from the long-line biographies, Dos Passos' Camera Eye passages shared the repetition of key details and the unification of an underlying rhythm. In these admittedly subjective and autobiographical prose-poems, however, Dos Passos drew on avant-garde signals for stream-of-consciousness effects: he replaced traditional punctuation with spacing within lines; capitalized only thematically important words; enjambed single words; and used formal figures of speech that might have seemed too poetic in the idiomatic rhythms of the biographies. The Camera Eye passages are accordingly short, even fragmentary in their lack of explicit connections, and often powerfully evocative.

> skating on the pond next the silver company's mills
> where there was a funny fuzzy smell from the dump
> whaleoil soap somebody said it was that they used in

> cleaning the silver knives and spoons and forks putting
> shine on them for sale   there was shine on the ice early
> black ice that rang like a sawblade just scratched white
> by the first skaters   I couldn't learn to skate and kept
> falling down   look out for the muckers everybody
> said   Bohunk and Polak kids put stones in their snow-
> balls write dirty words up on walls do dirty things up
> alleys their folks work in the mills
>   we clean young American Rover Boys handy with
> tools Deerslayers played hockey Boy Scouts and cut
> figure eights on the ice Achilles Ajax Agamemnon   I
> couldn't learn to skate and kept falling down (FSP, p. 101).

Early versions of this moving recollection of Dos Passos' boyhood fears show that the key statement, "I couldn't learn to skate and kept falling down," was originally underlined whenever it appeared. More important, the names of the comparative figures in the last paragraph were added later: the words *Boy Scouts* and the Greek fallen heroes did not appear in the first version.

At times changes from early versions were in the form of additions (and, as in this case, the additions attempted to make personal experiences wider, farther-reaching); again, Dos Passos deleted material from early versions (and that deletion pattern suggests that he was again trying to stay away from detail that had only personal relevance). Versions of the Camera Eye 25, re-creation of Dos Passos' Harvard (bellglass) years, illustrate the latter kind of change. The published version reads,

> those spring nights the streetcar wheels screech grind-
> ing in a rattle of loose trucks round the curved tracks of
> Harvard Square dust hangs in the powdery arclight glare
> allnight till dawn can't sleep
>   haven't got the nerve to break out of the bellglass

In the earlier draft, however, spacing and line indentation played more significant roles, as Dos Passos referred to authors whose lives were contrasts to his own during these college years.

> those spring nights the streetcar wheels screech grind-
> ing in a rattle of loose trucks round the curved tracks of
> Harvard Square.
>
> > Byron?
> Dust hangs in the powdery arclight glare allnight till dawn.
> > Shelley?
> Can't sleep. Dostoyeffski? [sic] Haven't the nerve to break
> out of the bellglass,
> > Browning (Paracelsus)
> > > Couperus (Small Souls)
> > > > Ibsen (Emperor and Galilean)
> > > > > Strindberg (The Dream Play)
> > > > > > Compton Mackenzie (Youth's Encounter)

What remains of the earlier draft is the cohesive and evocative
(and ironic) reminiscence ("grow cold with culture like a cup of
tea forgotten" and "and all the pleasant contacts will be useful in
Later Life say hello pleasantly to everybody crossing the yard"),
building to the staggered-line conclusion. In draft, Dos Passos
adds specifics that he later deletes, probably as cluttering his
tempo. The draft concludes

> it was like the Magdeburg spheres the pressure outside
> sustained the vacuum within
> and I hadn't the nerve (paralysis)
> or the intelligence (amnesia)
> or the knowledge (aphasure) . . .

whereas the published version reads more simply,

> and I hadn't the nerve
> > to jump up and walk outofdoors and tell
> them all to go take a flying
> > Rimbaud
> > at the moon (*FSP*, 311-312).

The verbal effects of enjambement and position, the differences
in line length and arrangement—Dos Passos is playing with

groups of words here, in ostensible prose, just as much as any poet ever played with those effects in his work (and one is reminded of the close friendship between E. E. Cummings and Dos Passos, from these Harvard years on). Of interest, too, is the fact that in both these Camera Eye sections, the persona is again the ill-at-ease advantaged boy who envies tougher and usually uneducated people.

Satisfied with the composition of the various kinds of writing in *U.S.A.*, Dos Passos kept to the same techniques in later books. His prose poems serve as epigrams for some novels; as interlude for others. But they do not appear with anything like the earlier quality or intensity until the 1975 chronicle, *Century's Ebb.* Titled *Century's End* in manuscript, this posthumously edited and published book may have been of more comfort to Dos Passos than he had anticipated. Not only did he change the title of the book itself to one less pessimistic; he also changed the title of the long opening biography of the man he had come to consider his mentor from "Warnings from Whitman" to the affirmative "Strike up for a New World." The question Dos Passos asks Whitman, in the prelude to the biography, is essential:

> what would you say, Walt, here, now, today,
> of these States that you loved,
> Walt Whitman, what would you say?

The answer is found, as one might suppose from Dos Passos' constant aesthetic of juxtaposition and imagery, in the whole book itself—segment of American life slapped against segment, the total effect one of mis-use and waste, salvaged somehow by the optimism and beauty that occurs even at the most unexpected times and places. There are quotations from Whitman (most often, from *Democratic Vistas*) as epigram as well as within the biography, but the chief affirmation comes from Dos Passos himself as he concludes the book with an account of the 1968 Christmas on the moon, an image in his eyes of the continuing promise of human curiosity. But that image would have been less forceful had he not set the entire fictional montage in the context of Whitman's impassioned quest, presented in some of the best of Dos Passos' prose-poem writing:

> Born of a rundown family on a rundown farm on the
> high dry hills of Long Island,
> Walt could well lay claim to the title
> of average man—less than average:
> bottom of the heap—;
> but, from their saltbox at West Hills the Whitmans could
> see to the north the silver streak of the Sound already
> furrowed by steamboats,
> and to the south on clear days, scallopings of the surf on
> the Atlantic beaches . . .[30]

As some of his best later writing suggests, Dos Passos' poetic methods were developed early, and were then used frequently, and purposefully, throughout his career. In some ways, his adherence to the principles of poetry may have been responsible for some of Dos Passos' most effective prose.

NOTES

1. As W. C. Blum noted in his review of *Three Soldiers* (*Dial* 71, Nov. 1921, 606-608): "Like novels by Zola or Frank Norris, *Three Soldiers* is frankly a book with a thesis."
2. Among the most interesting of Dos Passos' comments as critic in *The Harvard Monthly* are his stress on characterization (review of Louis Couperus' *Small Souls*, Feb. 1915, p. 169 and Joseph Conrad's *Lord Jim*, July 1915, 151-54) and his positive view of *Des Imagistes* in contrast to *The Catholic Anthology*, the poems of which he found weak because of the poets' "desolating attempts to be new, to be bold, to be smart, to be naughty" (review of *The Catholic Anthology* and *Georgian Poetry*, 1913-1915, May 1916, 92-94).

3. Charles W. Bernadin gives excellent detail about this period in his "John Dos Passos' Harvard Years," *New England Quarterly* 27, March 1954, 3-26.

4. *The Best Times, An Informal Memoir* (New York: The New American Library, 1966), 23.

5. *Occasions and Protests* (New York: Henry Regnery Co., 1964), 5.

6. "Translator's Foreword" to Blaise Cendrars, *Panama, Or, The Adventures of My Seven Uncles* (New York: Harper and Brothers, 1931), vii.

7. In the same foreword, Dos Passos termed the years of Imagism "a period of virility, intense experimentation and meaning in everyday life." The fullest statements of the Imagist credo are to be found in "A Few Don'ts by an Imagiste" and "Imagism," both in *Poetry*, I, No. 6, March 1913, 99-201; Ezra Pound's "Vorticism," *Fortnightly Review*, 96, Sept. 1, 1914, 469; and Stanley K. Coffman, Jr., *Imagism* (Norman, Okla.: University of Oklahoma Press, 1950).

8. "Foreword" to John Howard Lawson's *Roger Bloomer* (New York: Thomas Seltzer, 1923), vi.

9. Labeled *A Pushcart at the Curb*, the folder holds most of Dos Passos' poems—those sent in letters to friends but never published (some available now in *The Fourteenth Chronicle, Letters and Diaries of John Dos Passos*, ed. Townsend Ludington, Boston, Gambit, 1973); others published but not in book form; others never published. Permission to quote from the latter, courtesy of Alderman Library, The University of Virginia, Charlottesville, Virginia and Mrs. Elizabeth Dos Passos.

10. *A Pushcart at the Curb* (New York: George H. Doran Co., 1922), p. 43. Subsequent references cited in text as *PAC*.

11. *Fourteen Chronicle*, 26.

12. *Ibid.*, 42.

13. *Ibid.*, 33.

14. *Ibid.*, 118.

15. *Ibid.*, 33.

16. *Ibid.*, 26-27.

17. *Ibid.*, 38.

18. *Ibid.*, 52.

19. *Ibid.*, 74

20. This phrase occurs only in the early draft of the poem, found in a March, 1920, letter to Rumsey Marvin, published in *Fourteenth Chronicle*, 283-284; it is deleted from the *PAC* version, 151-152.

21. Until his father's first wife had died—having been institutionalized for many years—he and Dos Passos' mother could not marry—hence,

his childhood abroad, where Lucy Addison Sprigg Madison and John Roderigo Dos Passos could travel together on occasion. His name was John Roderigo Madison through his years at Choate School, until in 1910, when his parents were married and he could assume the name of Dos Passos.

22. University of Virginia manuscripts collection, essay titled "Contemporary Chronicles," p. 2, p. 1.
23. As stated in "An Interview with John Dos Passos" by Frank Gado, *Idol (Union College,* Schenectady, New York), 1969, p. 18.
24. "The Art of Fiction, 44: John Dos Passos," *Paris Review,* 46 (1969), with David Sanders, 171.
25. University of Virginia manuscripts collection, essay titled "Biographical statement," p. 1-2.
26. "300 Agitators Reach Passaic," "A Passaic Symposium," *New Masses,* I, No. 2 (June 1926), 8.
27. "The Pit and the Pendulum," *New Masses,* I (August 1926), 10-11, 30, and " 'They Are Dead Now—' ", *New Masses,* II (October 1927), 7.
28. *The Forty-Second Parallel* (New York: New American Library, originally published by Houghton Mifflin, Boston, 1930), 50-52. Cited in text as *FSP.*
29. University of Virginia Alderman Library collection of Dos Passos materials, folder labeled *A Pushcart at the Curb.*
30. *Century's Ebb* (Boston: Gambit, 1975), 5.

Rabbit Redux Reduced: Rededicated? Redeemed?

JOSEPH WALDMEIR

In 1974, I was fortunate enough to publish an essay on *Rabbit, Run*[1] in which I argued that it was John Updike's intention in that novel to delineate and examine the forces in conflict which both constitute and direct the quest for order and value upon which most contemporary American fiction is built. I tried to show that Updike casts the conflict in terms of the two idealisms, pragmatic and transcendental, which have dominated American intellectual life since Colonial days. But, I argued further, Updike's intention does not include an attempt to resolve the conflict in the direction of either idealism—nor, indeed, in the direction of any other intellectual/philosophical construct—for he does not believe that it is resolvable.

He dismisses vulgar pragmatism out of hand, but he also rejects the social reform aspects of applied pragmatic idealism as well, on the grounds primarily of its sterility; for, despite its righteousness, its busyness, it is far too smugly sure of itself, too short-sighted to fix or improve anything, let alone what it aims at. Likewise, though he implicitly sympathizes with transcendental idealism, with belief in and profession of absolute, essential value, he rejects it too, as vague in its credo and direction, and as impotent in its struggle with pragmatic reality. The only viable alternative is organized Christianity, and it ultimately is unworthy.

Thus, because he cannot in all honesty resolve it, Updike focuses his own and the reader's attention upon the conflct itself, in all its twists and turns and ramifications. I pointed out the artistic problems he faced in fulfilling this intention—problems entailing the maintenance of distance from, of strict uninvolvement on his and the reader's past with, his characters, and not the least, the problem of a necessarily inconclusive ending. And I tried to show that his main method of dealing with the problems was through an appeal to irony. But Updike did let himself become involved with the Harry Angstrom of *Rabbit, Run*, did care what happened to him, relinquishing his and our precious detachment to such an extent that no appeal to the ironic mode could reestablish it for him. And consequently, as I concluded in that essay, *Rabbit, Run* is both his best and his most flawed work.

In all of the novels since *Rabbit, Run* however, as in *Poorhouse Fair* which preceded it, Updike has scrupulously detached himself from his people, making possible that at once intense and dispassionate examination of the conflict which lies at the heart of his work; and which, inconclusive and irresolvable though it may be, is the principal reason for the work's existence. Any of the later novels amply illustrates these points; however, partly at least because it is an announced sequel to *Rabbit, Run*, I have chosen *Rabbit Redux*[2] for extended discussion here. If the deck seems to be stacked by my choice, I beg the reader to keep in mind that, while I have done the choosing, John Updike has done the stacking.

Superficially, the novels are very closely related. The locales are the same; the cast of major characters, with the significant exception of Tothero and Eccles and the equally significant promotion of Mim to majority status, is the same; the vulgarity of the American scene is the same. There is even a similarity in the plots—someone runs, sexually motivated; someone stays behind and due to irresponsible self-indulgence causes the death of a daughter. But, largely because Harry Angstrom and Updike's attitude toward him are vastly different, *Rabbit Redux* more closely resembles the other previous novels in the Updike canon than its namesake.

While the former Rabbit was an intuitive transcendentalist joined in fruitless battle with the forces of social pragmatism, this Rabbit is truly committed to neither idealism. He consciously rejects his former transcendentalism in pragmatic terms, telling Jill " '. . . I once took that inner light trip and all I did was bruise my surroundings. Revolution, or whatever, is just a way of saying a mess is fun. Well, it *is* fun, for awhile, as long as somebody else has laid in the supplies. A mess is a luxury, is all I mean.' " (172) But he unconsciously reasserts its basic tenet at the end of the novel, saying to Janice " 'Confusion is just a local view of things working out in general;' " (405) and it would seem to be hardly accidental that at this point he is impotent, that "lately he has lost the ability to masturbate; nothing brings him up . . .' " (403) including, as it turns out, a very willing Janice.

In a turnabout reminiscent of the Peter Caldwell-Joey Robinson switch in that other, disguised, original and sequel: *The Centaur* and *Of the Farm*, Rabbit seems to have shifted toward pragmatism. Jill accuses him of it, calling his cynicism " 'tired pragmatism' "; (228) and Skeeter, meaning very much the same thing, tells him " 'You still cluttered up with common sense. Common sense is bullshit, man.' " (263) But at best, Rabbit is a pragmatist *manqué*. In the first place, his pragmatic conclusions are built either on faulty evidence or faulty interpretation of the evidence. Janice puts it succinctly, saying to Stavros

"Maybe he came back to me, to Nelson and me, for the old-fashioned reasons, and wants to live an old-fashioned life,

but nobody does that any more, and he feels it. He put his
life into rules he feels melting away now. I mean, I know
he thinks he's missing something, he's always reading the
paper and watching the news." (53)

Those news reports, liberally sprinkled throughout the novel
(". . . the papers and television are full of the colored riots in
New York, snipers wounding innocent firemen, simple men on
the street, what is the world coming to?" [57]) along with the
expressed attitudes of his elders, Pop and Mr. Springer, buttress
his fear not only of blacks who have turned Brewer into a ghetto
through which a man is afraid to walk at night with a white girl
(see pp. 137-38), but of rebellious youth in general: " 'I guess I
don't much believe in college kids or the Viet Cong,' " he says
to Babe. " 'I don't think they have any answers. I think they're
minorities trying to bring down everything that halfway works.
Halfway isn't all the way but it's better than no way.' " (131)
And his patriotic support of the Vietnam war, expressed most
vehemently (for reasons which partially lie outside the discussion)
to Charlie Stavros—" '. . . it really burns me up to listen to
hotshot crap-car salesmen dripping with Vitalis sitting on their
plumped-up asses bitching about a country that's been stuffing
goodies into their mouth ever since they were born,' " (44)—is
based on the outmoded belief that America is "His garden.
Rabbit knows it's his garden and that's why he's put a flag decal
on the back window of the Falcon even though Janice says it's
corny and fascist;' " (13) that "Wherever America is, there is freedom, and wherever America is not, madness rules with chains,
darkness strangles millions." (47) And the belief is reinforced as
Rabbit takes the familiar path of an Updike protagonist, into his
sports-loving youth. At the baseball game with Nelson and Mr.
Springer, he muses:

There was a beauty here bigger than the hurtling beauty
of basketball, a beauty refined from country pastures, a
game of solitariness, of waiting, waiting for the pitcher to
complete his gaze toward first base and throw his lightning,

a game whose very taste, of spit and dust and grass and sweat and leather and sun, *was America.* (83 emphasis supplied)

In the second place, Rabbit's instinctive pragmatism is weakened by his hesitant, dimly understood awareness that his conclusions are given the lie by the evidence. He senses that "something has gone wrong" at the baseball game. The crowd is "sparse, loud, hard . . . their catcalls are coarse and unkind . . . Rabbit yearns to protect the game" for them. (83) But there isn't any game to protect anymore; "The eight-team leagues of his boyhood have vanished with the forty-eight-star flag. The shortstops never chew tobacco anymore. The game drags on. . . ." (84) He is reminded constantly that his old-fashioned reasons and rules no longer apply. He is surrounded by the slick, the superficial, the artificial. Downtown Brewer, besides being black, is garish and cheap. His house sits over a broken sewer line and

The furniture that frames his life looks Martian in the morning light: an armchair covered in synthetic fabric enlivened by a silver thread, a sofa of airfoam slabs, a low table hacked to imitate an antique cobbler's bench, a piece of driftwood that is a lamp, nothing shaped directly for its purpose, gadgets designed to repel repair, nothing straight from a human hand, furniture Rabbit has lived among but has never known, made of substances he cannot name, that has aged as in a department store window, worn out without once conforming to his body. The orange juice tastes acid; it is not even frozen orange juice but some chemical mix tinted orange. (71-72)

Likewise, like Piet Hanema, he is a craftsman; and like Piet he is shunted aside, offset by slicker mechanical methods. He sees his mother's pain eased by L-Dopa, a drug that offers no cure, only relief; and his father

. . . whittled by the great American glare, squinting in the manna of blessings that come down from the government,

> shuffling from side to side in nervous happiness that his day's
> work is done, that a beer is inside him, that Armstrong is
> above him, that the U.S. is the crown and stupefaction of
> human history. (11)

The Armstrong reference is to the moon landing, which takes
place during the time of the novel, "this unique summer of the
moon," (201) and is the overriding image of American techno-
logical ascendancy. But ironically, the moon is dust: arid, lifeless,
empty. Reaching it is the supreme achievement of pragmatic
know-how; but it is useless, except as a sign of that ascendancy.
" 'The moon is cold, baby.' " Rabbit tells Jill during an argument. " 'Cold and ugly. If you don't want it, the Commies do.
They're not so fucking proud.' " (170) And significantly, Rabbit
lives on Vista Crescent, and at one point sees Jill and himself
as "moonchild and earthman." (202)

Rabbit's lack of commitment to either idealism leads to his
depressive self-awareness— " 'Let's face it,' " he says to Mom. " 'As
a human being I'm about C minus. As a husband I'm about zilch.
When Verity folds I'll fold with it and have to go on Welfare.
Some life.' " (97)—and both in turn account for his aggressive
fears—of Communism, blacks, the youth culture—even of the
former Rabbit. He tells Charlie Stavros, "You know, you're
just like me, the way I used to be. Everybody now is like the
way I used to be.' " (182) But in an Updikean apparent paradox,
this complex of fears and self-pity leads him to accept Jill and
Skeeter into his home. It is his one truly pragmatic action in the
novel. He does it, or Updike makes him do it, in order that he
might be exposed to, might experience in a sort of controlled
learning situation, those ideas, points of view, attitudes which
Jill and Skeeter represent and which Rabbit hitherto has feared
and despised. And most importantly, that he might observe, and
Updike might report on, the most complex conflict between the
two idealisms present in any of the novels. For, beyond all else,
Jill and Skeeter represent the warring factions—Skeeter as revolutionary pragmatist, Jill as transcendentalist whose sole essential

value is Love. Furthermore, the conflict rages within each of them as well, so that Skeeter's pragmatism is corrupted by his transcendent apocalyptic vision, and Jill's essentialism is corrupted by her pragmatic necessity for drugs. However, to complicate matters still further, Skeeter's vision of apocalypse is dependent upon the pragmatic necessity of war; and the practical fulfillment of Jill's needs induces her awareness of essential value: she sees God while under the influence of drugs.

And Rabbit? Rabbit is simply observer, dispassionate, uninvolved, non-responsible, a participant only on his terms and only when he feels like it. He is closer to being a representative of Updike than any of his other protagonists. He is a very unsympathetic character, far more unsympathetic than his namesake; he has to be, if Updike is to avoid the trap that caught him in *Rabbit, Run* and concentrate his and the reader's attention on the conflict. He keeps Skeeter on in the house despite the veiled threats of his neighbors, despite the pleas of Jill and Nelson to send him away, despite his own foreshadowing foreboding at the outset of the novel that he had better hurry home "in case it's burned down. In case a madman has moved in." (9) He knows that Skeeter has hooked Jill on drugs, but he neither protests nor does anything for her. At the climax of the struggle, as the two idealisms merge, each driven by its own necessity, Rabbit is invited to participate; and out of fear, he refuses. (298) He fears involvement, responsibility, commitment. Later that night, in bed with Jill, he relents, offering to get her a doctor for her drug habit, to take her back to her mother, get her car out of hock. " 'It's too late' Jill tells him. 'It's too late for you to try to love me.' " (301) And, despite knowing that he has exposed them all to serious danger, the next day he leaves to indulge himself sexually with Peggy Fosnacht.

Neither idealism is equipped to cope with hard pragmatic reality, vulgar though it may be. Skeeter, in his evangelical fervor, eschews politics and revolutionary activism, though he foresees chaos as the first step toward a new social order. Vietnam is both sign and symbol of chaos for him, hence like Rabbit, though for obviously opposite reasons, he defends the war. But even as he defends it, he sees it abstractly, comparing it to a black hole in space which promises not only infinite contraction but infinite expansion as well—incidentally making clear the references early and late in the novel to Stanley Kubricks "2001"—thus promising the chaos out of which may come a new beginning. But violence *per se* does not interest him; " 'That it's gonna blow up we can *assume.*' " (245) Nor does the politics of violence. " 'People talk revolution all the time but revolution's not interesting, right?' " (245) he says; and again, " 'I confess that politics being part of this boring power thing do not much turn me on' "; (295) and yet again, " 'As to Robert Seale, any black man who has John Kennel Badbreath and Leonard Birdbrain giving him fund-raising cocktail parties is one house nigger in my book.' " (275) Thus, for all his surface toughness, Skeeter is more mouth than muscle, more skeeter than guided missile. And of course, he is incapable of defending himself and Jill against the forces of social righteousness. Jill, flower child, love child, moonchild, is even more defenseless. She cannot even defend herself against Rabbit and Skeeter, who are at least as guilty of her death as those who set the fire—the one because he rejected his responsibility to defend her, the other because he is responsible for her unrousable narcotic stupor. Nelson adores her, is converted by her, and is her only mourner—indeed, Nelson's main function in the novel appars to be to express Updike's sympathetic approval of Jill, yet another of his admirable though impotent essentialists, this one gentle and unselfish, a wounded bird and, inevitably, a victim. When Rabbit asks her why she has sex with Skeeter though she doesn't like it, she replies " 'Because whatever men ask of me, I must give, I'm not interested in holding anything for myself. It all melts together anyway, you see.' " (214) The statement is remarkable not only because of the transcendentalism inherent in the last sentence, but also because of the Christianity implicit in what goes before.

This Rabbit's day is as "bothered by God" as was the former's. Skeeter's evangelism is, as I have said, apocalyptic.

The Four Horsemen ride in Vietnam; the black hole " 'is where God is pushing through,' " (261) and " 'chaos is God's body. Order is the Devil's chains.' " (275) The millenium will bring " 'The new Jesus [who] will liberate the new money-changers. The old Jesus brought a sword, right? The new Jesus will also bring a sword. He will be a living flame of love.' " (275) " 'And you're the black Jesus going to bring it in," Rabbit mocks. 'From A. D. to A. S. After Skeeter. I should live so long. All Praise Be Skeeter's Name.' " (245) But for Skeeter, the metaphor is serious. The North Vietnamese are merely " 'one more facet of the confusion of false prophecy by which you may recognize My coming in this the fullness of time.' " (295)

However, it is Jill who truly opens both Rabbit and Nelson to an awareness of God and Christianity—and as is usual in Updike, it is a non-religious, in terms of churches and organization, awareness. Rabbit has no Bible, " 'we've kind of let all that go' "; (142) he feels he " 'ought to go to church but he can't get himself up to believe it.' " (148) He asks Jill to describe God as she perceived him in her narcotic-inspired mysticism or intuitionism. " 'Oh, God,' " she says. " 'He changed. He was different every time. But you always knew it was Him. Once I remember something like the inside of a big lily, only magnified a thousand times, a sort of glossy shining funnel that went down and down. I can't talk about it.' " (146) But she can talk about it to Nelson, more abstractly and about as foggily as most transcendentalists. " 'Anything that is good is in ecstacy.' " she says. " 'The world is what God made and it doesn't stink of money, it's never tired, too much or too little, it's always exactly full.' " She goes on to describe the order of the universe in terms of Pythagorean music of the spheres, and asserts that our egos make us deaf to the notes—" 'it's like putting a piece of dirt in our eye,' " for " 'without our egos the universe would be absolutely clean.' " When Rabbit the cynic asks why God simply does not clean up the universe, she answers " 'I'm not sure He's noticed us yet. The cosmos is so large and our portion of it so small.' " When she proceeds to argue that the planets need not be *used* for anything, that they may exist only to teach man to count or to give him an awareness of the third dimension, the cynic responds " 'Pretty thoughtful of God . . . if we're just some specks in His mirror;' " and the intuitive essentialist rejoins " 'He does everything . . . by the way. Not because it's what he has to do.' " (159-61, *passim*)

Jill's arguments are insubstantial, even, as I say, foggy; but they are also convincing. At the end of her section, before Skeeter comes on the scene, Rabbit prays unselfishly: *"Make the L-Dopa work, give her pleasanter dreams, keep Nelson more or less pure, don't let Stavros turn too hard on Janice, help Jill find her way home. Keep Pop healthy. Me too. Amen."* (199, Updike's italics)

But the Christian religious level of *Rabbit Redux* is handled quite differently from the way it is handled in most of Updike's other novels. There are no organized churches here or men of the cloth for him to snipe at or side with—no Eccles or Kruppenbach, no church with a golden cock on its steeple and a Reverend Pedrick in its pulpit. Instead, Christianity functions metaphorically here, and is intended to clarify the relationship of the three characters, to establish the distinction between Jill and Skeeter, and to affirm as well Jill's ascendancy over Skeeter. Jill's "Beatitudes of Skeeter" about half way through his section playfully reinforce both the distinction and the ascendancy:

> Power is bullshit.
> Love is bullshit.
> Common sense is bullshit.
> Confusion is God's very face.
> Nothing is interesting save eternal sameness.
> There is no salvation, 'cepting through Me.
>
> (264)

And in a remarkable exchange at the end of Skeeter's section, the religious metaphor sets forth once and for all the complex set of relationships upon which the action has thus far been built.

Rabbit spirits Skeeter out of town, and drops him off at an inter-section marked Galilee 2—"Otherwise it could be nowhere." He gives Skeeter thirty dollars, and "wonders now what would be proper. A Judas kiss?" Skeeter spits solemnly into the palm of Rabbit's proferred hand, and Rabbit, choosing "to take the gesture as a blessing . . . wipes his palm dry on his pants." As they part, Skeeter says " 'Never did figure your angle' "; and when Rabbit answers, " 'Probably wasn't one,' " Skeeter "cackles" his final line: ' 'Just waiting for the word, right?' " (336)

Not uncommonly in Updike, the passage is fraught with ambiguity and apparent paradox. The one truly consistent identity is Jill, the Word that Skeeter recognizes Rabbit had been waiting for. But the identities of Skeeter and Rabbit shift and squirm and float interchangeably. Galilee 2 is an obvious reference to the Second Coming which Skeeter prophecies; and Skeeter assumes the role of Jesus, blessing Rabbit with his spit as Jesus has blessed the blind man to restore his sight.[3] But just as obviously, Skeeter is Judas here, accepting the thirty dollars as his due for turning Jill over to the mob. And Rabbit, who may see himself as Judas, giving rather than accepting the kiss (one recalls that it was he who turned on the light and identified Jill for the mob), is more nearly a Pilate figure, Judas' paymaster. This identity fits better his characterization as an objective ob-server, uncommitted, who washes his hands of responsibility in Skeeter's spit. What seems most paradoxical in the scene is the sympathetic treatment of both figures which Updike extends even into the dual identification of Skeeter as Jesus and as Judas. But even this is consistent in terms of that portion of the Chris-tian legend alluded to. Paradoxically, the Falls of Judas and Pilate were indeed Fortunate, for without their betrayals, the sacrifice of Jesus could not have been consummated. Nor could Jill's, without the falls of Skeeter and Rabbit.

But what purpose does the sacrifice of Jill serve? It is a dis-turbing question. One might argue that it enables Rabbit to distinguish and choose between the forces in conflict that Jill and Skeeter represent. Updike prepares us for such an interpretation when he tempts Rabbit with the naked, black, masturbating Skeeter, then sends him running to Jill instead, "up the varnished stairs, into the white realm where an overhead frosted fixture burns on the landing. His heart skips. He has escaped. Narrowly." (283) Rabbit has made the distinction, but he rejects the choice. Even with Jill, he finds "nothing to breathe but a sour gas bottled in empty churches, nothing to rise by," (284) and he turns his back to her. Later of course, he refuses to partake of her even as Skeeter does; and immediately after this, as I pointed out above in a slightly different connection, Jill tells him that it is too late for him to try to love her.

But despite Jill's sacrifice, Updike does not let Rabbit choose between the conflicting forces—though he does let him lean, as do all Updike protagonists, toward the essentialism which Jill represents. He cannot let him choose and remain true to his intention: the portrayal of the conflict in all its inconclusiveness. The sterility of Skeeter's pragmatism must be matched by the impotence of Jill's transcendentalism; neither the spit of the one, nor the death of the other can be permitted to give Rabbit sight or to redeem him, any more than the sacrifice of Rebecca could identify him or give direction to his running in *Rabbit, Run*.

Thus, one might conclude that the purpose of Jill's death is to clear the air and the stage, to reestablish whatever distance we may have lost by our involvement with the characters and with the somewhat bizarre nature of the action thus far, and to prepare us for the reconstruction of the battlelines of the philosophic conflict which is the subject of the last section of the novel. Updike establishes the distance and points up the conclusion by first alienating us from Jill with narcotics, then, unlike Rebecca, sacrificing her offstage, so that even if we care, our caring, like his own and even like Rabbit's, is more intellectual than emotional, the hysterics of Nelson the convert notwithstanding; and by the ironic intellectual gamesmanship of the religous metaphor itself. As we finish Skeeter's section, we are ready to move onto the plane where conclusions may be drawn, where resolutions may be proposed.

Rabbit Redux Reduced: Rededicated? Redeemed?

We are ready for Mim, *deus ex machina* from the dark side of
the moon, sexual machine and uncompromising pragmatist from
Las Vegas, the gambler's moon crater, epitome of artificiality
and sterility. We never get to know Mim, never get inside of
her, become involved with her in any way. We know only that she
is an unphilosophical social meddler, determined to put matters
right as she sees the right. Furthermore, because she functions
on a strict day-to-day basis, Mim is, more than most Updikean
pragmatists, prone to wrongheaded oversimplification; and, like
Conner or Eccles or the switching couples, she can achieve little
more than the merely superficial, little more than stopping
Janice's running and keeping Rabbit from starting off again—
little more, that is, than a landing on the moon. Thus, she is
ideally suited both to reconstitute the battlelines of the philosophic conflict, and to justify half of Updike's unwavering conviction that any resolution of the conflict is necessarily inconclusive.
The other half of the justification is borne by Rabbit—but only
after Mim has worked him into position.

She conducts Rabbit back through his guilt. Jill, she says,
" 'let herself die. Speaking of that, that's what I do like about
these kids: they're trying to kill it. Even if they kill themselves
in the process.

> "Kill what?" Rabbit asks.
> "The softness. Sex, love; me, mine. They're doing it in.
> I have no playmates under thirty, believe it. They're burn-
> ing it out with dope. They're going to make themselves
> hard clean through. Like, oh, cockroaches." (361)

Her generalization may be accurate, but any application of it
to Jill is simply wrong. And Rabbit doesn't argue, even though
he must know better; the statement neatly reinforces his prior
belief and excuses his irresponsibility.

Mim takes him back to his belief in the war, the belief that
Jill and Skeeter had shaken. He learned from them, he says at
one point that " 'the country isn't perfect.' " But "even as he

says this he realizes he doesn't believe it, any more than he be-
lieves at heart that he will die." (358) And shortly thereafter, he
can reaffirm that " 'Anybody with any sense at all is for the damn
war. They want to fight, we *got* to fight. What's the alternative?
What?' " (366) And Mim, prompted by Charlie Stavros, inter-
prets this commitment precisely opposite to the way Janice had
interpreted it earlier. Janice had told Charlie that Rabbit had
" 'put his life into rules he feels melting away now' "; (53) but,
according to Mim, Charlie's " 'theory is . . . you like any disaster
that might spring you free. You liked it when Janice left, you
liked it when your house burned down.' " (366) That is to
say, both Mim and Charlie see Rabbit as he was ten years
earlier. And when he offers no demurrer, Mim is free to pursue her
oversimplified course, to negate specifically Janice's argument,
and in effect, by conducting him even further back, to reconstruct
him as the original Rabbit:

> "Why don't you tend your own garden instead of hopping
> around nibbling at other people's?" Mim asks. . . .
> "I have no garden," he says.
> "Because you didn't tend it at all. Everybody else has a
> life they try to fence in with some rules. You just do what
> you feel like and then when it blows up or runs down you sit
> there and pout."
> "Christ," he says, "I went to work day after day for ten
> years."
> Mim tosses this off. "You felt like it. It was the easiest
> thing to do." (370)

That Janice is right and Mim is wrong is attested to by everything that Rabbit does in the novel. It is true that he has rejected
commitment and that he accepts only minimal responsibiliy for
any of the "disasters" that strike; but the fact remains that he
did give shelter to Jill and Skeeter, and to Nelson. " 'Black,
white, I said Hop aboard. Irregardless of color or creed, Hop
aboard. Free eats. I was the fucking Statue of Liberty,' " he says

to Mim; and adds, " 'I did what felt right.' " (358) And the further fact remains that he groped persistently for whatever answers, whatever rules, Jill and Skeeter might have given him. However, he allows himself to be placed unprotestingly into that semblance of his former identity that Mim marks off for him. And once she has him there, Mim effectively gets rid of Charlie Stavros by overstimulating his heart (significantly, his weakest organ) thus making possible Janice's return. Then she remounts her machine and returns, pragmatic god that she is, to the never-never moon-scape of Las Vegas.

She leaves behind a Rabbit Angstrom who is " 'still pretty screwed up' "; (403) a Rabbit whose idealistic vacuum she has helped inadvertently to refill with transcendent value—whose belief, cited earlier, that " 'Confusion is just a local view of things working out in general,' " is only slightly less transcendentally muddy than his namesake's belief that " 'There's something out there that wants me to find it.' " She leaves him that is, right where Updike wants him: inconclusive, uncertain, leaning toward an essentialism which is both intellectually and physically im-potent.

Right where Updike wants him, yes. Having maintained his distance throughout the novel by his characterization of Rabbit as dispassionate observer—indeed, having taken a further step away from involvement with his people by permitting the inter-vention of Mim—at the end, Updike focuses our attention where he always wants it to be: Upon the conflict that has been at the heart of the novel and upon its inconclusiveness. And he leaves the reader in a familiar void, an emptiness filled with Hook's unaskable question, with Peter Caldwell's unsayable thing, with the questioning sounds of the first Rabbit's running feet. He leaves us with a Rabbit cured of incipient pragmatism, purified of the cynicism that startles the ending of *Couples*. He leaves us with as many fears and as much hope as we can reasonably expect.

He leaves us with a human being.

O. K.?

Joseph Waldmeir

NOTES

1. "It's the Going That's Important, Not the Getting There: Rabbit's Questing Non-Quest," *Modern Fiction Studies* XX (Spring, 1974), 13-27.
2. John Updike. *Rabbit Redux*. New York: Alfred A. Knopf, 1971. Page numbers in parentheses refer to this edition.
3. Mark 8:22-26.

Notes on Contributors

John G. Cawelti is Professor of English and Humanities at the University of Chicago and author of various books and articles in American Studies and Popular Culture. He has been associated with Professor Nye in the Popular Culture Association for many years.

Professor Robert Falk, retired Professor of English at UCLA, is the author of *The Victorian Mode in American Fiction* (1964).

Louis Filler has published some 40 volumes. Two of them in the dynamics of education are: *Horace Mann and others*, by R.L. Straker (1963), and *Horace Mann on the Crisis in Education* (1965).

A former president of the Popular Culture Association, Marshall Fishwick has recently published two books in this field: *The World of Ronald McDonald*, and *Mass-Media Mosaic*. He is Professor Communication and Humanities at Virginia Polytechnic Institute and State University.

Norman S. Grabo is Distinguished Professor in English at Texas A & M University. He has written primarily on Colonial American Literature, especially the poet Edward Taylor, and was co-editor, with Russel Nye, of *American Thought and Writing* and *American Poetry and Prose.*

Victor Howard is Professor of English and Chairman of the American Studies and Canadian Studies Programs at Michigan State University.

Georges J. Joyaux, who has been teaching at MSU since 1946, is presently Professor and Chairman of the Department of Romance and Classical Languages and Literatures. His fields of interest are in XXth century French literature and in the literatures of the French-speaking world.

William McCann (ret.) edited *Ambrose Bierce's Civil War* (1956), and has been a contributing editor for the *Dictionary of American Bibliography.*

Hugo McPherson is former Commissioner of the National Film Board of Canada (1967–1970), currently Grierson Professor of Communications at McGill University, Montreal. Author of *Hawthorne As Myth-Maker* (Toronto, 1969); chapters in a dozen books on modern art and literature, and numerous articles.

C. David Mead is Professor of English at Michigan State University, and editor of *The Centennial Review.* His publications include *Yankee Eloquence in the Middle West* (1951).

Professor J.E. Morpurgo, former director of Britain's National Book League, holds the Chair of American Literature at the University of Leeds. Among his numerous publications is the *Penguin History of the U.S.,* written in collaboration with Russel B. Nye.

Gilman M. Ostrander is an historian of American culture. He teaches at University of Waterloo in Ontario and is author of *American Civilization in the First Machine Age, 1890–1940* (1970).

Until his retirement in 1972, A.J.M. Smith was Poet in Residence at Michigan State University. A distinguished Canadian poet and critic, he has recently published *The Classic Shade*, poems selected from his fifty year career.

Milton R. Stern is Distinguished Alumni Professor of English at the University of Connecticut. His numerous publications include *The Fine Hammered Steel of Herman Melville* (1957) and *The Golden Moment: The Novels of F. Scott Fitzgerald.*

Linda Wagner is Professor of English at Michigan State University. She has written widely on Modern American literature, both poetry and fiction. Recent books include *Dos Passos, Artist as American* and *Ernest Hemingway: A Reference Guide.*

Joseph J. Waldmeir is Professor of English at Michigan State University. His publications include *Recent American Fiction: Some Critical Views* (1963) and *American Novels of the Second World War* (1969).